AMERICAN
TRADE UNION
DEMOCRACY

AMERICAN
TRADE UNION
DEMOCRACY

by WILLIAM M. LEISERSON *orris, 1883-1957.*

with a Foreword

by SUMNER H. SLICHTER .

354 p.

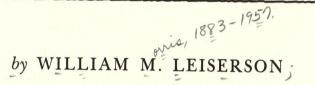

GREENWOOD PRESS, PUBLISHERS
WESTPORT, CONNECTICUT;

1976, c 1959.

ts on the

Library of Congress Cataloging in Publication Data

Leiserson, William Morris, 1883-1957.
American trade union democracy.

Reprint of the ed. published by Columbia University
Press, New York.
Includes index.
1. Trade-unions--United States. I. Title.
[HD6508.L43   1976]   331.88'0973   75-40926
ISBN 0-8371-8688-9

FOREWORD

NO BOOK could be more timely than Dr. Leiserson's study of the internal government of trade unions. The last few years have seen a rapid, if somewhat belated, appreciation of the great influence that trade unions exert over conditions in many shops, over the lives of their members, and on the economic and political life of the country. Quite naturally, the growing awareness of the importance of trade unions has been accompanied by an increasing interest in how unions conduct their affairs.

Up to now little has been done to satisfy the desire for information about the normal operations of trade union governments. There have been able studies of special situations (particularly situations where crime and corruption have occurred), there have been many historical studies of individual unions, there have been studies of limited aspects of trade union government, and there have been important studies of the changing structure of trade unions. But no one had as yet undertaken a broad examination of the normal operation of trade unions.

This need has now been admirably met by Dr. Leiserson's scholarly study. Research on trade union government cannot be based merely upon the study of union constitutions, convention proceedings, and other documents. It must be done by someone who knows the men who make union policies and who understands why they do what they do. Dr. Leiserson was the ideal man for this task. He had lived most of his life in close contact with union leaders, he knew intimately many prominent union leaders of the last generation, particularly in the railroad industry and the needle trades, and he enjoyed their confidence. He had opportunities to observe unions closely both at the local level and

at the national level, he guided some unions and employers in
the early stages of collective bargaining, and he also worked in
industries where unions and collective bargaining are well established. His wisdom and his insight as well as his experience
enabled him to know the problems of union leaders, how the
minds of the leaders worked, how they ran their unions, and
why they behaved as they did. But though he knew trade union
leaders intimately, he was not one of them. He was a member
of the general public, and he could view the actions of union
leaders with detachment as well as with sympathy and understanding.

Dr. Leiserson focuses attention in the main on the national
unions because they are the centers of power in the trade union
movement—though he examines the activities of both the locals
and the federations of national unions. Local unions are far more
important in the United States than they are in European trade
unions, but the federations of national unions (the AFL, the CIO,
and later the AFL-CIO) have had less authority and influence
than is possessed by the federations in most European countries.
But in both the United States and most European countries, the
most important decisions in the trade union movement are made
by the national unions.

Trade unions are in a sense private governments but, as Dr.
Leiserson points out, "they are no ordinary private governments."
They seek to challenge management's rights, to control the activities of nonmembers, and, at times, even to challenge the authority
of the government of the country. Through trade unions labor
strives to supplant business as the most influential interest in
the nation.

Trade union governments perform the three underlying functions of government—the legislative, the executive, and the judicial—but in trade unions these functions are not handled by
separate, specialized bodies. Indeed, absence of the separation of
powers is an outstanding characteristic of trade union government.

The most important body in trade union governments is the

convention which combines the functions of a constitutional assembly, a legislature, and a supreme court. In addition, in over two-thirds of the unions the convention elects the national officers. The executive power in unions is divided between the president and the national executive board or council. But the conventions do not reserve legislative powers to themselves. Hence, between conventions the executive boards exercise legislative as well as executive authority. There is no union with a judiciary that is independent of the administration in power, though two unions have provided for appeal under certain circumstances to outside neutrals. The judicial power may be exercised by various persons or bodies within the union from local trial boards to the convention. The principal judicial officer is usually the president who interprets the constitution subject to appeal to the executive board and ultimately to the convention.

Dr. Leiserson discusses at length the work of the union convention, and of the union executive and the operation of the judicial process in unions. All of these discussions are excellent, but the several chapters on the union convention are especially noteworthy—they give by far the best account of the union convention to be found anywhere in trade union literature. Dr. Leiserson discusses how conventions are organized, how they conduct their business, how the operation of conventions is affected by the growing size of unions, by the large size of many of the conventions, and by the growth of the committee system.

A few unions hold a convention every year; some, every other year; others, every third or fourth year; still others, at irregular intervals. Some conventions are "not much more than an audience registering approval of programs presented by the officers," while others are truly deliberative bodies with wide participation by the delegates in formulating, discussing, and adopting laws and policies. But even when the convention is a deliberative body, most of the real work is done in committees and in hearings before the committees. Some people deplore the fact that at most union conventions there is little debate on the floor and most actions seem to be routine and perfunctory. But this impression of perfunctoriness is often an illusion. In the sessions of the committees much hard work may be done, and in the hearings before the committees vigorous debate may ensue.

Dr. Leiserson provides interesting discussions of representation in conventions and the size of conventions. The problem of giving representation in the convention to small locals is a difficult one—and it grows in difficulty as the duration of conventions increases. Many a small local must wonder whether sending delegates to a large convention in which most delegates play only limited roles is worth the expense. At the 1950 convention of the Typographical Union there were 368 delegates, though the union had about 900 locals. At the Machinists' convention in 1945 less than one-third of the 1,700 local lodges were represented, and those that sent no delegates had almost half of the union's membership. A few national unions, of which the Federation of Musicians is one, pay all costs, including the time lost by delegates, out of the national treasury. The Upholstery Workers have a pool to which all locals contribute regardless of whether they send a delegate. The money in the pool is used to equalize the travel expense falling on the different locals. A few unions have experimented with fining locals that do not send representatives, but this remedy works such severe hardships that it often is not imposed.

Some unions attempt to save expenses by holding conventions only every third or fourth year. The cost depends upon the rules of the union and the length of the convention. The 1951 convention of the Brotherhood of Railway Clerks cost the union more than $650,000. This works out at about 7 percent of the union's receipts for the four years between conventions. This organization pays delegates for the time spent at the convention and for time lost enroute to and from the convention.

A number of conventions have become quite large. At the Steelworkers' convention in 1958 there were about 3,500 delegates; the Men's Clothing Workers and the Women's Garment Workers have about 1,000 delegates; the Hotel and Restaurant Workers about 1,200 delegates. The Textile Workers have had as many as 1,600 delegates, and the Auto Workers and Miners more than 2,000. Attempts have been made to reduce the number of delegates, but such changes are regarded as undemocratic and have failed. The large size of conventions is one reason, though not the only one, why the real work of most conventions is done in committees.

The key role played by the committees in conventions makes the method of appointing committees of great importance. Committees are generally appointed by the president or executive board subject to approval by the convention. In the days when conventions were small, committees were commonly elected by the delegate body. New organizations have experimented with this method, but they have usually abandoned it in favor of appointment.

The matter of representation on the committees is naturally of considerable interest to the delegates. If committees are to be kept of workable size, it is unavoidable that a majority of local unions have no representation on any committee. This state of affairs often produces complaints. Some unions provide that no delegate shall be eligible to serve on more than one committee. Appointing committee members rather than electing them does not avoid dissatisfaction, but by and large it seems to result in the fairer representation. In unions where there is a closely knit officialdom, the same men may be chairmen of committees convention after convention. Study of the proceedings of conventions shows that the recommendations of committees are rarely changed or rejected.

The rules governing the work of the committees are important. Some of the largest former CIO unions, which copied their constitutions more or less from the United Mine Workers, follow the rule of that union that committee reports may not be amended on the floor of the convention. Only by rejecting a proposed section of the committee report may the convention amend or recommit the recommendation of the committee. Among the unions following this rule are the Auto Workers, the Steelworkers, the Oil Workers, the Men's Clothing Workers, and the Rubber Workers. Some other unions bar amendments but do consider motions to recommit.

Between conventions the supreme power in most unions is vested in the officers and the executive council or executive board. Sometimes the officers are members of the council or board; sometimes they are not. The authority of the board, as was pointed out above, is executive, legislative, and judicial.

On paper the executive board has authority over the president and may modify or reverse his decisions and even suspend him from office on proven charges. In practice in most unions the executive board is pretty much under the influence of the president just as the boards of directors of corporations are usually under the influence of the president. The president's activities in handling the affairs of the union from day to day give him superior understanding of the problems of the union. Hence, the members of the board defer to his judgment and expect him to make decisions and recommendations. His authority falls considerably short of the authority given to heads of business concerns, but union presidents who are able, industrious, and conscientious have as much influence over the affairs of their organizations as the heads of corporations have over their organizations.

Dr. Leiserson is of the view that the concentration of power in the hands of union presidents is pretty much a result of the struggle that unions must carry on with employers. This certainly is one of the reasons, but there are other reasons as well. In addition to the fact that the president's duties give him superior knowledge of union problems, there is the fact that in some unions (the Printing Pressmen and the Musicians, for example) strong leadership is needed to keep economic differences among different classes of members from causing trouble.

The least satisfactory aspect of trade union government is the judicial process. It is possible (though not usual) under many union constitutions to discipline members for such vague offenses as "conduct unbecoming a union member," "creating dissension," or "slandering officers." At the local level investigation of charges may be by the local executive board or a special committee. If the investigation does not lead to a settlement of the case, the member is usually tried either by the local executive board or by a special trial committee. The trial body recommends a disposition of the case to the local membership meeting, and from the decision of the local an appeal may usually be taken, if desired, to the national president, the national executive board, and the national convention. But in a majority of unions an appellant must accept a decision against him (such as paying a fine or suspension from membership) pending appeal.

This procedure has two obvious defects: (1) at the local level there is no clear separation between those doing the prosecuting and those doing the trying, since each group is likely to represent the local officers; and (2) the decisions both at the local level and the ultimate national level are made by political rather than judicial bodies.

Unions have been confronted with a difficult dilemma in working out trial procedures. By taking great care to protect the rights of defendants they would make it more difficult to get rid of "crooks" and "stool pigeons." But unions are now sufficiently well established so that they can afford to take the risks that would accompany the establishment of procedures that give better protection to the rights of defendants. An extension of the practice of conducting trials by national representatives would often assure fairer trials and might lead to an earlier discovery of irregularities at the local level. An ultimate appeal to an outside neutral has merit. The president of one of the two unions that has introduced appeal to outside neutrals believes that this arrangement has enhanced the confidence of the members in the fairness of the union's judicial process. Appeals to the neutrals in this union are almost never made, but the fact that appeals may be made has reassured his members.

Are trade unions on balance an influence for democracy in American culture? Dr. Leiserson believes that trade unions on the whole are an expression of the American democratic spirit. Unions are democratic in the sense that they have limited the powers of employers and have made the "management of em-

ployees" a "government of laws instead of an absolute government with arbitrary authority." But he points out that labor organizations exercise great power over their members. Hence, he
asks whether "workers may merely be substituting dictatorial
rule of union officials for the arbitrary authority of the employer
or his managers." May not the democratic spirit with which unions
start be lost in the processes by which organized labor achieves
its goals?

Dr. Leiserson points out that there is evidence of lessening of
popular control in unions, but adds that the evidence is mixed
with contrary currents and is not definitive. Certainly at the
local level there is much evidence of democracy. It is true that
attendance at union meetings is poor and the affairs of most
unions are handled by a few officers and a handful of devoted
and interested members. But the officers and active members are
close to the rest of the union members and hear from them what
they want. As a result, the majority of members are content with
the way the union is being run and stay away from the meetings.
Hence, at the local level the members of most unions directly
or indirectly exercise a good deal of control over what the union
does. But this kind of grass-roots democracy has not been particularly successful in breeding vigorous local leaders who are
interested in molding the national policies of the unions.

Dr. Leiserson believes that we cannot rule out the possibility
that unionism which was created to rescue labor from the
tyranny or overlordship of industrial kings and corporation managements may also become the chief enemy of freedom for the
workers. He points out that no one knows enough about the
American union government to give a definitive answer to the
question of whether organized labor is becoming a menace to
freedom. His whole book is designed to help the reader make
up his own mind, for as Dr. Leiserson observes, clues to the
answer must be found by examining how trade unions conduct
their affairs.

But Dr. Leiserson's admirable study does more than furnish
clues to the answer. It helps mold the answer itself—for by lucidly

and realistically setting forth the facts about trade union government, it arms the friends of democracy with the knowledge and understanding they need to improve the governmental processes within trade unions and to combat the dangers against which Dr. Leiserson so wisely warns.

SUMNER H. SLICHTER

Harvard University
January, 1959

PREFACE

EXCEPT FOR an absolute minimum of grammatical and other minor editorial corrections, the manuscript of *American Trade Union Democracy* is being published as found in my father's papers after his death in February 1957. Work on the book extended over the last twelve years of his life, beginning in 1945 with three years of intensive library and field research: interviewing union leaders, personal observation at union conventions, analysis of union constitutions and proceedings, etc. This phase of the study was financed by a grant from the Rockefeller Foundation administered by Johns Hopkins University with which my father was affiliated as a Visiting Professor. In 1948 he returned to arbitration, consulting, and other professional work. Analysis and writing was interspersed with these activities on a part-time basis throughout the following years.

Accumulating physical ailments prevented him from finishing the work according to his original plan. He was not able to make any changes in the first thirteen chapters which had been written prior to the merger of the AFL and CIO in 1955. Such revisions would probably have been minor in any case and I have taken the liberty of inserting the designation of the merged AFL-CIO in those instances where it is clear from the context that reference is being made to national labor federations in general.

More important is the fact that the manuscript must be published without the concluding chapter (or chapters) which he had barely begun to draft when he became ill. The concluding section was intended to be an explicit interpretation and focused evaluation of trade union government as of mid-century. It was here that he apparently meant to return to the "trend" and "value" questions elaborated in Chapter IV, armed with the descriptive analysis of the main body of evidence provided in Chapters V–XIV. The book is in this sense incomplete.

Eager theorists and impatient partisans will find neither the abstract formulations nor the policy prescriptions they seek. I am confident, however, that the serious citizen and responsible student of organized labor will find much to learn and reflect upon in the substance and method of the work.

All his life, my father distrusted "ideal type" theories and abstract "model" explanations of human behavior. His method emphasized the empirical and inductive, with findings and generalizations continually being referred to observations of how men actually behaved in addition to (or contrasted with) what they said or believed they did and wanted. Emotional commitment and sincerity, ideology and logical inference were, he insisted, inadequate together or singly for understanding the acts and policies of workers. His own commitment to the growth and improvement of collective bargaining as an institution never, throughout his career as an arbitrator, public official, and student of labor relations, interfered with factual recognition of undesirable developments within the union movement whenever they occurred.

Events during the years of organized labor's unprecedented power and influence, 1940–45, apparently precipitated his concern with disturbing trends within the labor movement. The reader is referred to an article on "The 'Growing Pains' of the American Labor Movement," *Annals of the American Academy of Political and Social Science* (November 1942), for the setting and frame of mind in which the research underlying this book was begun. The goal of the study was to provide an objective foundation for union and governmental policies to forestall and control the "undemocratic" tendencies within labor organizations. His point of departure was to investigate unions in a political context as private governments rather than in the traditional categories of economics and sociology.

The book devotes relatively little attention to the burning controversies of recent years over Communism and racketeering.

To Billy Leiserson these were "old aches," not new problems of the labor movement. Unlike many economists, to whom problems of union management and administration are either uninteresting, unimportant, or a "simple matter of decency and honesty," he directed his inquiries at what he considered the fundamentals: the institutional norms, the structural assumptions, the functioning processes of union control, policy, and decision-making. He steadfastly believed that dispassionate appraisal and straightforward expression would serve both the unions and the public better than apologetic generalities in dealing with the negative criticism and sensational alarms when some of the unsavory particulars of unionism were inevitably brought into public view. His premonitions concerning the impact of a public display of some unions' "dirty linen" have been amply justified. Time and circumstance prevented him from realizing his faith that truth, wisdom, and justice would emerge from proper analysis of the facts.

I am not in a position to make adequate acknowledgement to all those who aided my father during the years devoted to this study. A complete list of those in labor, business, government, and the professions who were helpful to him would, I am sure, be a long one. For various periods of time Joseph Shister, Herbert Lahne, and Joseph Kovner were associated with the Johns Hopkins Labor Organization Study as research assistants. Their digests and research memoranda underlie much of the descriptive material in Part II, and in view of the extended period of writing these were utilized by them, with my father's permission, in the preparation of several independent articles in academic journals. Final publication has been made possible by the further generosity of the Rockefeller Foundation.

I would like to acknowledge the assistance of Frank Kleiler and my brother Mark Leiserson in preparing the manuscript for the publisher, and I am particularly grateful to Professor Sumner Slichter for his contribution of the thoughtful and stimulating Foreword.

AVERY LEISERSON

Vanderbilt University
February, 1959

CONTENTS

PART ONE

THE DEVELOPMENT OF
THE TRADE UNION

I

UNIONS AS GOVERNMENTS

AS WE SPEAK OF "the Church" in the sense of organized religion, so in common speech and public prints "labor" has come to mean organized or union labor. When organized labor reaches the proportions it has attained in the United States it becomes to all intents and purposes the government of the labor community. In the words of the sagacious political philosopher Charles E. Merriam, "The trade-union groups constitute a formidable world of quasi-political managements in themselves and tend to become centers of authority of the most important nature, with economic, political, social and cultural implications of vital significance." [1]

Organized labor in the United States is a complex of labor union governments functioning through representative institutions, federations, leagues, and congresses much like federated states. Constitutional assemblies organize authority and distribute it among various branches. Union constitutions allocate legislative, executive, and judicial powers, and organize administration. They define limits of authority and rights of members, describe the "jurisdiction" (occupations, industries, territory) over which each union claims suzerainty. They provide for internal tranquillity, for maintaining order and obedience within the union ranks, for protection against outside aggression, and for the general welfare of the members. Unions enact and publish laws, adjudicate controversies under the laws, punish offenders. They cherish and guard their autonomy much as nations do their sover-

[1] Charles E. Merriam, *Systematic Politics* (Chicago, University of Chicago Press, 1945), p. 15.

eignty. They work with the common tools of government: custom, myths, parliaments, councils, leadership, strategy, and violence.

Through these governmental methods and machinery, organized labor sets standards of work and pay, establishes "job security" and "union security," welfare, insurance, and pension funds. By common rules applicable to whole bodies of workers it maintains the reign of law in the trades and industries in which it functions, governing not only the relations of members to each other, but also of employers and employees. "All these regulations [The Webbs pointed out in their classic *Industrial Democracy*] are based on the assumption that when, in the absence of a Common Rule, the conditions of employment are left to 'free competition,' this always means, in practice that they are arrived at by Individual Bargaining between contracting parties of very unequal strength. . . . We find accordingly that the Device of the Common Rule is a universal feature of Trade Unionism, and that the assumption on which it is based is held from one end of the Trade Union world to the other." [2]

Union officials often speak of their organizations as "legislating for" and "representing" the workers within their jurisdictions. What appears to employers as arbitrary restrictions, organized workers see as legal enactments of their union governments, due process of law limiting the absolute powers of management and protecting the liberties of employees. To gain or safeguard the right to collective action and to enforce their rules or laws, union workers "withdraw their services," shut down not only private enterprises but essential public services as well.

Thus the complex of union governments synthesizes much more than the internal rule of labor organizations. It embraces also government of employees in their workplaces. Hence the term "Industrial Democracy" to describe the main objective of trade unionism. This end would hardly be achieved if unions confined themselves to governing their own organizations. So far as organized labor's own constitutional setup is concerned, it is not un-

[2] Sidney and Beatrice Webb, *Industrial Democracy* (London, Longmans Green, 1902), pp. 560–61.

like other large private associations. Its objectives, however, reach into the government of industry as well, and it asserts authority to extend its laws within domains which employers and the courts have considered exclusively within the jurisdiction of management. Employers often say that they are not opposed to unions, that they acknowledge the right of employees to form or join labor organizations, and that they maintain "open shops" employing union and nonunion men without discrimination.

Such statements are not always false pretenses as the unions charge, but rather reflect the employers' notions as to the proper province of labor organizations, which would confine them to their own internal affairs. It is the intrusion of unions into business organizations to challenge management rights and force changes in policies in terms of employment that they consider improper. In this view, until recent years, they were upheld by the United States Supreme Court, which saw no coercion in discharge of an employee for being a member of a union. "Conceding the full right of the individual to join the union, he has no inherent right to do this and still remain in the employ of one who is unwilling to employ a union man, any more than the same individual has a right to join the union without the consent of that organization" (*Adair v. U.S.*, 1908). The employer's right to discharge for any or no reason was equal to the employee's right to quit. But though organized labor insists that the right to quit is inalienable, it surrounds the employer's right to discharge—and to manage his labor force—with many limitations.

Moreover, one of the main purposes of organized labor is to raise the status of workers in the nation, and it is not content with participation in the public government through its members as citizens. It strives for and secures recognition as authoritative representative of the labor community or labor as a class. As such it gets its nominees seated in the government's inner councils and administrative agencies. When representatives of labor are needed to serve on public boards or on government advisory agencies, organized labor designates them. Organized labor thus regulates group conduct of working people outside the ranks of union organizations as well as those within. Its economic and political pressures force union rules, customs, and practices into the management of industry and into the law of the land.

THAT UNIONS ARE GOVERNMENTS is no new discovery. In a sense, of course, all voluntary associations—churches, fraternal organizations, professional societies, corporations, trade associations, even families—are governments. Private governments, political scientists call them, as distinguished from public governments. But American labor unions are so formally modeled along the lines of public governments, so exacting in the loyalties they require of their members and in the obedience they demand to their laws, so insistent on extending their rule over all workers and forcing nonmembers to obey their regulations, that they are no ordinary private governments. The effects of their activities and assertion of rights are so profound that they must be classed with those great private governments like the church and the ethnic, landed, and commercial groups which have challenged kings and emperors, and taken over public governments. Referring to such private governments Merriam, in his *Systematic Politics*, observes:

In point of fact these groups in great measure govern themselves, maintain a system of organization discipline and morale within their own ranks, with problems of social service and leadership, subordination, super-ordination, and co-ordination, and dictate to or resist the bearers of political authority. . . . Each of these groups possesses an inner organization and a form of inner government of its own and a disposition to dictate to government—at times becomes the government.[3]

Unions order individuals to work or not to work, punish those who refuse in ways that are prohibited to the American government. Their orders to stop work are usually obeyed while the public government is often helpless to prevent work-stoppages. Its appeals that crippling strikes be ended generally go unheeded until the union orders a return to work. The penalties for violating union laws are swift and severe, and extend to taking away the means of livelihood. But what distinguishes unions most from

[3] Merriam, *Systematic Politics*, p. 8.

other private governments is that they are not strictly voluntary organizations with respect to the members included in their ranks and others whom they have authority to represent and rule. Their success depends on compelling employers and managements to share the government of industry with them, as well as forcing nonmembers to abide by their working agreements and regulations.

These efforts to control industry and workers generally put organized labor in a special relationship to the State; and to some extent it takes on the character of a political party. Unions seek and get aid from the government to further their ends, but at the same time they strenuously oppose public regulation of their activities, which they consider unjustifiable attempts to interfere with the constitutional right of voluntary association and the internal management of their private affairs.

Workers are torn between loyalty to their union governments and loyalty to the public government, and the conflict of authorities develops features not unlike those that have marked the struggle between Church and State. As the Church in medieval times attempted to extend canon law to civil affairs, so organized labor today attempts to extend union law to apply not only to the "faithful" but to all workers, to their relations with managements and with public authorities.

DIVERGENT INTERESTS among various classes of workers prevent the acceptance of rule by an overall union government. Skilled craftsmen, men in related crafts or occupations, white collar groups, and production workers in a single industry or in related industries have their own self-governing unions. Some are affiliated with the American Federation of Labor and Congress of Industrial Organizations; others remain unaffiliated, independent unions. But all claim to be autonomous, sovereign in their own right. The AFL-CIO is a league or association of union governments like the original states under the Articles of Confederation and the member states in the United Nations. It is not a central government with authority bearing directly on the individual members or the affiliated organizations. The right of secession or disaffiliation is recognized, and unions are suspended or expelled for nonpayment of dues or for other reasons. At times the various organizations declare and carry on open war against each other.

Nevertheless, there is a unity of common interest, feeling, and opinion among the members of all union organizations, which is shared to a large extent also by unorganized workers. Hence the familiar use of the terms "labor community," "organized labor," or simply, "labor." In the same way we speak of the "Western world" to express the common heritage and outlook of occidental nations. And just as the concept of One World has led to movements to establish a world government, so American labor history has been marked by attempts to organize "One Big Union" to govern all labor and express its basic unity. But the results of these efforts have been much the same as those in the realm of world politics.

Though its voice is divided organized labor speaks for all workers, as the Church with divided voice speaks for all believers. Like the Church too, the American Federation of Labor, earliest and largest of existing labor federations, claimed to be the original "House of Labor," and it invited the Congress of Industrial Organizations and other dissidents to come "home." But labor unity, like church unity, remains an unfulfilled dream. Unions amalgamate and federate, they secede, reaffiliate, remain independent, or join another central organization. The AFL and the CIO did merge in 1955, but if history is any guide there will continue to be some independent unions, some dissident labor movements, so long as individual workers retain the freedom to choose and to form their own organizations. This failure of labor to unite workers under one government may well prove to be the source of its success and strength. Nevertheless "Labor United" continues to be the goal of organized labor.

The strength of organized labor is not lessened by its divisions. Split into two main centers in 1936, the AFL and the CIO together had doubled union membership four or five years later. In another five years, the total membership in all organizations including independent unions had tripled. Compared with 1933 it had multiplied five times. Suspended or seceding unions, and others operating independently, continue to grow, as do the affiliated unions. Unions raid each other for members; by means of government-conducted elections they contest each other's right to represent employees and bargain for them. Such interunion rivalry is generally condemned as a source of weakness, but there is ample evidence to the contrary. Stirred to active campaigning by the rivalry, unions enlist hitherto unorganized workers and keep their officers alert to the needs of their members.

Nor is the number of union members a measure of the influence and power of organized labor. In 1955 all American labor organizations, including independent unions as well as those affiliated with the AFL-CIO, had close to 17 million members. By reason of statutes which provide that the majority of employees in an appropriate collective bargaining unit may choose a union to represent all employees in the unit regardless of membership, several million more workers are covered by union agreements. In addition, whenever a union wins better wages or improved conditions for the employees it represents, the employer usually finds it necessary to grant similar improvements to its supervisory, clerical, and other employees with whom he does not bargain collectively. Foremen and other subordinates of the management staff often learn to their dismay (and enlightenment) that they cannot expect raises in the levels of their salaries unless the organized production workers have first won wage increases.

Employment standards set by union agreements become patterns which unorganized industries tend to follow in order to hold their best workers and in attempts to discourage the spread of unionism among their labor forces. Unions are constantly under the necessity of protecting their gains against competition of non-union labor with lower standards, and their organizing departments put on campaigns to force conformity to the patterns. Unorganized workers having no means of community or political expression naturally turn to union organizers—the ever-present missionaries of organized labor—whenever they have serious grievances and when they feel themselves lagging behind union standards.

Union organizations are also mobilized voters who can effectively bring pressure on the government to help safeguard and spread their gains. The Fair Labor Standards Act with its minimum wage, maximum hours, and time and a half for overtime, bolsters union standards and extends them throughout industry and commerce. The same objective is achieved by federal, state, and municipal laws regulating wages and employment on public works, and on work let out on public contracts. Legislation restricting and regulating the employment of women and children, providing for safety in workplaces, workmen's compensation for injuries and accidents, social security, and other labor protections, works to the same end.

Such legislation usually is inspired by the needs of workers expressed in countless union meetings. The basic provisions take shape during debates in the higher councils of labor, details are worked out by the research staffs and professional employees or consultants, and the proposed laws are delivered to leaders in the federal, state, or municipal government for appropriate action. Despite fluctuations in the political strength of organized labor, its legislative offerings seldom lack sponsors in the Congress, the state legislatures, of the city councils, and much of it finds its way to the statute books. Thus organized labor's standards, rules, and laws tend to govern nonunion as well as union labor. Court decisions defining rights of labor and managements aid in the process.

BY FEDERAL LAW and some state enactments, a union which has the support of a majority of the employees in any craft, plant, or business becomes the "statutory representative" of all the employees in the unit regardless of whether they are union members or not.[4] Provision is made for government-conducted elections in

[4] "The majority of any craft or class of employees shall have the right to determine who shall be the representative of the craft or class for the purposes of this Act." (Railway Labor Act [as amended in 1934] Section 2 [fourth].)

"Representatives designated or selected for the purpose of collective bargaining by the majority of employees in a unit appropriate for such purposes, shall be the exclusive representative of all the employees in such unit for the purposes of collective bargaining in respect to rates of pay, wages, hours of employment, or other conditions of employment." (National Labor Relations Act, 1935, Section 9 [a].)

The Labor-Management Relations Act of 1947 did not change this section, although it drastically revised the 1935 Act in other respects.

cases of doubt as to the union's majority, and every employee in the unit by virtue of his employment (not because he is a member) is entitled to vote. As many as 49 percent of the employees may have voted against the union, but if a majority is registered for the union, the government agency must certify it as the "exclusive representative" of all workers in the bargaining unit.

The laws obligate employers to bargain exclusively with any union in behalf of the labor force in an appropriate unit, if it can demonstrate its majority; and, by ruling of the U.S. Supreme Court, agreements reached must be put in writing.[5] The collective agreements thus made, with their standardized wage scales and rules governing the employees, are legally binding on management and unions alike. They apply not only to members of the recognized union, but also to nonmembers, and to any workers in the bargaining unit who may belong to other labor organizations.

The full significance of these provisions has been generally overlooked. The bargaining units are something more than mere election districts for choosing representatives. In effect they are local units of industrial government with "home rule" powers. The union as majority representative is authorized by law to bind the minority, to act in the name of all workers in the unit. In this respect the units are comparable to town governments, school districts, or the drainage, reclamation, and conservation districts familiar in our Western states.

Although the laws compel bargaining, they do not compel agreement. This the union must win by negotiation, strike threats, mediation, or actual strikes. As expected, however, the effect of taking away management's right to refuse to deal with unions has been to extend collective agreements to all the major industries of the country where the employing corporations formerly reigned supreme. Once the employer—individual or corporation —enters into an agreement with a union, management preroga-

---

Among the states having similar provisions are Mass., R.I., Conn., N.Y., Penn., Wis., Minn.

[5] H. J. Heinz Co. v. NLRB, 311 U.S. 514 (1941). The Railway Labor Act from its original enactment in 1926 imposed the duty to bargain collectively on workers and managements alike. The Labor Relations Act of 1935 placed the obligation only on employers. The 1947 Law made it applicable to both management and labor.

tives are restricted. Its absolute rule over employees becomes a limited government. The agreement is a charter, a constitution for the bargaining unit; the working rules, wage scales, and grievance machinery define rights, duties, privileges, and immunities of the employees. The workers in the bargaining unit share sovereignty with the employer. A joint government is maintained; the management may veto proposed union work and pay rules, the union may veto management regulations affecting employees. The two must agree on legislation in contract negotiations.

The industrial government units thus operate like constitutional monarchies with bicameral legislatures. The employer retains the executive power and he designates the management representatives whose functions are similar to those of an upper house of a legislative body. Union representatives elected by the employees constitute a lower house. The grievance procedures embodied in the agreements, usually topped by a neutral arbitrator, provide courts and an independent judiciary.

Long before the national and state governments thus formally enfranchised the workers in industrial government units and ordained joint control of labor relations within them, organized workers by their own efforts had been forcing employers to establish such constitutional rule over portions of their labor forces. They did this wherever they could by withholding their labor, not unlike the early European burghers who forced the establishment of parliamentary, political governments by withholding taxes. But whereas unions can tax their members by virtue of their own governments, they could not ordinarily tax the nonmembers included in the bargaining units. On this point employer resistance was much stronger than on according recognition to unions as representatives of employees.

Nonmembers, however, enjoy the benefits of the industrial government set up by unions without contributing to its costs, and they are a danger to the security of union organizations. They weaken union bargaining power, and employers encourage their loyalty to management against the organizations that represent them. Hence from the beginning of unionism organized workers have insisted on making membership a condition of employment —in other words, on the closed or union shop.

Without government aid the stronger unions have been able to win this "union security" directly from employers, and thus tax all the workers they represented. But in most bargaining units, unions have had only the authority of exclusive representatives, with nonmembers free of financial obligations to the unions. When in 1935 Congress first clothed the bargaining units with governmental authority, it did not help organized labor in this respect; it left union-shop policy to collective bargaining. During World War II the National War Labor Board went a step further and ordered the inclusion of "maintenance of membership" clauses in collective agreements in all but a few cases where union security was an issue before the Board. These clauses required employees who were members when an agreement was signed, and those who voluntarily joined afterward, to remain members until the termination of the agreement on pain of forfeiting their jobs.

Then in 1947 the Labor-Management Relations Act (Taft-Hartley) took a long step toward making unionism compulsory and adopting substantially the union security policy of organized labor. Congress apparently did this unwittingly, for the Act outlawed the "closed shop" and prohibited employers from deducting union dues or assessments without specific authorization from the individual employees. However, the law also provided that a special government-conducted election, a majority of the eligible voters in a bargaining unit, might adopt a rule making union membership a condition of employment. The employer was then legally authorized to agree with the union to maintain what is called a "union shop." There is reason to believe that the sponsors of this provision thought that in free elections most workers would vote against making membership a condition of employment.

From the point of view of compulsory unionism, there is little difference between closed and union shops. Both make it obligatory to be a union member, one before the worker is employed, the other within thirty or sixty days of his employment. The main effect of the union-shop elections has been to extend the union shop widely through the mass production industries where the large industrial unions actually prefer this form of union security. In the face of clear majorities, ascertained by secret ballot and certified by a government agency, with public opinion likely to be on the side of the union under such circumstances, management resistance to compulsory unionism was rapidly broken down.

Today a substantial majority of collective agreements provide for the union shop, and those still granting only exclusive representation or maintenance of membership are rapidly being converted to this form. Nor have closed shops actually been abolished. They continue to operate, though many have been renamed "union shops." Perhaps because of the possibly unintended result of the Labor-Management Act within a year after its adoption, its sponsors began to advocate repeal of the provision for union shop elections. But the unions succeeded in getting the section strengthened. This experience makes plain that not only direct pressures of organized labor, but even the attempts of public authorities to curb its powers, may result in turning its rules and practices into public policies. At any rate Congress early in 1951 amended the Railway Labor Act to eliminate the prohibition against making union membership a condition of employment, and authorized union shops without requiring elections. In the same year the Taft-Hartley law was amended to eliminate the requirement of a majority vote of employees before an employer could legally agree to make union membership a condition of employment.

FROM THE TIME when union organizations late in the eighteenth century first attempted to dictate the labor bargain and then to force joint control over it, this process has been going on. Workers' organizations originally were treated as criminal conspiracies. The courts, whose duty it was to punish them, in time changed the law to authorize collective action by workers to better their own conditions. They continued to punish members who pursued illegal means to further these ends, but they did not disband the organizations. Then they justified the force exerted by unions on employers as legitimate economic pressure like the pressure of employers on workers because of their superior economic position. Sometimes they referred to the pressures as competition between employers and workers. Later the union agreements wrested from employers were held to be contracts, establishing valuable property rights, and therefore enforceable at law.[6] As unions multiplied and disputes arose between members and union officials, or between local unions and the national organizations of which they were a part, the courts began to interpret and enforce the constitutions of the union governments in the same manner as they interpret and enforce state constitutions or the Constitution of the United States.

While this was going on, a growing body of labor legislation was bolstering union standards, and incorporating into law many of their policies. This was more often due to the agitation and activities of social reformers than of the trade unions. The organizations feared the effects of government action on unionism and they concentrated on the narrower problems of strengthening unions for bargaining purposes. But the depression of the 1930s turned organized labor wholeheartedly to politics. It began to support social legislation actively, instead of confining its political efforts mainly to securing legal protection for union activities and outlawing court injunctions in labor disputes, which had been the official policy of organized labor previous to Franklin Roosevelt's administration.

As a result, employers' labor forces, or appropriate portions of them, have been institutionalized as industrial government units by legislative enactments, and unions have become statutory representatives with legal authority to govern nonunion minorities. Organized labor's programs for achieving job security and union security are encouraged and supported by the government. Social security against unemployment and old age has been established by national laws, and steps are being taken toward providing health insurance. At the same time the unions strive to increase benefit payments and to supplement them with health, welfare, insurance, and pension funds secured by collective bargaining with employers. These latter efforts are but a continuation and enlargement of the mutual aid and beneficiary features which have characterized trade unionism from the beginning.

In these developments we see the processes by which union

[6] Under British law union agreements are not legally enforceable contracts. They are treated as "gentlemen's agreements."

laws and practices, policies, and programs find their way into the public laws of the nation. Organized labor rules not only the members won by its own efforts, but additional millions included in its bargaining units by virtue of legislative enactments. These units, first established by private contract with employers, and bounded only by the jurisdictional laws of the unions, become industrial government areas defined by public authority. Not by its power to withhold labor alone, but as a matter of legal right enforceable in the courts, labor shares with employers the government of its labor forces, limiting the prerogatives of management and establishing a kind of constitutional government in industry. Through these means the pattern of conduct for all workers is set, and organized labor becomes the recognized agent of the labor community in dealing with other groupings of the population, as well as with public authorities.

II

THE ROOTS OF
UNION GOVERNMENT

LIKE OTHER POLITIES, union governments grow out of common needs, experiences, traditions, and aspirations of groups of people. Unionism is rooted in the customary practices and social habits of wage earners at their work long before formal organizations appear among them. To protect their customary ways of living and working, cliques and other informal groups of workers habitually adjust employers' shop regulations to bring them into line with their own traditional codes of behavior. Union rules and collective bargaining agreements, as we now know them, are in effect legislative enactments, bearing the same relation to the unwritten customs and codes of working people that statutes do to common law.

In shops untouched by unionism, informal organizations of workers develop spontaneously and unconsciously to control and regulate group conduct. Mathewson, an engineer, described these, without fully realizing their nature, in his study of the methods used by nonunion workers to restrict production according to standards they considered reasonable.[1] He was led to his investigations by his experience as Personnel Director at Antioch College where his duties were to place students in industrial and commercial establishments to work in alternating periods with class work on the campus. He found that most students returned from their initiation into the working world with one lesson learned in common: they must not turn out any more work than the

[1] Stanley B. Mathewson, *Restriction of Output among Unorganized Workers* (New York, Viking Press, 1931).

quotas informally set by the groups with which they worked. Usually in some secretive way the students were informed by fellow workers that they would be "spoiling the job," hurting their shopmates, if they did not keep their output within the bounds considered proper by the others.

Mathewson worked as a laborer, machine operator, bench and conveyor assembler, and skilled mechanic in nonunion plants scattered through the Middle West. Wherever he worked, and despite ingenious incentive wage payment plans to stimulate employee output, he found his shopmates fixing for themselves a daily stint of production considerably below what it was possible for them to turn out. This did not necessarily mean that their output was unreasonably low. They merely differed with the management as to what was a fair day's work for the pay they were getting. In many cases the lower ranks of supervisory employees cooperated with the men under them by advising them as to how much work could be turned out without risking retiming of jobs by management, and cutting incentive or piece-work rates. Mathewson's observations and conversations with fellow employees convinced him that their seemingly universal practice of circumscribing production was due to fear of unemployment and rate cutting.

Roethlisberger and Dickson, in their account of the notable experiments in industrial research carried on at the Hawthorne Works of the Western Electric Company, delved deeper for an explanation. They analyzed in scientific detail what they described as the "Social Organization of Employees."

From examining the social environment within the factory, it became evident that the worker is far from being an isolated individual at work. He is in constant association with other workers and his superiors; he is a member of a particular social group. . . . The individuals in the various groups and the various groups themselves are bound together by certain codes of behavior. These codes and customs define the attitudes of the workers to one another, to their supervisors, and to the Company as a whole. . . . The behavior and beliefs of the members of an industrial plant were at any given time in a relation of mutual dependence to a system of sentiments expressing their social organization. Many of their complaints had to be understood in terms of disturbances of this social equilibrium. It became clear that [the workers' behavior] was neither logical nor irrational. . . . It was essentially social behavior.[2]

The studies at the Hawthorne Works revealed that nearly all the activities by which individual employees related themselves to one another were contrary to the rules of management. By management standards it was wrong for a faster worker to help a slower one, wrong for one operator to attend another's machine, wrong for any group of workers to relax and converse before quitting time. Each individual was supposed to devote himself exclusively to his assigned duties from the beginning to the end of the scheduled workday. There was no time for neighborliness. But the employees pursued the ways that seemed natural to them. Habitually they "visited," talked about their own affairs, engaged in horseplay, discussed the amount of work they were turning out and what was the proper quantity.

Various groups of them had their own standards of seemly social conduct in the shop, and they had ways of bringing pressure on individuals who deviated too much from those standards. However informal their methods, the groups determined norms of individual output, and they subjected production to controls according to their customs. To management this was nothing but "restriction of output," for as Roethlisberger and Dickson observed, management sets individual tasks on the basis of an efficiency that is limited only by fatigue. To the working groups, however, their social customs were additional limiting factors to production, and they instinctively applied them.

Long before union organizations rationalize worker control of production by formal rules, unorganized workers thus informally modify management efficiency regulations in accordance with their own codes and standards of proper social conduct among fellow employees. Both management and workers regulate and restrict production, but the values they seek are not entirely the same. Workers pursue their values regardless of how false these may appear in terms of business or economic logic. They continue

[2] F. J. Roethlisberger and William J. Dickson, *Management and the Worker* (Cambridge, Harvard University Press, 1947), p. 575.

their practices of limiting production according to their codes, regardless of logical and scholarly demonstrations that in so doing they are reducing efficiency and decreasing opportunities for employment.

In the recorded history of the printing trades other illustrations may be found of the way in which unionism is rooted in the informal organizations of employees at their work, and how unions carry on traditions and customs of the informal organizations. In 1683, one Moxon described the "Ancient customs used in a Printing House" in London.[3] "Every Printing-house is by Custom of Time out of mind, called a Chappel; and all the Workmen that belong to it are members of the Chappel; and the Oldest Freeman is Father of the Chappel. . . . There have been formerly Customs and By-Laws made and intended for the well and good Government of the Chappel, and for the most Civil and orderly deportment of all its Members while in the Chappel; and the Penalty for the breech of any of these Laws and Customs is in Printers Language called a Solace. And the Judges of these Solaces, and other Controversies relating to the Chappel, or any of its Members, was a plurality of Votes in the Chappel."

Then he goes on to describe the offenses for which Solaces were imposed, and how "These Solaces were to be bought off, for the good of the Chappel," at various prices (fines). "But if the Delinquent proved Obstinate or Refractory, and Would not pay his Solace at the Price of the Chappel; they Solaced him. . . . The manner of Solacing thus: The Workmen take him by force, and lay him on his Belly athwart the Correcting-stone, and hold him there while another of the Workmen, with a Paperboard gave him . . . Eleven blows on his Buttocks; which he laid on according to his own mercy."

Today the union-shop organizations in American printing plants are still known as "chapels," and penalties in the form of fines are imposed for violation of chapel rules by majority votes. But expulsion from the union for refusal to pay fines has been substituted for physical punishment. The chapel originally was a

---

[3] Reprinted in *The London Compositor* by Ellic Howe (New York, Oxford University Press, 1947), pp. 23–27.

mutual benefit society as well as an organization for enforcing customs of the trade and settling controversies, and American printing trade unions continue to maintain mutual benefit funds. Neither in Great Britain nor in the United States, however, were there any organized unions of chapels until the latter part of the eighteenth century.

Some idea of how deeply rooted such methods of social control are in the folkways of working people may be gathered from the fact that in the entirely different environment of the Western Electric Works near Chicago, the investigators discovered customs among the employees not unlike those of the printing chapels in London three centuries earlier. By a practice known as "binging" the group attempted to control the behavior of individual employees. Like solacing this involved physical punishment for violation of customs. Having no union to enforce established rules, the practice was for one man to hit another as hard as he could on the upper arm, and "the one hit made no protest." In addition to its use as a penalty, binging was also used to settle disputes; but "one of its most significant applications . . . was to regulate the output of some faster workers." [4]

Binging and solacing are but illustrations of innumerable other informal methods of worker-control of group conduct in places of employment. "By custom of time out of mind" such methods have been used to enforce common rules or standards developed to guard the interests of laboring people before unionism or legislation took over this function. When in the course of time trade unions are established, they formalize the rules, and get them embodied in working agreements with employers, or in legal enactments.

No union rule is better known than that of the Typographical Union, which restricts local interchange of plates or papier-mâché mats, so that if they are used by another employer, the type must be reset, read, and corrected as in the original form. This "bogus work," as it is known, is of course designed to protect printers against loss of work; but to employers it is unnecessary "featherbedding." The rule, however, is no mere invention of a "bad"

[4] Roethlisberger and Dickson, *Management and Worker,* pp. 421–22.

union. It has a long and respectable heritage in the printing industry, dating at least from the sixteenth century. In 1587 "A Copie of Certen Orders Concerning Printing" issued by the Stationers' Company provided: "ffyrst that no formes of letters be Kept standings to the preidice of Woorkmen at any time." And in 1635 this was further elaborated in answer to a petition from the journeymen printers: "that yf anie standinge form shall on necessary occasion be used (yf anie compositor in that house want worke at anytime) he shal be paid for that forme, as yf he had composed it . . ."

Ellic Howe, who edited the "Documents relating to Wages, Working Conditions and Customs of the London Printing Trade" from which these quotations are made writes: "The regulations of 1587 and 1635 were clearly for the protection of the new class of permanent journeymen, unable to rise into the ranks of the masters and still, withal, strongly conscious of its rights as freemen. They were mainly designed for the prevention of unemployment. . . . The orders of 1587 are, indeed, of the greatest historical importance, since they record the right of the compositors to any advantage accruing from the existence of standing formes. It was set forth that such formes, from which an impression had been taken, and which had not been broken up or distributed, should not be used again without some compensation to the journeymen, since their regular use materially lessened the amount of work available for the workmen." [5]

THERE IS A COMMON MISCONCEPTION that trade unionism arose with factory production. As the size of business units grew, the assumption is, employers lost the close touch they formerly had with their employees, and they could no longer settle differences amicably as they did when the owners knew the workers by their first names. This prevalent notion is mainly myth. The first unions both in the United States and in Great Britain were made up of skilled mechanics who worked in small shops. While there were strikes before the end of the eighteenth century, earliest of the continuous organizations of wage earners appear to have estab-

[5] *The London Compositor*, pp. 15 ff.

lished themselves during the last decade. They were known as "Trade Societies." Journeymen shoemakers and printers were among the first to organize, soon followed by tailors, coopers, carpenters, cabinetmakers, hand weavers, and similar craftsmen. Although about 100,000 persons worked in cotton mills in 1820, no unions of factory operatives had yet been organized. The trade societies which then existed were in effect closely restricted craft unions, small in membership and local in character.

The organizations established authorities to enforce the customs and standards of the crafts which were threatened by changes in work methods introduced by employers under the stress of competition in markets wider than the locality. The members bound themselves to strict rules and regulations and rigid discipline. They adopted wage scales, and swore to abide by them and to refuse to work with anyone who accepted less than the scale or who was not a member. Only journeymen were eligible to membership, and the closed-shop device was directed also against employers' efforts to break down the apprentice system.

Thus the organization of labor separate from the employer and in opposition to his unilateral control began more than half a century before large-scale machine production or the factory system became the prevailing form of industrial enterprise. Moreover the primary self-rule objectives and defense methods of labor unionism as they were worked out by these original organizations of artisans and mechanics have continued to this day, though with elaborations as greater numbers of less-skilled workers were brought into the fold of organized labor. Many of the earliest unions began as mutual aid societies, providing sickness and death benefits, and reverted to these forms when they were weakened or destroyed by unsuccessful strikes. Today most labor organizations carry on similar mutual benefit and insurance activities.

Although the first trade societies did not attempt direct joint negotiations with employers, they soon had to resort to this basic method of labor unionism—collective bargaining. They tried at first to follow the methods of the employers who formally or informally agreed on price lists and on the wages they would pay. Similarly the journeymen's societies adopted "price lists" (wage

scales), and then attempted to impose these on individual employers. But when employers resisted and strikes became necessary, the societies were forced into negotiations and settlements
by mutual agreement. Offers of compromise became common,
joint conferences were arranged between the masters' and workers'
societies, and agreements reached in the modern manner.[6]

It is significant, also, that those in the lowest ranks of labor
were not the first to organize. The untrained workers, the common
laborers, the lowest paid, and those with the worst working conditions, lacked the cohesiveness and resources to maintain organizations. This may explain why the factory operative who required
little training and no apprenticeship lagged in establishing unions.
Artisans and mechanics who had standards and a status above
ordinary laborers were the pioneer unionists. Indeed what led
them to form protective organizations was usually the threat to
their standards from the competition of lower grades of labor.
"It seems that their only motive for organizing was to protect their
standard of life as skilled mechanics." At every stage in the development of organized labor this pattern of the better paid,
higher grades, of workers organizing first was repeated.[7] When
really durable organizations were established in the 1880s, again
it was the skilled trades that organized first, and these formed the
American Federation of Labor.

One might suppose that large aggregations of employees working in close proximity in factories would have better opportunities for organization than craftsmen scattered among many small
shops, and they had the added incentive of lower wages and notoriously bad working conditions. Early in the nineteenth century,
however, women, children, and recent immigrants were largely
used at machine production; not until hierarchies of skilled workers, with usages and standards that marked their status developed
among them, did union organization take hold in factory industries. Later, when improved machinery and processes broke down
skill hierarchies based on apprentice systems, and when most pro-

[6] John R. Commons & Associates, *History of Labor in the United States* (New
York, Macmillan, 1918), I, 121.
[7] Commons, *History of Labor*, I, 104.

duction workers were trained on their jobs, industrial unionism began to grow, joining all workers in a single organization. Here again it was the upper crust of skilled groups that took the initiative in organizing unions.

THE GROWTH OF UNIONISM in mass production industries has stimulated psychological and sociological studies of human relations in industry, and these have thrown new light on the sources of unionism. The concepts developed by these investigations make easily recognizable the kind of soil from which union governments sprout. The basic concept is that every industrial plant is a social organization, a social system. It has a "social structure: a network of reciprocal rights and obligations, supported by sentiment and formal rule. . . . The actual patterns of social relationships, whether formal and official . . . or informal and unofficial [reflect] the prevalent sentiments and attitudes about the organization in general, or about particular rules and personalities." [8] The whole structure forms a social status system.

The patterns of relationships are outlined in the familiar business organization charts. "In most companies or factories there is one Big Boss and below him rank after rank of smaller bosses . . . increasing in numbers as they decrease in importance . . . down to the very bottom where we find those who are so numerous and so unimportant that their names never appear on the organization's charts—the workers." [9] The charts show the positions occupied by people and indicates functions and duties. This is the formal organization as established by the management for production of goods and services.

Not shown on the charts, however, is another pattern of relationships growing out of personal contacts among people who work together in groups, or who are otherwise brought together in the course of their employment. These relationships tighten into cliques and larger groupings carrying on a variety of associated activities not contemplated by the management, often inter-

[8] Wilbert E. Moore, *Industrial Relations and the Social Order* (New York, Macmillan, 1946), pp. 7–8.

[9] Burleigh B. Gardner, *Human Relations in Industry* (Chicago, Richard D. Irwin, 1945), p. 8.

fering with its operations, and largely beyond its control. They make up what is known as the "informal organization." The formal structure is imposed from above, while the informal organization develops from below without conscious or deliberate intent.

Gardner, who was trained in social anthropology and who directed employee relations research at the Western Electric Company for five years, describes the informal group activities:

Now these informal relations are not merely a matter of friendly association and conversation unrelated to work behavior. Numerous studies have shown that they play a major role in determining the attitudes and behavior of workers with respect to their work, their superiors, and the company. In fact, the most powerful controls over the individual lie in the hands of the group itself and are expressed through the informal structure. Thus we see the work group deciding upon the proper standards of output and taking pains to see that the newcomer understands and conforms to these unofficial standards. . . . Or we see the individual forced to choose between his superiors and the group. As one worker said, "You gotta decide whether to go along with the group or to stand in with the boss. And if you don't go along, the gang can make it mighty unpleasant." [10]

A new employee is initiated and is tested by his fellow workers to see if he will fit into the group. In a clothing factory he is sent to his foreman to ask for a sleeve stretcher, in a lumber mill for a board stretcher, in a machine shop for a left-handed monkey wrench. In a railroad shop his ability to chew tobacco is tested: "Everybody here chews tobacco," said the master mechanic of such a shop, "and when we had women workers during the war, they chewed tobacco too." An experienced worker taking a new job soon asks: "How much is a day's work?" He knows that there must be a standard fixed by the group with which he is to work, and to be accepted by his fellow workers he expects to conform to group-imposed patterns of conduct in this as in other matters.

The informal organizations substitute group ends for the competitive individual ends the management expects workers to pursue, and which it tries to stimulate by promotions and demotions, merit pay increases, incentive wage plans, and labor cost controls.

[10] "The Factory as a Social System," Chapter II in *Industry and Society*, edited by W. F. Whyte (McGraw-Hill, 1946), p. 7.

The groups value their joint activities and strive to preserve the social relationships thus established; they will not be singleminded in their devotion to technical duty. The interests of the various groups merge in defense against the expectations and demands of their bosses. They try to keep information from the management and especially to hold their group activities under cover. In this way the divisions and differences in social status created by the hierarchy of positions in the formal organization of the plant are sharpened by the informal organization. Differences in outlook are intensified, modes of social behavior and group thinking spread wider apart. This cleavage within the plant organization is interrelated with the social status of the managerial and laboring personnel outside the plant. The tendency of bosses to belong to organizations which in social status are on the same level as their status in industrial plants, and of workers to do the same, has often been noted. Thus the status pattern and the cleavages within plant organization parallel those in the social life of the community.

Although there are cleavages between different layers of supervisors, between office and shop workers, and also between different grades of manual workers, the most important cleavage is that between order givers and order takers, between the management hierarchy and the labor force. Between these the most vital antagonisms arise, the clash of interests is greatest, differences in attitudes and sentiments most pronounced, and ways of thinking and living farthest apart. We still speak of "the employer" as if he were an individual person or in the sense of the legal fiction of corporate personality, meaning that the shareholders are the employer. In reality, however, it is the management organization, the staff of bosses, that is the employer. Although the lower supervisory ranks merge into the working force through "straw bosses" or lead men, the management acts as a unit, and its differences with the great body of employees outside its ranks constitute our main problems of industrial relations.

One of the most important effects of this cleavage is the way it interferes with communications within the industrial plant. What holds the production organization together is a system of communications by which information goes upward from the lowest layer of bosses through the next higher supervisors step by step to the top executives, and from these orders come through the same channels down to the bottom. We have already noted that the management hierarchy tends to think in terms of efficiency while the workers think in terms of social behavior. What happens is strikingly described by Roethlisberger: [11]

The top of the organization is trying to communicate with the bottom in terms of the logical jargon and cold discriminations of the technical specialist, the engineer, the accountant, etc. The bottom of the organization, in turn, is trying to communicate with the top through its own peculiar language of social sentiments and feelings. Neither side understands the other very well. To the bottom the precise language of efficiency, instead of transmitting understandings, sometimes conveys feelings of dismay and insecurity. The bottom, in turn, instead of transmitting successfully its fears of social dislocation, conveys to the top emotional expressions of petty grievances and excessive demands.

THE ROOTS of union government thus reach into the social organization of the industrial plant. They are nurtured by the social behavior of the laboring population in and outside the plant. The informal organization is the breeding ground from which unionism grows. The activities carried on by informal groups, the standards they set, and the unwritten regulations they use (illicit in the eyes of management) for controlling group conduct, are the beginnings of worker-group governments which in their maturity break away from the factory or plant organizations. As they grow they determine their own constitutional structure with organs of government for establishing standards, adopting working rules and regulations for controlling behavior of members, and carrying on the variety of other activities which characterize union organizations from time to time.

In rudimentary form we find in the informal plant organizations not only control and regulation of production as carried on by unions, but also the initiation ceremonies, the pledges to secrecy about activities of the organizations, the methods of disciplining members for unsocial behavior, the mutual aid and pro-

[11] F. J. Roethlisberger, "The Social Structure of Industry," address before Professor Cabot's Business Executives' group (Boston, December 5, 1936), pp. 15–16.

tection, group bargaining, etc. When threats to group standards spread widely through a plant and the informal organizations prove inadequate to protect them, the cleavage between workers and management widens and deepens, the workers are ready to set up "outside" organizations of their own, or they gravitate toward and are absorbed by existing union organizations.

Usually this final break results from some crisis that has developed in the relations between the supervisory hierarchy and the wage earners. Warner and Low studied and analyzed a typical case—a city-wide strike of shoemakers in a New England community.[12]

They struck with little or no warning; struck with such impact that all the factories closed and no worker remained at his bench. Management had said their workers would never strike because the workers of Yankee City were sensible and dependable, and had proved by a long peaceful history that they always stayed on the job. Union men outside the city said the Yankee City workers would not strike because Yankee City had never been and could not be organized and, furthermore, the shoe workers of Yankee City were obstinate and "always stupid enough to play the management's game." Many of the workers told us that there would be no strike. . . . But foreigners and Yankees of ten generations, men and women, very old and very young, Jews and Gentiles, Catholics and Protestants—the whole heterogeneous mass of workers left their benches. . . . Not only did they strike and soundly defeat management, but they organized themselves, joined an industrial union, and became some of its strongest members.

The study posed the question—"Why did it happen?"—and the staff set out to find the answers. They got the usual replies from people they interviewed. Managers said times were bad, you couldn't sell shoes without reducing costs, cutting wages. Workers said it was low wages; you couldn't feed a family with what was paid. Other workers thought it was a plot: the rich are never satisfied with their profits, they want to take everything away from the workers. Management representatives charged it was a "Red plot": there would have been no trouble if it hadn't been for the union agitators. But there had been depressions and low wages

[12] W. Lloyd Warner and J. O. Low, *The Social System of the Modern Factory* (New Haven, Yale University Press, 1947).

before, and there had been no strikes and no unions. On the other hand there were strikes when wages were high and times were good. "Although these economic arguments supplied important and necessary reasons for the strike and the unionization of the workers, they were insufficient to explain the strike and why unionization occurred." [13]

The causes were multiple, of course, but they extended beyond the mere conflict of economic interests between employers and workers. The social status of the wage earners below the management staff and the different logic that dominated the thinking of each group were basic factors. Even the skill hierarchy among the workers had been broken, practically all were on a single level of operatives—hence their preference for industrial unionism. Another primary factor was the constant changes in the techniques of shoemaking. New machines and new processes often required readjustments in the social organization of the factories. This increased the feelings of insecurity. The factories themselves could not provide new jobs for displaced workers, though some might be transferred to lower paying jobs. More powerful protection was needed than informal organizations of groups of employees in the plants could give. Fundamental to all, however, was the wide gap between the thinking of the workers and that of the owners and managers.[14]

In some quarters debates are still going on as to whether labor unions are desirable or not, as if this were a question that could be determined by argumentation. If, however, union organizations and their policies are expressions and formulations of the collective beliefs and sentiments which give rise to spontaneous, informal

[13] Warner and Low, *Social System of Modern Factory*, p. 21.

[14] This is well illustrated by the suggestion of a laborer for preventing unemployment quoted by Warner and Low. He thought that machines should not be working while men stand around and look. As times get bad the machines should be stored away, and men put to work. They would earn money and spend money, and pretty soon there would be so much work there would be a shortage of labor. Then the machines could be put to work again. "They should save the machines until they don't have enough men, then they could use them." To men who must compete with machines for a living such ideas seem no more absurd than the logic of industrial management which requires breadwinners to be laid off—stored away—when business is bad until good times return. A really objective observer—a man from Mars—might well consider the thinking of both equally quaint.

organizations in shops and factories, then of course logical disputation as to the merits of unionism are as irrelevant as they are futile. Attempts to evaluate their customs, practices, and rules in terms of technical efficiency, productivity, or economic effects, without reference to the traditions of the workers' own organizations for social control, are of little more worth.

III

TRADE UNIONS AND THE
LABOR MOVEMENT

THE FORMS AND CHARACTERISTICS of "outside" unions (as employers call them) are shaped by the same social habits reacting against management that create spontaneous social control groups in shops and factories. Changes in technology and industrial administration upset social equilibriums outside as well as inside places of employment, threaten workers' existing standards and hopes of advancing them. Unions respond with new protective measures, new practices, new rules. They alter their structures, contrive new activities, proclaim new policies and programs. Present-day unions are as different from the local trade societies of the early nineteenth century as the modern industrial or commercial establishment is from the combined shop and store of the master workman of that time.

From the breeding ground of unionism in the informal wage earners' organizations surrounding their work, new people are constantly coming into established unions, or they join the ranks of organized labor as new unions. They bring with them new problems, new methods, varying ideas as to the kind of organization and activity that will most effectively keep them united for protection and for improving employment conditions. At the same time existing unions grow older. Some have had a long history, have learned to adjust methods and policies to new developments in order to survive and grow. This process of change, growth, and stability has been going on ever since the first union organizations appeared in the United States a century and a half ago.

The last two decades witnessed spectacular changes in union

organization brought about by the development of mass production industries. As the workers in these industries broke away from the domination and tutelage of the great employing corporations, old established organizations helped them financially, politically, and otherwise, to challenge successfully the unilateral control of labor relations by the managements. Not only were new industrial unions established on a firm basis, but the older organizations too were transformed.

Unions changed both in structure and in the ordering and management of their affairs. Their functions expanded, their aims were enlarged. They have become more political in character. Their leaders have found places at the council tables of the nation. Their staffs of employees have multiplied, an administrative bureaucracy has grown up, and something like a civil service is taking form. Increasingly they have found it necessary to employ lawyers, economists, statisticians, and other experts. Self-organization by the workers has been largely supplanted by businesslike, high-pressure organizing campaigns planned and directed from the top down. Greater powers are being exercised by the national unions and by their interunion organizations.

A similar profound change took place during the last quarter of the nineteenth century when national craft unionism established itself as the typical form of labor organization. This period marked the beginning of what we may call permanent unions—the railroad brotherhoods and many of the AFL unions have maintained a continuous existence since that time. Previously unions were ephemeral things, springing up in prosperous times when cost of living rose, maintaining a brief existence, and disappearing or turning into political or social reform organizations in every economic depression.

The earliest unions were local societies of journeymen mechanics with no connections outside their home towns. They were as much mutual benefit societies as trade unions. They paid relief benefits as well as strike benefits. When business was on the upswing they resorted to strikes and made some gains. On the downturn, when strikes proved futile, they disintegrated or barely kept themselves alive by reverting to mutual aid. When business activity revived, there was a resurgence of strikes mainly by a crop of new organizations.

When property qualifications for voting were abolished, the unions began to turn to politics for relief, usually with disappointing results. Later, disillusioned by their political efforts, they sought refuge in movements for social reform and economic reorganization as depressions overwhelmed them. This pattern of active union organization followed by disintegration and fading into political and social movements with the turns of the business cycle repeated itself again and again down to almost the end of the nineteenth century when a stable unionism was achieved.

THE CIRCUMSTANCES that bring a union into existence are not limited to a particular trade or industry. So from the first we find unions appearing in waves of organization spreading over wide areas through many occupations and industries; and it is not long before they develop interunion organizations and connections with other workers' associations both economic and political. Just as a worker is not an isolated individual in his place of employment but part of a factory social organization, so a union is but a link in the chain of organized activities of wage earners referred to as organized labor or the labor movement.

John R. Commons and his associates in the first thoroughgoing history of labor in the United States wrote: "We place the beginning of American labour movements in the year 1827 at Philadelphia. In that year and place American wage-earners for the first time joined together as a class, regardless of trade lines, in a contest with employers." [1] Prior to this time there were sporadic strikes and transient unions, but not until journeymen separated themselves from the masters' organizations and recognized the common interests of the workers in all trades did the unions join in a concerted movement for mutual protection and to challenge prerogatives of employers.

But no sooner had a trade union movement appeared than a political labor movement also developed. Within a year the Phila-

[1] Commons & Associates, *History of Labor in the United States* (New York, Macmillan, 1918), I, 25.

delphia Mechanics Union of Trade Associations turned itself into a Workingmen's Party, and similar parties spread through Pennsylvania, New York, and New England. This political movement lasted two or three years, but when business revived in the 1830s workers renewed and extended the trade union movement. The number of trade societies greatly increased; in more than a dozen cities they were combined in General Trades' Unions on the Philadelphia model, and by 1834 these formed a nation-wide delegate body known as The National Trades' Union. Disillusionment with the political ventures was reflected in the constitution of this organization which provided: "No party or political questions shall be agitated or acted upon in the union." But the revived union movement was as short-lived as the political movement. It disappeared in the Panic of 1837.

During the long depression that followed, what labor organizations there were took the form of mutual benefit societies, or "Protective Unions" which set up cooperative shops owned and operated by the workers, and they engaged also in cooperative buying and selling of goods needed by workers' families. There was no distinctly labor political movement, but philanthropists, intellectuals and social reformers promoted experiments in economic reorganization, established labor reform and land reform associations designed to uplift the working classes which enlisted support from wage earners. With the return of prosperity in the early 1850s, an exclusively trade-union movement revived, and for the rest of the century the earlier experience of alternating emphasis on trade unionism in prosperous periods and on mutual aid, politics, and cooperation during business recessions was repeated, only on a larger scale. But whatever the emphasis, the organizations were in the main short-lived.

Toward the end of the century, however, skilled craftsmen, finding they could improve their own conditions by trade union action separated themselves from the unskilled whose bargaining power was weak and who consequently looked to politics and social reform for amelioration. The craftsmen managed to establish relatively strong and stable national organizations of their trades which the earlier trade unionists had attempted but without success.

This became the typical form of union organization in the first two decades of the present century. And it remained for the industrial unionism following the great depression of 1930–33 to bring the unskilled and semiskilled within the fold of organized labor.

One effect of this development has been to unite under the aegis of organized labor the three lines of activity which formerly were considered substitutes for one another and tended to develop separate labor movements. Political action is now an essential part of labor unionism. Although cooperation has had little success in this country, due largely to mass production and chain stores, many unions sponsor consumers' cooperatives and provide various social services. Occasionally they still promote cooperative workshops. The tendency today is to make organized labor synonymous with the labor movement, whereas in the last century the political and cooperative movements were usually separate from the union movements and were generally inspired and led by intellectuals, social theorists, and reformers, rather than by union leaders.

THE LABOR MOVEMENT had its origin in the system of capitalist enterprise which created a class of free wage earners with a social status lower than that of their employers. Although there was free labor (as well as bound and slave labor) through most of the American colonial period, so long as masters and journeymen worked side by side, both were mechanics with little difference in social status. Local governments regulated both in the interest of consumers and to protect the trades. Journeymen became masters, masters went back to work as journeymen, both belonged to the same organizations to protect their common trades, and for fraternal purposes. Such organizations resembled the craft guilds of European countries;[2] they were not labor unions.

Merchant-capitalism was the first stage in the development of capitalist enterprise, and it produced the first labor movement in the United States. The merchant-capitalist who became the typical entrepreneur early in the nineteenth century was the catalyst who

[2] "In theory at least the medieval guild had united journeymen and masters, treating them not as fixed classes but as two stages in the development of any competent artisan." (Henri Hauser, "Journeymen's Societies" in *Encyclopedia of Social Sciences*, VIII, 425.)

separated the merchant function from the master workmen, turned him into a labor contractor or boss to whom he let out the production of finished goods. The boss was a managing employer.[3] He split crafts into parts, diluted the trade with less-skilled workers, created a labor force of wage earners. His profits came from the difference between what the merchant-capitalist paid him and what he paid to the workers. Journeymen's unions combined in strike movements to protect the standards and status of their crafts, and in political movements to secure legislation for the benefit of all workers. Merchant-capitalism developed a substage of jobber-capitalism when the contractor-boss became a foreman in a capitalist factory or a manufacturer on his own account who sold his products to a jobber-capitalist who maintained distribution organizations.

Employer-capitalism was ushered in when manufacturers broke the jobbers' control of markets by establishing their own distribution organizations and making credit available directly to their customers. The employer became both producer and distributor again as he was when he was a master-workman, but wage earners were further separated from those who employed them in income and social position. Nevertheless capital was generally raised in the locality where the factory was located, owners and employers usually lived in the same town with their employees, and their relations were to a certain extent governed by local community custom and opinion. Machines increasingly supplanted manual labor, and the proportion of unskilled and semiskilled workers greatly increased compared with the skilled. It has been said that merchant-capitalism arose with extension of markets and employer-capitalism out of technology.

Finance-capitalism began to succeed employer-capitalism when financial institutions started underwriting mergers of manufacturing establishments, transportation, and other businesses. Combinations and trusts multiplied rapidly, arousing public opinion against the dangers of monopoly. To get around the law which forbade

[3] "The first use I have found of the Dutch word 'Bos,' meaning manager of a group of workmen, is in the organ of the New York Trades' Union, 'The Man,' 1832, Vol. VI." (J. R. Commons, *Documentary History of American Industrial Society* [Cleveland, 1910], III, 43.)

combinations of competing establishments to restrict trade, the holding company device was developed. Investment bankers financed such companies to buy outright the plants and properties of various businesses. Thus have grown the factory branches, divisions, and subsidiaries of great parent corporations operating in many states. Headquarters of the corporations were moved to the financial centers of the country, and ownership became widely scattered among large numbers of shareholders who have as little say in the management of the companies as the great bodies of employees. Thus has developed what we know as Big Business which in turn has produced a labor movement characterized by Big Unions.

This is the dominant form of capitalism today. Enterprise is mainly private, but it is typically corporate enterprise, not individual enterprise.

Signs are not wanting, however, that a new stage of capitalism may be developing. The government first found it necessary to regulate public service corporations, then other big businesses, and more recently it has begun to regulate labor unions. It has established public corporations to develop river areas and power systems, provide public housing, and even to operate some businesses. The national government lends money to corporations through the Reconstruction Finance Corporation, and it controls credit through the Federal Reserve Board and the U.S. Treasury. It has practiced nationalization of industries when it took over and operated the railroads, coal mines, and some other businesses during the war as strikes threatened to tie them up. It has established marketing and price control organizations for dairy and other farm products. Cities own and operate transportation systems, states join in incorporating public port authorities. Such are the signs indicating that we may be at the threshold of a new stage perhaps "State Capitalism," certainly an economy in which government investment planning and control will play an increasingly important part.

As the different forms of capitalism developed the character of the labor movements has changed. Under merchant-capitalism union activity was stimulated mainly by reductions in pay, by attempts to protect the integrity of the mechanical trades, and by the desire to bolster the dignity and status of the trained mechanic. At the same time the unions agitated for legislation to ameliorate conditions of the unorganized factory and sweatshop workers. When unionism failed in the face of declining prices and depressions, political and cooperative movements were directed to the same ends. Free education, mechanics' training, restriction of "boy labor," abolition of prison labor, shorter working hours, and demands for easy access to the land were the main features of platforms designed to remove abuses, keep opportunities for self-employment open, afford the worker freedom of choice, and maintain his independence. Increasing poverty made attractive the theories and doctrines of social reformers, however contradictory, and workers joined intellectuals in movements for social and economic reorganization as these promised various utopias.

Through all the years of merchant-capitalism in the United States most wage earners did not give up their hope of becoming independent proprietors. But employer-capitalism dimmed that hope. Increasing numbers of workers began to feel that they were likely to spend their lives as wage earners. This feeling stimulated more permanent union organizations among them. But so long as there was free land, rapidly developing new small industries, and opportunities for wage earners to move up in the economic scale during periods of prosperity, the ideal of independent proprietorship pervaded the American labor movement.

It was not until free land had disappeared toward the end of the nineteenth century that a labor movement developed based on the outlook of workers who expected to remain wage earners throughout their working lives. Led by skilled craftsmen in nationally organized trades, this movement relied on unionism to raise the status of wage earners as a class rather than to create opportunities for individuals to get out of the class. It eschewed politics, except to protect the right to organize and to strike. It had no faith in producers' cooperatives as a way out of wage earning. The national craft unions grew in strength and numbers, and emerged as the dominant labor movement of the period of employer-capitalism.

Little progress was made, however, in organization of specialized machine workers and unskilled labor. A certain antagonism developed between the upper and lower grades of labor due in part to the predominance of immigrant workers and Negroes in the latter. The craftsmen found their own bargaining power weakened when they joined with the unskilled; they came to think these unorganizable. They distrusted the will and ability of immigrant and unskilled workers to maintain organizations strong enough for effective bargaining with employers. They disliked the tendency of such workers to espouse government legislation and social reform in preference to union laws for regulating wages and working conditions.

It remained for finance-capitalism to stimulate a labor movement bringing all grades of workers into the ranks of organized labor on a large scale. Industrial unions were necessary to accomplish this, and such organizations now include more members than those organized on a craft basis. There were large industrial unions both in the AFL and CIO, and many of the craft organizations have extended their jurisdiction to miscellaneous factory workers and unskilled labor. With this movement has come also increasing organization of white-collar workers and the lower grades of professional and supervisory employees. Many, such as factory clerks and minor supervisors, join the unions of manual workers in their industries; others whose work is more professional in nature have set up separate unions as independents or affiliated with workers' federations.

The movement toward big unionism could not get started, however, without the aid of the government. The great employing corporations were able to prevent unionization of mass production plants, first by direct suppression, then by welfare work and improved personnel management, and finally by offering them "something better"—company unions. Until the industrial collapse of 1930–33, unionism was practically confined to the traditional crafts and the smaller competitive industries. The depression, however, reduced skilled and unskilled workers, as well as salaried employees, closer to a common status. Then, although no formal political labor movement was organized, all labor rallied to the New Deal, and the government responded with legislation protecting workers' organizing rights against interference or coercion, outlawing company unions, and compelling employers to bargain collectively with bona fide labor organizations. Franklin Roosevelt's administration was referred to by friend and foe alike as a "Labor Government."

The new unions particularly were politically minded, but the older unions too, as they grew in numbers and strength, became more and more active in politics. All realize their dependence on a favorable administration in Washington. Thus began the combination of trade unionism with politics which achieved in 1938 the century-old goal of political labor movements—national legislation fixing maximum work hours. At the same time the most helpless workers were protected by a statutory minimum rate of pay, while time and a half for overtime was made mandatory for all workers from the lowest to the highest paid. Other legislation inaugurated a social insurance system against the hazards of unemployment and old age.

These effects of a labor movement adapted to finance-capitalism emphasize the trend mentioned above toward a government-directed economy. Whether this will be state-capitalism, socialism, or go by some other name, it promises to be marked by a government-directed economy with increasing public enterprise. Organized labor officially still avows its devotion to the private enterprise system, and many unions fear the effects of government ownership on their organizations and activities. But the pressure of the labor movement is toward more government control of business and prices, toward economic and social planning, and the use of government capital and credit to finance production facilities in order to maintain full employment. At the same time business and agricultural interests press for government financial aid to their own activities and regulation of organized labor, its policies and practices.

DESPITE THE TREND toward a unified American labor movement expressing the common outlook of wage earners and combining unionism with political action, the ideal of organic unity remains unachieved. Conflicts of interest among the unions often break out into open warfare; unions raid each other for members, engage in election contests for the right to act as sole collective bargaining agents, establish closed shops against members of other unions as well as nonunionists, and strike against each other in jurisdictional disputes. Within the individual organizations, too, divisions among the memberships are frequently occasioned by conflicts of interests and outlook similar to those that divide the national unions; various groups of workers strive for autonomy inside the unions, locals assert home-rule rights and quarrel about their jurisdiction.

Explanation of the continual divisions in a labor movement dedicated to the unity of all workers must be sought in the nature of labor unionism. Despite its traditional motto: "An injury to one is an injury to all" and its constant call, "Labor United," diversity and conflict persist. Seeking understanding of the union behavior, labor economists have classified and analyzed unions in two ways: according to their structure and according to their function. The time-honored classification distinguishes craft, industrial, and mixed or general labor unions. More significant are the "functional types" differentiated by Professor Hoxie: uplift or welfare unionism, business unionism, revolutionary unionism, and predatory unionism.

The first classification is based on the kinds of workers a union admits to membership, the second on the ends it seeks and the nature of its activities. Naturally the two are interrelated. Thus craft unions tend particularly to be marked by business unionism. Composed mainly of skilled mechanics, better paid and with a common apprentice training, they have found it relatively easy to organize, to win improvements from employers, to maintain set standards, and to regulate the conditions under which they will work. They have confidence that their goals of security and advancement can be secured by collective bargaining and strikes, and have little faith in movements for changing the economic or social order. They tend to favor private enterprise, look askance at government regulation of the labor bargain, and are usually content to deal with employers on a business basis.

Industrial unions, on the other hand, though also devoted to collective bargaining, customarily place greater emphasis on government legislation as a means of regulating and improving labor conditions, and they stress political action as a necessary union activity. The all-inclusive nature of their membership makes detailed working rules for their numerous occupations difficult, and the management of mass production industries necessarily exercises more control over work standards and operations than is possible in the trades where craftsmen prevail. Industrial unions therefore have less confidence in the sufficiency of collective bargaining to gain their ends. They tend to be reformist in their policies, are lukewarm about private enterprise, and not unfavorable to government ownership. They are more tolerant of admitting nonmanual workers to membership, readily accept guidance from intellectuals, and are more attractive to reformers, socialists, and revolutionaries.

Mixed or general labor unions are rare in the United States. Local unions of this type are often set up temporarily and attached directly to the AFL-CIO until the membership can be assigned to appropriate national unions. But when mixed or general unions are formally established on a national basis, they are apt to be revolutionary in character. Revolutionary unionism is little concerned with what union structure will be most effective for bargaining with employers. Its main interest is to unite people regardless of occupation or industry for the purpose of changing the economic or political system. To hold their following among union members revolutionary leaders must try to win improved conditions from the employers, but this is incidental to their primary purpose.

Uplift or welfare unionism and predatory unionism are hardly types at all. Mutual aid, insurance, education, and other welfare activities are features of every kind of labor union. In times past unions emphasized these features when their effectiveness as bargaining agencies was destroyed, and later "beneficial unions" were established as a sort of a camouflage to make them appear harmless when employer opposition was too strong for them. Company unions formed by employers also stressed uplift and welfare.

Racketeering and violence on occasion appear in the most respectable unions. These evils are not confined to labor organizations. They occur most frequently in trades where cutthroat competition prevails, particularly in cleaning and dyeing establishments, restaurants, building contracting, etc. Officials of employers' associations and union officers often join the practices in order to "police the industry," as they put it.

Some measure of violence, however, seems to be inherent in labor unionism. Peaceful picketing is protected by the courts as an exercise of freedom of speech or the press. But workers do not look upon picketing merely as a method of publicizing their side of the issues in a strike. In their own conversations and publications, picketing is regarded as a means of keeping "scabs" from going to work and struck plants shut down. Picket lines and particularly mass picketing make this purpose obvious. When strikers get into disputes with nonstrikers they do not always limit themselves to intellectual argumentation. On the other hand there is abundant evidence of employers hiring professional strike-breakers and thugs to beat up men on picket lines and active strike leaders. At times violent elements in unions have carried on a sort of guerrilla warfare against employers without thought of extortion. The MacNamara brothers case is an example. These officers of the Structural Iron Workers Union systematically dynamited properties of employers who fought unionization of employees. During the latter part of the last century anarchists in unions similarly conducted their campaigns of "propaganda by the deed."

The different types of unionism stem from unequal technological development of trades and industries and from variations in the social composition of the working forces. Different ethnic groups and the occupational groupings of employees on the basis of skill, training, and responsibility vary not only in their backgrounds, but in beliefs, sentiments, attitudes, and general outlook. Variations in economic opportunity among the groups have stirred clashes of interest between skilled and unskilled, immigrant and native labor, between Negro and white, men and women workers, and between migratory, homeless, workers and those with stakes in established communities. The conflict of interest and belief find expression in preferences for different forms of union organization, emphasis on different methods and goals of union activity.

But the habitual reactions to continuous order-taking create a common outlook and psychology among all those whose destiny is a life of wage working. The cleavages among laboring groups tend to narrow while the division between the managements and the labor forces grow wider and deeper. Organized labor becomes correspondingly stronger and more influential. The trend may be traced in the merging or amalgamation of unions, in their growing structural uniformity, and in the blending of different types of unionism in single organizations.

There are now few strictly craft unions. Most of them are multi-craft and semi-craft organizations, or they are semi-industrial or multi-industrial. Technological developments split old crafts, create new ones, specialize operations into quasi-trades, and increase the need for helpers and machine operators. Correspondingly craft unions split, new unions are created, then combined into amalgamated or federated organizations. In the process semi-skilled helpers and specialists, formerly excluded from craft unions, are admitted to membership. In time, unskilled labor working close to mechanics are also accepted. Thus have craft unions approached the industrial unions in composition and structure, and it becomes difficult to draw the line between them. The multiple names of many of the unions reflect the trend toward uniformity.[4]

Nevertheless the idea of craft unionism remains a fixed principle in the minds of many workers as does industrial unionism in others. But the conflict of principles tends more and more to be fought out between groups within the same union rather than between separate organizations built on different principles. Skilled workers and other differentiated groups within industrial and semi-industrial unions often complain that their interests are disregarded or subordinated by the majority of less-skilled mem-

[4] For example, Brotherhood of Boilermakers, Iron Ship Builders and Helpers of America; Molders and Foundry Workers Union; Brotherhood of Railway and Steamship Clerks, Freight Handlers, Express and Station Employes; United Automobile, Aircraft, and Agricultural Implement Workers; United Rubber, Cork, Linoleum, and Plastic Workers; Brewery, Flour, Cereal, Soft Drinks & Distillery Workers; Marble, Slate & Stone Polishers, Rubbers and Sawyers, Tile & Marble Setters, Helpers & Terrazzo Helpers.

bers. They struggle for autonomy and freedom to pursue their own policies, and usually some compromise is arranged between the minority groups and the larger majority.

Similarly the functional types of unionism are rarely to be found in a pure state in separate organizations. As Hoxie pointed out many years ago:

The conflict between functional types goes on within one and the same union organization, taking the form of a struggle for control between two or more factions holding vitally different social view points and interpretations. As a matter of fact this internal conflict is a characteristic feature of unions, and at any moment there is almost always some factional compromise and some practical admixture of functional type programs. Official union programs therefore rarely exist true to type.[5]

Today practically all American unions are basically business unions, that is to say their primary purpose is to make labor contracts with employers, to regulate the working conditions of their trades, occupations or industries, and to enforce uniform application of their rules by collective bargaining and strikes. While some are craft-minded and some industrial-minded because of their origin, most of them are expanding their memberships to include all grades of workers, and skill distinctions are subordinated to the necessity of providing equal protection for all members. At the same time most unions are also uplift or welfare organizations, pursuing workers' education programs, paying various kinds of benefits and insurance. Although few are openly revolutionary, some are controlled by Communist officers and leaders who at times divert the union bargaining and strike techniques to their propaganda and political purposes. Other unions are led by socialists whose revolutionary social doctrines appeal to many members. But the foundation of all union organizations today is business unionism which provides the resources and the mass support for effective pursuit of larger programs. The American organized labor movement, in its maturity, does not recognize as coming within its fold any organization that is not at bottom a bona fide bargaining or business union.

[5] Robert F. Hoxie, *Trade Unionism in the United States* (New York, Appleton, 1917), p. 70.

ALTHOUGH the organized labor movement arose with capitalism and has changed its forms and programs with the changes in capitalist enterprise, there is no reason to believe that it will disappear should any other economic system come to prevail. So long as industry will require labor forces of wage earners and salaried employees regimented and directed by management staffs, we are likely to have some kind of unionism and labor movement, regardless of whether enterprise is private or public, free or controlled, or who owns the industries. Organized labor may not remain free, as experience in other countries has shown, but it will be organized. Free unions will doubtless continue to alter their objectives and structures as new economic and political developments make this necessary; others will have their goals and functions changed for them.

Even totalitarian states have their unions and labor movements. Just as modern dictators find it necessary to legitimize their rule by something like a vote of the people, so their governments feel the need of an organized labor movement as a pillar of the state. Nazi Germany had its labor front, Fascist Italy its corporate labor organizations, and Soviet Russia has its plant, regional, and all-Russian trade unions integrated as part of the apparatus of Communist government. Dictatorships do not get rid of organized labor; they take it over, liquidate its leaders, and transform it into an agency of the state. Like the company unions which our industrial corporations sponsored before they were outlawed, these government labor organizations promise workers something preferable to outside or disloyal unions, and emphasize promotion of management production programs as the main function of labor unionism.

On the other hand in Great Britain and the Scandinavian and Low Countries where democratic institutions are treasured, Labor and Socialist political parties backed by organized labor have become the governing parties and have attempted to maintain free unionism while nationalizing key industries and pursuing programs of economic planning and gradual social reorganization. Such labor governments consider their goals of "social democracy" as the only practical alternative to Communism, and a good part of the world agrees with them. "I shall make a government of Laborite orientation," said President Getulio Vargas of Brazil in an interview, "on the example of what is occurring today in some of the most civilized and advanced countries of the world. I refer specially to England and the Scandinavian countries . . . , which are considered nations of model organization." [6]

But these labor governments have found it necessary to regulate and control union activities to an extent still considered incompatible with free unionism by American organized labor. The right to strike has been restricted, compulsory arbitration imposed by law, and directly or indirectly free collective bargaining for increased wages is discouraged by the governments because of its upsetting effects on the planned economic programs. Under such governments, the labor organizations are not united in opposing compulsory arbitration and determination of wages and working conditions by public authorities, doubtless because the governments are considered favorable to the workers. But whether self-governing unions can survive if the goals of socialized industry and planned economy are achieved—even though the countries are ruled by labor or social democratic (socialist) parties—remains a serious question. Communist totalitarian governments, too, identify workers' interests with their own, and rule in the name of labor.

In our own as in other countries, organized labor's relations with the national government have been changing. Within the last two decades we have seen free unionism and collective bargaining first extended by government action and then subjected to the restrictions and controls of the Taft-Hartley Law. The power of the State grows as a vigorous labor movement challenges the strength and influence of great employing corporations controlled by financial institutions. When Big Labor is pitted against Big Business in giant struggles that paralyze basic industries and public services, the government cannot stand idly by. Restoration of the use of court injunctions in labor disputes and damage suits against unions has solidified union organizations for political

[6] New York *Times*, October 14, 1950, p. 7. Vargas had previously become President by revolution and ruled for five years pretty much as a dictator. This time he was legally chosen in a free election, vowing his devotion to democracy.

action, and both labor and management reach for governmental authority to aid them in their struggles.

The government responds by aiding first one of the contestants and then the other. It grows stronger in the process, taking on new functions and powers. When it helps business, labor accuses it of fostering price fixing, promoting monopolies, increasing profits and the sway of wealth. When it helps labor with old age pensions, unemployment insurance, minimum wage laws, and full employment policies, business accuses it of undermining the free enterprise system and promoting the Welfare State. As agriculture becomes more and more commercialized it develops the need for increasing numbers of seasonal and migratory farm wage earners, and its labor relationships take on the character of industrial relations. Big Business enters the field and insists on importation of alien labor to meet the need, as improved conditions of industrial employment drains the supply. Organized labor, finding it difficult to enroll these workers in unions, demands government legislation in their behalf—to protect their right to organize, to legalize union or closed shops, to fix minimum wages and maximum hours for them, to provide decent housing and safeguard their health, and to extend the benefits of social security legislation to them.

Thus the government becomes increasingly involved in the detailed problems of labor and management, and as it strengthens the position of one vis-a-vis the other, it tends to subject both to increasing regulation and control. The necessities of war production and, since the Korean War, of defense production, with their controls of prices and wages, have of course accelerated these tendencies.

In addition the government's proprietary functions, its publicly owned corporations, its power and atomic energy authorities, housing, transportation and other public enterprises are expanding, making it a large-scale employer of labor in its own right. The management of its enterprises involves it in disputes with employees and the unions that represent them similar to those in privately owned industries, but it can hardly act as a neutral between labor and management in such cases; and strikes against public enterprises are strikes against the government, much more serious than those against privately owned public service corporations. At the same time unionism among public employees is growing, and as organized labor becomes an increasingly important factor in the political life of the nation, its relations with the government take on a character not unlike those between the labor movements of West European countries which have laborite or social democratic governments.

IN THE UNITED STATES, then, as in other countries, a continuous and growing organized labor movement has now been established committed to both trade union and political action which is powerful enough to influence and direct changes in the national economic and governmental system. And its growth and success in winning its goals, together with the efforts of the opposition movements it stimulates, necessarily increases the power of the state, not only over business corporations and agricultural associations, but over labor organizations as well.

What are the portents of these developments? Promising? Threatening? Or what?

"The American economy," says the far-seeing Professor Slichter, "is a laboristic economy, or at least is rapidly becoming one. By this I mean that employees are the most influential group in the community and that the economy is run in their interest more than in the interest of any other economic group. A community composed almost entirely of employees must be expected to have its own distinctive culture—its own scales of value, its own industrial institutions, its own public policies, and its own jurisprudence. The fact that employees are supplanting businessmen as the most influential group in the community means that basic and far-reaching changes are impending in the civilization of the United States. Employees have great and growing influence, because three out of four persons who work for a living in the United States are employees, and less than one out of four are self-employed." [7]

But as labor strives to supplant business as the most influential interest in the nation, organized business does not stand idly by. Both seek favorable laws and a favorable government administra-

[7] Sumner H. Slichter, *The American Economy* (New York, Knopf, 1948), pp. 7–8.

tion to safeguard and advance its position. In the contest between them freedom becomes the stake, not merely freedom for the employees as organized labor thinks, or freedom for business enterprise and management as employers claim, but free government and individual freedom for all. Will we in the United States find a better solution for this major problem of Western civilization than European countries have been able to devise, one that is more in keeping with our democratic institutions and traditional concepts of individual liberty?

We cannot stop the rising power of organized wage earners and salaried workers, though it may be retarded from time to time. The prophetic words of De Tocqueville written just a hundred years ago, and so largely fulfilled, must not be forgotten. In the preface to the twelfth edition of his classic *Democracy in America,* he wrote: "There will be found on every page a solemn warning that society changes its forms, humanity its condition, and that new destinies are impending. Would it be wise to imagine that a social movement the causes of which lie so far back can be checked by the efforts of one generation? Can it be believed that the democracy which has overthrown the feudal system and vanquished kings will retreat before tradesmen and capitalists?"

Humanity is indeed changing its condition and a new destiny is pending. But what kind of destiny is ahead for us? If "the democracy" to which De Tocqueville referred is today the wage earners and salaried workers of the country, what changes are they likely to bring about when they are united for effective action and triumph as a majority? As organized labor pursues its drive to equalize the status of employees with those of employers and managers, and for a dominating place in the government of the nation, what kind of rule does it promise? What economic orderings and new social arrangements may we expect? Toward what kind of society are we moving?

Some see the centralization of power in the national government resulting from the pressures of nation-wide labor organizations leading us to state capitalism, socialism, or communism. Others say we are becoming a laboristic society or a Welfare State as the proportion of employees in the population grows and increasing public provision is made for their economic security and material well-being. These names, however, tell us little about the destiny of the individual, whether he be wage earner, salaried worker, supervisor, manager, or what. Whatever form the economy or the government toward which we are moving may take, will the individual be a freer person, or even as free as he has managed to be up to the present? Will his personal freedom be enlarged by greater opportunities for choosing his own career, for intellectual cultivation and freedom to think and express himself according to his own convictions? In his economic organizations and in government will he enjoy free elections, civil liberties, equal protection of the laws, inviolability of the person, and other such characteristics of what Americans consider democratic institutions?

If we were to judge by the lip service given to the word "democracy," the whole world would seem to be striving for more and more of it. But apparently democracy can be all things to all men, for everywhere it is being prefixed by an adjective. So we hear of economic democracy, industrial democracy, people's democracy, and so on. What kind of democracy, then, is it reasonable to expect if, as seems probable, labor supplants business as the dominant interest in the nation, as in its turn years ago business supplanted agricultural interests? We turn, therefore, to review in a general way the concepts and practices of union democracy.

IV

UNION DEMOCRACY

ORGANIZED LABOR sums up the ends for which it strives as "industrial democracy," and the term is variously used to refer to its own internal government, to the industrial governments set up by union agreements with employers, and to its general political ideal, "free unions under a free government."

That labor unionism in the United States is an expression of the American democratic spirit working itself out in industry is hardly to be doubted. Its beginnings coincided with the period when the free colonies were establishing state governments, and the principles of the federal Constitution were subjects of great political debate. It developed stretch in Jefferson's administration, and grew to a full-fledged labor movement during the presidency of Andrew Jackson. Workmen's clubs, unions, were part of the movement of "Republican-Democratic Societies" which marked "the Rise of National Democracy" in the early decades of the nineteenth century.

The American ideal that swept away the vestiges of government by an elite class also freed wage workers of property qualifications for voting, and of court restraints on their freedom of association. The same democratic movements that fashioned the ideas and methods of establishing the nation as a government of, by, and for the people also gave rise to trade unionism as a means by which worker self-government and participation in the government of workplaces might be achieved. "When the full story of self-government in America is written, . . . pages on the cellular growth of local craft unions will be placed beside the records of town meetings; while chapters on the formation of national labor structures will complement the sections on the origin and development of the federal Constitution." [1]

But trends in the development of American labor organizations suggest the query whether this democratic spirit may not be lost in the process by which organized labor achieves its goals. The effects of unionism are undoubtedly to democratize industrial management in the sense that autocratic powers of employers are restricted by rules and regulations negotiated with representatives of the workers. Management of employees becomes a government of laws instead of an absolute government with arbitrary authority. There are indications, however, that the participation of the workers in this government is hardly free and untrammelled. The union which represents them, and through which they share in the rule-making power, may itself be undemocratic and disregard individual freedom and rights of employees.

If labor organizations also exercise autocratic powers over their members, then workers may merely be substituting dictatorial rule of union officials for the arbitrary authority of the employer or his managers. Does "industrial democracy" tend to maintain the traditions and liberties of American democratic government, or is it moving in the direction of what in other countries is called "people's democracy"? Increasingly, as organized labor grows in power and influence, questions are being asked as to the kind of democracy that is being furthered by the economic and political programs of union organizations.

"In the Anglo-Saxon world of today," the Webbs wrote more than half a century ago, "we find trade Unions are democracies: that is to say, their internal constitutions are all based on the principle of 'government of the people by the people and for the people.' . . . These thousands of working-class democracies spontaneously growing up at different times and places, untrammelled by the traditions or interest of other classes, perpetually recasting their constitutions to meet new and varying conditions, present an unrivaled field of observation as to the manner in which the

[1] Charles A. Beard, *Rise of American Civilization* (New York, Macmillan, 1929), p. 214.

working man copes with the problem of combining administrative efficiency with popular control." [2]

But Robert Hoxie, writing in the United States two decades later, found it necessary to distinguish between the effects of labor organizations on industry and the nature of their internal government. He observed: "While unionism in its ultimate effect on industrial organization and conduct of industry is democratic . . . unionism in its own organization and conduct is hardly to be called democratic." He quoted a union leader: "As a democracy no union would last six minutes." [3] More recently another union leader, well known and with much experience, wrote: "What they [the leaders] find is that to a certain extent democracy in [union] management is unworkable and often detrimental to the interests of the workers." Many of them would prefer democracy "if they could make it work." [4]

If it is indeed true that democracy in union government and administration is unworkable, can we then reasonably expect that such organizations could be the means of achieving the democratic ends? John Dewey remarks in his *Human Nature and Conduct* that of no other engine than the human do we expect perfect products to be turned out by defective machines. "Everywhere else we recognize that the design and structure of the agency employed tells directly upon the work done." However much union aims and programs may be directed toward democracy in industry and in the state, could organized labor's efforts produce these results if its own governmental machinery operated on undemocratic principles?

Little study has been given to the relation between the internal government of union organizations and the ultimate effects of labor unionism on industry and on individual freedom. Most students of organized labor in America have accepted the Webb's view that unions are essentially democracies, though they often criticize undemocratic tendencies "in some unions." The aims of

[2] Sidney and Beatrice Webb, *Industrial Democracy* (London, Longmans, Green, 1897), Preface to first edition.

[3] Hoxie, *Trade-Unionism in the United States* (New York, Appleton, 1928), p. 180.

[4] Quoted in Herman Feldman, *Problems in Labor Relations* (New York, Macmillan, 1937), p. 245.

unionism being to democratize industry, and its effects working in this direction, it has generally been assumed that the means used —the labor organizations—must necessarily also be democratic. "Unions are the most democratic organizations in the world" says an editorial in *The Pilot,* official paper of the National Maritime Union. This is generally the public position of organized labor, though many leaders may be convinced that it is necessary to forego democracy in the organizations in order to achieve their democratic ends.

THAT AUTOCRATIC arrangements and practices are to be found in union organizations is, of course, generally known; but these are commonly considered exceptions—undemocratic spots such as are to be found in all democratic governments. Public opinion also shares this view. Despite its condemnation of "labor czars," denial of individual members' rights, and other union abuses, it feels that freedom of workers to combine in labor organizations is somehow connected with the maintenance of democratic political institutions. No better proof of this public feeling is needed than the policy of the United States in defeated Italy, Germany, and Japan.

Among the first steps taken to build democracy in the former Nazi and Fascist countries was to proclaim freedom for workers to form and join unions. Revival of suppressed free labor movements was stimulated, and organization of new self-governing unions encouraged. Apparently the framers of the policy felt that democracy could not be built in those countries without unions like those that thrive under free governments. American military governments and the Economic Cooperation Administration (Marshall Plan) continue to pursue this policy with practically no public opposition. The fact that the Taft-Hartley Law of 1947 continued the legal protections of the right of workers to organize contained in the Wagner Act of 1935, though it gave some counterrights to employers, was a reflection of the same public feeling.

But while there is general approval of the organization of labor in principle, there is at the same time much public uneasiness about unions establishing "labor monopolies," restricting "the right to work," arbitrary power of "union bosses," discriminatory

and other undemocratic practices within the unions. This uneasiness is to some extent stimulated by employer opposition to
unions and by newspapers which reflect management viewpoints.
But it is not confirmed to people who are influenced by antiunion
propaganda or by their own economic interests. It extends to those
who are sincere "friends of organized labor," to disinterested labor
economists, and to many union members as well.

For example, in 1943 the American Civil Liberties Union in
the course of protecting civil rights was confronted with appeals
from trade union members to test in the courts suspensions or
expulsions from unions for criticism of union officials or denial of
the democratic right to oppose the union's administration. "To
these complainants the exercise of their rights as members of unions
was even more important than their rights as citizens," said the
ACLU, "for it involved the conduct of their unions in relation to
their livelihood." [5] Concerned that the "continuing complaints of
autocratic practices" furnish ammunition to the "enemies of trade
unions," this organization appointed a committee to study union
practices and to suggest remedies for undemocratic procedures.

The committee's 1943 report listed and analyzed arbitrary practices, and made recommendations designed to promote democracy
within labor organizations. It concluded: "American trade unions
are doubtless growing more democratic. This growth is not uniform; there are unfortunate and glaring exceptions. In many
unions democratic growth is by no means compatible with their
strength and power. Democratic standards, while general, are not
sufficiently strong to furnish the friends of trade-unions with un-
questioning assurance regarding the future."

If indeed the organizations are really growing more democratic,
and if, as the committee added, autocratic practices are merely
"exceptions to the generally democratic methods of most unions,
then additional assurance as to the future would hardly be necessary." The committee assumed but offered no evidence of a trend
toward more democracy. Its inquiry was limited to "typical instances involving individual rights and liberties," and did "not

[5] *Democracy in Trade-Unions*—A survey with a program of action (American
Civil Liberties Union, New York, 1943), p. 7, 9. But see later reports in 1949 and
1952.

deal with all undemocratic practices in trade unions." The opinion of the committee hardly squared with the recommendations in the report and its proposals for legislation to regulate internal union affairs submitted by the Civil Liberties Union to Congressional committees.[6] There may be as much reason to believe that union governments are tending toward less as toward more democratic rule.

It is true that restrictions on admission of new members by "closing the books," by high initiation fees, and unreasonable limitations on the number of apprentices are being relaxed. The policy of monopolizing work opportunities for relatively small groups of organized workers is giving way to programs of "organizing the unorganized." It is true also that discrimination against women, foreign-born workers, and Negroes is also gradually being eliminated from union constitutions and rituals. Such restrictions have been particularly characteristic of skilled craftsmen's unions, and as these extend their jurisdiction to include less-skilled workers, the tendency to remove discrimination grows. To gain their ends, unions now seek strength in all inclusive numbers rather than in monopolizing opportunities for groups of favored workers.

In these respects, progress toward more equality in unions seems to be steady, although much remains to be done.[7] The same cannot

[6] House Committee on Education and Labor: Hearings on bills to amend National Labor Relations Act, 80th Congress, 1st session, pp. 3633–43 (1947). The same proposals were submitted in March, 1949, to a subcommittee headed by Representative Jacobs of Indiana which was investigating undemocratic practices in unions.

[7] Elimination of discrimination on account of race, color, sex, and nationality is not necessarily a sign of increasing democracy. The totalitarian "people's democracies" of eastern Europe pride themselves on equal treatment of all races and nationalities. They discriminate only against those who think wrong! Such governments may well find inconvenient social and economic distinctions that arise out of the prejudices of the population. Their concern is that there shall be no deviation from official doctrines or policy, no opposition to the ruling power, no unorthodox individuals or groups questioning or departing from the course of action adopted by the rulers. So in unions which have concentrated power in their national officials, equality of the sexes, races, and nationalities is apt to be emphasized as they come to consider opposition to the administration the most serious offense. This is particularly true of Communist controlled unions. It is also noticeable that the organizations in which rank and file control is more effective are slowest in eliminating racial and similar discrimination.

be said of membership control of union affairs, however. The evidence of lessening popular control is not definitive. It is mixed with contrary currents, and must be extracted, weighed, and considered in connection with the normal functioning of union governments and the changes worked in its constitutional structure by informal as well as formal action. This we attempt in later chapters; only a general indication of the nature of the evidence can be given here.

As unions have grown in membership and in the territory and occupations they cover, and as they have taken on new functions, the relations between the officialdom of the organizations and their members have become more and more like those between the government of a nation and its people, or between the management of a great corporation and its stockholders and employees. Like the State, the union becomes something of an abstraction. No longer can the typical union and its membership be identified as one and the same, as it could be when action of the organization was directed by the members in the manner of a small town meeting. The officials to whose care the institutions of unionism are entrusted tend to value and conserve interests of the organizations above those of the individual members. The union must be safeguarded, perpetuated, even at the cost of sacrificing those who happen to be members at any time. The permanent interests of the union often conflict with immediate interests of individuals and groups of members; and the life of officials grows apart from that of the workers they represent.

With these trends the problems of union democracy grow and become more complex. Settling differences between officials and rank and file by discussion and compromise becomes more difficult, and debate takes valuable time. Impatience with the delays of democratic procedures leads to arbitrary action, especially in the face of real or imagined emergencies. Thus the Civil Liberties Union Committee reported: "The chief complaints by rank and file members concern lack of opportunity for full participation in the conduct of a union's affairs, tending to the perpetuation in office of entrenched officials; the difficulty of organizing an opposition to the leadership; the lack of adequate machinery for review of expulsions and suspensions; the penalties imposed by varied means on critics of the leadership; the lack of control over expenditures and assessments in many unions; discrimination in assignment of jobs; and exclusions from membership based on race, sex, or political connections."

But it must not be assumed that the leadership alone is responsible for these objects of complaint. Rank and file majorities are not free from guilt. The progress that has been made in removing race and sex discrimination in recent years has been largely stimulated by union officers, often against formidable rank and file opposition. Some union conventions have voted down proposals for removing bars against Negroes and for affording them equal treatment within the organization; and local union meetings have resisted the changes after they have been approved by national conventions. On the other hand convention delegates elected by local memberships have been generous in conferring arbitrary authority on national officers by constitutional provision and resolutions.

In 1946, the Theatrical Stage Employees, involved in a jurisdictional dispute in the motion picture industry, gave its president "full power to act in the Hollywood situation to add, alter, or amend any portion of the constitution or by-laws he deems necessary." This was considered an emergency. But all unions face emergencies from time to time, and the tendency is to leave it to the executive to determine what is an emergency. Beginning with temporary authorizations or with convention approval of acts already taken, exercise of summary powers thus becomes one of the usages of the office, and sometimes formally legalized by constitutional provision.

Whenever in the opinion of the president of the Musicians' Union an emergency exists:

He is authorized and empowered to promulgate and issue executive order, which shall be conclusive and binding upon all members and/or locals; any such order may by its terms (a) enforce the Constitution, By-Laws, Standing Resolutions, or other laws, . . . or (b) may annul and set aside same or any portion thereof (except financial provisions) and substitute therefore other and different provisions of his own making . . . the power so to do is hereby made absolute in the President when, in his opinion, such orders are necessary to conserve and safeguard the interests of the Federation, the locals and/or members; and the said power shall in like manner extend to and include cases where existing laws are inadequate or provide no method of dealing with a situation.[8]

All laws so passed [by the convention of this union] must be referred to the Executive Board and chairman of convention committees who may sanction or veto same, their action to be final.[9]

The Operating Engineers vest their president "with unlimited discretion in the application and administration of his powers and duties." [10] These include "all the administrative powers of the organization, [and] to interpret the provisions of the Constitution and decide questions of law arising there under." Specifically he is also given full power to suspend or remove local unions, local officers, or members "whenever in his opinion the best interests of the organization require it, or [they] shall be deemed by him to be incompetent, negligent, or to have failed in carrying out their respective duties." He is also empowered to appoint local officers in place of those he has suspended or removed. In addition he is vested with such "other powers and duties as the General Executive Board may from time to time specifically delegate to him." [11]

The authority of the national executives to suspend and discipline local unions, district, and other subordinate organizations and their officers is a necessary one. Most union constitutions so provide, and if accompanied by requirements of due process of law, there can be no objections to such provisions on democratic grounds. A tendency is noticeable, however, to subordinate due process to the opinion or judgment or discretion of the executive. Thus, among the powers of the president of the Brotherhood of Electrical Workers, are the following:

[8] Constitution, By-Laws and Policy, American Federation of Musicians (1949), Art. I, p. 19.

[9] Constitution, Art. V, p. 8.

[10] Constitution of the International Union of Operating Engineers (adopted 1938, as amended in 1940 and 1944), Art. VI, pp. 19–21.

[11] Similar powers and duties are conferred on the president of the Hod Carriers and Building Laborers' Union by its constitution. These and a long list of definite duties were spelled out in the constitution after New York courts had ruled in a series of cases that the previous instrument did not authorize the president to set aside the autonomy of local unions. (Rodier v. Huddell, 332 App. Div. 531, 250 N.Y. 336; Rowan v. Possehl, 173 Misc. 898; 18 NYS [2d] 574, 1940.)

To suspend the cards and membership of any member who, in his judgment, is working against the welfare of the [Brotherhood] . . . , or for creating dissension among members or among Local Unions. . . . .

To take charge of the affairs of any Local Union when in his judgment such is necessary to promote or advance the interests of its members and the (Brotherhood).[12]

Similarly, the Carpenters' constitution provides: "Whenever, in the judgment of the General President, subordinate bodies or the members thereof are working against the best interests of the United Brotherhood, or not in harmony with the Constitution and Laws of the United Brotherhood, the General President shall have power to order said body to disband under penalty of suspension." [13] The Teamsters' President has similar constitutional authority. When he "has or receives information which leads him to believe that any officers of a local union are dishonest or incompetent, or that the organization is not being conducted for the benefit of the trade, he may appoint a trustee to take charge of and control of the affairs of the local." [14]

A grateful convention of the International Longshoremen's Association has virtually permitted life tenure for its president. To make this possible the constitutional limitation to a four year term for all officers was amended by adding: "except as may be otherwise provided, with respect to any particular officer, at the convention at which he is elected." [15]

Although all national officers of the United Mine Workers are elected by referendum vote of the members, the president of this union "may suspend or remove any National Officers or appointed employee for insubordination or just and sufficient cause." Most constitutions, including the Miners', provide for trials of such officers upon charges of delinquency or malfeasance, but since this union broke the ground in giving its president summary powers to remove popularly chosen officers, other unions have been following its example. The suspended or removed officers do have a right of appeal to the executive board, but in

[12] Constitution, International Brotherhood of Electrical Workers (as amended 1941), Art. IV, p. 9.
[13] Carpenters' Constitution (adopted 1941, as amended 1944), p. 11.
[14] Constitution (1940), Art. VI, p. 19.   [15] Constitution (1943), Art. VIII, p. 12.

the Miners' Union that board meets when convened by the president (except when a majority of its members authorize the secretary-treasurer to convene it),[16] and there is little chance that the board, with Mr. John L. Lewis presiding, would reverse Mr. Lewis.

With respect to the appointing power of the unions' chief executives, the tendency is to remove requirements of review or restrictions of his authority. In early years this power was often limited by constitutional provision fixing the number of organizers, representatives, and other employees in the national union, or by requiring convention authorization of additions to staff. Later it became customary for the union's executive board to determine the size of the employed staff and to approve appointments and dismissals. Now there is a distinct trend toward making the president's appointing power absolute, to leave him free to decide how many employees or staff members the union needs, and to hire and discharge at will. He is being authorized, in other words, to decide for himself the amount and character of the patronage at his disposal.

The United Steelworkers' constitution, for example, empowers its president "to appoint, direct, suspend, or remove such organizers, representatives, agents, and employees as he may deem necessary." Although this constitution is modeled on that of the older United Mine Workers, which also authorizes the president to appoint and remove as he deems necessary, the steel union made a significant change toward eliminating control of the appointing power. It omitted the provision of the miners that "all appointments suspensions and removals . . . shall be approved by the Executive Board," and made subject to such approval only the appointees' compensation which the president fixes.[17] The Electrical Workers' Brotherhood, in its 1941 constitution, made no provision for approval or consent of either appointments, or com-

[16] Constitution (1944), Art. IX, Sec. 30. Elsewhere the constitution states that the president "may in his discretion" travel in this country and abroad "for the purpose of conserving his health," among other reasons, with all expenses paid including "full and complete maintenance of his wife . . . and all secretarial help and services he deems necessary . . ." But this constitutional provision applies "only to the present incumbent."

[17] Constitution (1944), Art. IV, Sec. 7.

pensation by its executive council. And this practice was followed by the International Longshoremen's Association, the Hod Carriers and Building Laborers, and some other organizations.

Accompanying this trend toward granting unrestricted appointing powers to chief executives is another new development which is particularly useful in building a patronage machine. Persons not eligible to membership because they lack the ordinary trade or industrial qualifications become eligible by virtue of the fact that they have been put on the organization's payroll by the president. For many years the general counsel of the CIO was secretary of its powerful Convention Committee on Resolutions, and he exerted great influence on the policies of that organization as well as of the United Steelworkers whom he also served as counsel.

As a lawyer he would not be eligible for membership in the Steelworkers' Union, since he was not an employee doing iron, steel, or similar work. But he could become a member under the following additional clause in the union's constitution: "Staff representatives or employees of the International Union are eligible." [18] Being a member he was eligible for election as delegate both to the union's and to CIO conventions, and it would not be surprising if he had a good deal to do with adding this provision to the eligibility qualifications for membership. Other unions have also adopted the policy of authorizing those employed by the organizations to become members on an equal basis with those who work in the industry. With the increasing employment of attorneys, labor economists, researchers, accountants, publicity men, legislative representatives, and other staff employees—usually appointed by the union executives—it can easily be seen how the power and influence of the officers over the membership tends to grow.

THE AUTHORIZED extraordinary powers exercised by union executives are not to be confused with mere abuses like racketeering. They are of profounder significance. Something like government by decree is established by constitutional or legislative action, or by administrative practice, apparently with the consent of the

[18] Constitution, Art. III.

governed. It is to be noted also that union constitutions almost universally do not provide for an independent judiciary, but lodge the judicial power in the membership at local meetings and in the higher executives, with final appeal to the national conventions. This primitive judicial system inevitably mixes political considerations into trials and decisions. It tends to build powers in the executive superior even to those of the convention in which all powers of the union are usually lodged.

Union constitutions often make it an offense against the organizations, punishable by fines or expulsion with consequent loss of jobs, for members to create dissension, work against the interests of the union, slander an officer, act dishonorably, or do anything to injure the union or the labor movement. Many prohibit members and local unions from circulating material about union affairs without permission of the chief executives. Such provisions are relics of the days when unions were small and weak, and copied many of the features of fraternal benefit associations. But the vaguely defined offenses, which seemed appropriate in earlier days, linger on in the laws of great nation-wide labor organizations, and are easily used to suppress legitimate criticism, to get rid of troublesome opposition, and to deny civil rights to dissenting individuals or groups within the unions.

These tendencies are too deeply rooted to be reversed by mere warnings from friends that they "furnish ammunition to the enemies of trade unions." Nor are they likely to be anything but intensified by legislation to "curb the power of labor bosses." When the president of the Musicians' Union was questioned about his unlimited powers by a congressional committee, which was considering legislation aimed directly against his activities,[19] the union responded in characteristic fashion. A thousand delegates representing the entire membership, in convention assembled, resolved to "give our President a sincere vote of confidence, . . . concur in all former acts of our honored President, . . . [and] we pray that the rich blessings of God Almighty be upon him, giving him strength, wisdom, and understanding that

[19] The Lea Bill, enacted into law in 1948, was later declared unconstitutional by the Supreme Court.

he might continue the great work before him." They denounced "the enemies of organized labor, the press and syndicated newspapers and periodicals, who have sought along with many others high in the government of our country, to discredit his acts."

Such approval and support of arbitrary authority for the union president can hardly be due merely to his own efforts to build up his power. It is too common in labor organizations to doubt that the rank and file of union members do not share the feeling of the leaders that dictatorial rule is often necessary for their protection and advancement. Yet the usual explanation of undemocratic practices in unions run in terms of a drive for autocratic powers on the part of many labor leaders. Something in the conditions of labor leadership is supposed to make them want to be dictatorial bosses.

This explanation is at best only a partial one. While labor leadership has its special problems, the personal qualities of the men who rise to the top in organized labor do not differ essentially from those that lead to dominating influence in politics, in business, or in community life generally. Plenty of ex-labor leaders have achieved commanding positions as business executives and political leaders. The drive for power is not limited to union leaders; and our familiar political bosses, business barons, and labor bosses are brothers under the skin. If the power motive of labor executives were the only factor leading to undemocratic methods in unions, there might be no more reason to question the fundamentally democratic character of organized labor than there is to doubt the essential democracy of American political institutions because of the autocratic rule of political bosses in many of our large cities, or the denial of civil rights in some sections of the country.

The behavior and attitudes of the rank and file of organized labor may be responsible for as serious threats to freedom and democracy in union organizations as the desires of labor leaders for autocratic powers. Perhaps it is because of an assumption that what majorities do is necessarily democratic that most students of labor organizations consider undemocratic practices in unions exceptional. What is usually overlooked in centering attention on autocratic practices of union leaders is the evidence that they often protect rights and liberties of individual members against intolerant majorities. In the course of their duties as judicial appeal agencies, union presidents and executive boards frequently reverse arbitrary and prejudiced decisions made by majorities in local unions, or by local officials with majority approval. Partly ignorance, and partly the prejudice of the rank and file against individuals who vary from type, often lead some members in local meetings to disregard procedural requirements, deny fair hearings, arbitrarily find men guilty of offenses, and impose drastic penalties. Moreover, the feelings of apprehension which most workers have for the safety of their unions makes them impatient of dissent which seems to threaten the unity of the membership.

The executive board of the United Steelworkers found it necessary in 1946 to adopt a resolution emphasizing that it was not obligatory on individual members to support political candidates indorsed by the union. Apparently the top officials were concerned about attempts of local organizations to discipline members for not going along with the political recommendations of the union. Similarly, race and nationality discrimination by local majorities are not uncommon despite prohibitions in union constitutions and contrary to the orders of national officers. And members of local unions, fearing increased competition for available jobs, continue attempts to restrict admission of new members after such practices are forbidden by the constitutions of the national organizations.

The rank and file admire and rather prefer "strong" leaders who win victories for the workers without being squeamish about constitutional authority to exercise the powers they deem necessary. Such leaders "bring home the bacon," and the members are content to leave to them the determination of policies and actions of the union. So long as the leaders keep the union strong, raise wages, or secure other gains, the members are usually content to follow them in whatever direction they want to go. If in the process, these leaders ruthlessly suppress opposition, there is little protest. Like an army at war, the membership feels the need of united support of its commanders in their battles with employers.

Thus, masses of American workers with no particular social philosophy loyally back up "rightist" leaders like John Lewis of the miners and William Hutcheson of the Carpenters, or "leftist" leaders likes James Matles and Julius Emspak of the United Electrical Workers, and Harry Bridges of the West Coast Longshoremen.

In so far as union officers exercise autocratic powers, whether by constitutional authority or by administrative assumption, the rank and file appear no less willing to grant them than the officials to have them. This is not to say that leaders are not responsible for undemocratic trends in unions, but to direct attention to the equal if not greater responsibility of the memberships. They are not as unwilling followers as the common criticisms of labor bosses imply. When the conditions are examined that make both leaders and rank and file behave as they do, it becomes quite doubtful that democratic standards are as general as the friends of trade unions believe; and the portents of popular control of unions' governments do not appear as promising as these friends see them. One may well wonder whether such loyalty and support could not as easily be transferred from right to left and vice versa as new leaders arise who promise more and are in a position to deliver.

THE DANGERS to liberty and democracy in union organizations are basically the same as those that lead to arbitrary rule and suppression of freedom in nations—insecurity, threats of war, fear of attack from the outside, rebellion within. Among American unions the sense of insecurity is pervasive; they seem to live in constant fear for the safety of the organizations. Ever present they see dangers of attack from employers, threats of antiunion laws, court injunctions, jurisdictional wars with competing organizations, internal disorders causing disunity, and the necessity for strikes to protect gains and win improvements. It is a commonplace of history that democracy does not live and thrive in such an atmosphere.

It used to be said that union officials acted like war leaders in the early stages of an organization's growth while employers were still fighting to destroy them. But after management accepted the union, recognized and dealt with its officers as proper representatives of employees, they began to feel secure, and then a process began which gradually eliminated truculent, warlike leaders because they could not survive in an atmosphere of industrial peace. Either they changed to follow more peaceful methods or they were supplanted by conciliatory and businesslike leaders. Especially was this held to be true when employers granted union security in the form of the closed or union shop. Now, however, the organizations that have such security clauses in more or less continuous agreements with employers appear as haunted by anxiety for their safety as those that are not so fortified.

Anyone who follows the speeches and public statements of union leaders must be impressed by their emphasis on threats to the security of the organizations. While leaders may stimulate such fears for their own advantage, the fact is that the membership by and large shares the feeling of apprehension for the safety of their organizations. Despite union security clauses, and notwithstanding the legal protections which federal legislation has thrown around the unions, they still feel themselves vulnerable to attack. The prohibitions against employer restraint and coercion, the outlawing of company unions and discrimination against union members, and the legal obligation placed on management to bargain with union representatives have not allayed the fears for the unions' safety. Nor has their phenomenal growth in membership, power and influence made them feel any more secure.

The stronger the unions have become the more dangers to their existence they seem to see. Hardly a union convention has been held since the end of World War II in which there was not some proposal advanced to authorize summary expulsion of members, suspension of locals, or other arbitrary powers for the president, with "whereases" to the effect that the life of the union is in jeopardy. Although such proposals are frequently rejected in the original form, they often find their way into union constitutions modified to apply in cases where the executive finds it necessary to protect the life of the national or a local organization.

To their ordinary anxieties about employer opposition has been added in recent years fear of antilabor legislation, as Congress and state legislatures have begun to regulate and restrict their activities. In a Labor Day speech in 1948, Philip Murray, President of the CIO said, referring to the Taft-Hartley Law enacted the previous year: "Today organized labor is burdened with legal shackles . . . that threaten its eventual destruction." William Green, President of the AFL, only used different words to express the same thought; and at numerous meetings throughout the country lesser leaders reiterated similar warnings.

This political rallying to defend unions against unfriendly legislation, together with the overwhelming votes in favor of making union membership a condition of employment mentioned in a previous chapter, leaves little room for doubt that the leaders express the feelings of the memberships in their constant emphasis on the dangers that threaten the existence of the unions. That the leaders overemphasize the dangers and may whip up scares is true enough, but this would profit them little if it did not strike a responsive chord in fears that pervade the memberships which elect them to office.

It is in this feeling of insecurity that the explanation for undemocratic trends in union governments must be sought. Autocratic practices of union officials would not be tolerated to the extent of alarming the friends of organized labor, members would hardly be willing to grant arbitrary powers to their executives and support or approve those who assume such powers, were it not for the persistent fears that their unions were in danger of destruction or weakening to the point of ineffectiveness. From this feeling of insecurity stems the belief, common to rank and file and union officers alike, that unity of labor is the all-important consideration, that dissenters whether members or nonunion workers endanger the existence of the unions and the industrial governments they force on employers.

Nothing illustrates this better than the traditional closed or union shop policy of organized labor. Compulsory unionism is a firm tenet of practically all American labor unions, despite affirmations in some of their constitutions that they are voluntary organizations, and despite the fact that unions generally look upon themselves as voluntary in nature. Every union worthy of the name aims to compel all who work in the trade or industry in which it functions to become a member. It strives to make union membership a condition of employment, considering this essential to the effective functioning and safety of the organization. Although the railroad brotherhoods built powerful organizations capable of imposing unwanted rules on the carriers without closed or union shops, they too urged and in 1951 secured from Congress an amendment to the Railway Labor Act legalizing provisions for making membership a condition of employment.

Before the larger industrial unions were able to get union shops by agreements with the managements, they developed the practice of establishing picket lines around plants to check on dues paying. Periodically the pickets would be at the gates for several days at a time, and workers who were not members were kept from entering the plants. A leader of a steelworkers' local estimated that only about 6 percent would be in the union and pay dues if membership was voluntary, but "with dues inspection and pressure" the union had over 95 percent. He thought that 100 percent would join if they were required but did not have to pay dues.[20] Thus the closed or union shop is identified with "union security," although when achieved the organizations seem to feel just as insecure as before. In earlier years when the pattern of collective bargaining was local in character and agreements were generally made with individual employers, this was defended as quite consistent with voluntarism, since a group of union employees had the right to refuse to work with nonmembers who were obnoxious to them; the employer was merely being asked to choose between union and nonunion workers. Also, as a private employment agency might do, the union would not supply him with any help if he persisted in hiring labor from other sources.

But as unions have enrolled in their ranks major portions of the experienced workers in their jurisdictions, and extended their collective agreements to cover most employers in their trades or industries, this argument became less and less valid. Today we

[20] J. Seidman, J. London, and B. Karsh, "Leadership in a Local Union," *American Journal of Sociology*, Vol. 56 (1950), pp. 229–37.

hear little of it. A new defense of compulsory unionism has taken its place. Compelling workers to become members on pain of losing their jobs is now justified as democratic on the ground that the minority of nonmembers ought to be bound by the wishes of the majority. And this justification apparently was the basis of the original provision in the Taft-Hartley Act authorizing unions and employers to enter into union shop agreements when a majority of the workers employed at the time the election is held vote in favor of such compulsory membership (in 1951 the requirement of an election was repealed).

There is much merit, of course, in other reasons the unions give for the closed or union shop policy: nonmembers get the benefits of union bargaining without contributing to its costs or being subject to its responsibilities, and managements tend to favor them and use them to undermine the organizations. But the grounds for these justifiable complaints can be removed in other ways than by forcing workers into the unions. Already the Labor Relations Acts prohibit employers from discriminating in favor of nonunion men or against unions and their members, from establishing company unions, and other antiunion activities.

So far as enjoying benefits without paying fair share of costs is concerned, there is no reason why those who object to joining a union cannot be made to contribute to the costs without compelling them to become members. Aliens in the United States are not forced to become citizens, but must pay taxes and obey the laws. A similar arrangement might be worked out by which nonmembers who are governed by a union agreement and enjoy its protection and benefits could contribute to its costs and obey its rules without forcing on them the obligations of membership. "Union security" jeopardizes the "job security" of suspended and expelled members, and those who refuse to join, just as "open shops" jeopardized job security of union men. And generally overlooked is the fact that union security for one organization often endangers the existence of others. The union that wins an election compels the members of others to give up their membership and join the winner. Perhaps, if organized labor showed some inventiveness in devising a method of safeguarding job security for all workers together with a way of making all pay for the benefits derived from union bargaining there would be less sentiment for the so-called "right to work" laws that many states have enacted.

BUT THE COMPULSORY union-shop policy may be so deeply rooted in the belief that labor must maintain a united front against employers as to permit of no such compromise with voluntarism. Implied in this belief is that there is no room for factions or parties in the governments of unions, and that democracy in industry requires something like a one party system of government. We are told as much by two former union officials who have written perhaps the ablest defense of making union membership obligatory under collective bargaining agreements. Golden and Ruttenberg, discussing "The Union Shop" in their persuasive study of union-management relations, state organized labor's position without equivocation: [21]

It is a fact of industrial democracy, written into the law, that it is a one-party system of democracy. . . . Because supreme power is divided between management and the union, the majority rule principle operates differently from the way it does in a political democracy —where supreme power is vested in one agency, the government. Industrial democracy functions through a one-party system. . . . All workers are represented by one union, and they are not citizens of industry until they belong to it.

The phrase, "written into the law," refers to the labor relations acts which provide that a union designated by a majority has the exclusive right to represent all employees in a bargaining unit. The argument is plain: the logic of majority rule requires the minority to join the union, even though the dissenters include loyal members of organized labor who belong to other unions, and some who are conscientiously opposed to all unions. Otherwise, the union "lacks the power to see that the minority abides by the rules."

[21] Clinton S. Golden and Harold J. Ruttenberg, *The Dynamics of Industrial Democracy* (New York, Harper, 1942), Chap. VII. Mr. Golden, who was one of the organizers and a vice-president of the United Steelworkers, may justly be described as a "dean of the American labor movement." He is respected by employers and workers alike.

The assumption is that though employees may vote as citizens in industry for one union or another, or for no union, once a majority has chosen a union to represent them, all must join the victorious party. The fact that democratic political governments find it possible to enforce their rules and laws against noncitizens, dissenters, and active opponents of the governing party, is disregarded, and entirely ignored is the supreme power of the general government to enforce the collective contracts which serve as the constitution for the industrial governments. But whatever may be thought of the validity of the argument, it undoubtedly expresses not only the reasoned convictions of organized labor's officialdom, but also the mass feeling among union members as shown by their overwhelming affirmative votes in the numerous union shop elections held under the repealed provision of the Taft-Hartley law.[22]

If worker-participation in industrial government is conceived as a one-party system of democracy, it should not be surprising to find such one-party rule also in the internal management of the unions. The sole example of a formal two-party system in American union governments is in the Typographical Union where the "Progressives" and the "Independents" openly oppose and carry on election campaigns against each other. This organization refers to itself as "America's oldest and most democratic union." It tolerates public criticism of its officers by members and opposing candidates in a way that is rare among labor unions. But the president, writing in the union's *Journal,* seemed to imply there was no need for two parties since there was unanimity in policy making. "To place a label on a delegate and expect him to follow a political leader is not democracy. Appeal is now being made to support men running as 'independent' candidates. No 'independent' policy was offered either in the 1947 or 1948 Conventions. The officers and delegates were unanimous in policy in 1947. There was no 'independent' plan or policy offered in 1948." [23] The Independent Party's candidate for President in 1947 publicly denounced the incumbent officers as dictators. "I charge President Randolph has deliberately practiced his tactics of confusion. Confusion is the

[22] *Annual Reports,* N.L.R.B., 1948–51.   [23] *Typographical Journal,* May 1949.

spawn of dictatorship. . . . Small local unions exist in constant fear of reprisals by the executive council under the new expulsion laws asked at the Cleveland Convention. . . . We cannot long survive under dictatorship. . . . How long are you going to follow the mandates, decrees and edicts of Dictator Randolph." [24]

Most unions would discipline or expel members for making false charges and working against the interests of the organization if they publicly criticized and denounced the administrators of their affairs as is done in the election contests of the printers' union. Factional divisions among the members in the manner of political parties are generally looked upon as inimical to union-ism. An organized opposition within the unions to the officials chosen to govern them is regarded as not essentially different from attacks by outside opponents. The overwhelming pressure is for unity, unanimity.

May it not be, then, that the autocratic practices which have been considered exceptional—the denial of the right to oppose the union's administration, the expulsion of members for criti-cising union officials, the granting of arbitrary authority to exec-utives, and the tendency to govern by decree—are indications of a trend toward one-party union government in conformity with the single party concept of industrial democracy? Is there any reason to believe that a one-party system of industrial government or union government is likely to be any less disastrous in its effects on individual freedom than such systems have been under political governments? And one may well wonder if the conviction that in-dustrial democracy must function as a one-party system can long prevail among so large a proportion of the population as organized labor represents without sooner or later having some influence on workers' concepts of political democracy.

The deep-rooted feeling of insecurity which pervades the unions keeps them on a war basis, and it would be surprising if their gov-ernments were continuing to grow more democratic in spite of the militancy engendered by fears for the safety of the organizations. "Freedom lives and prospers [says Shotwell, historian of civiliza-tion] only where society itself is confident of its stability. . . . In

[24] New York *Times,* Jan. 26, 1948.

proportion therefore as the war system pervades the civilized world, freedom is curtailed and the chances for its development are slight indeed." And philosopher Bertrand Russell finds that "One of the most important conditions of freedom in the matter of opinion as in other matters is governmental security." [25]

What is true of nations in this respect may also be true of unions. There is a certain parallelism between the demands for union security and the demands of the peoples of the world for national security. As we shall see in the succeeding chapter, the governments of national unions are sovereign powers like the governments of nations. Theirs is the supreme law, and there is no binding law that governs the relations of national unions to each other any more than of national states to each other. Thus there is a "nationalism" in the world of organized labor comparable to the nationalism in the world generally which is turning nations into armed camps and suppressing freedoms in order that democracy may be saved. This labor "nationalism" has a direct bearing on union security, and hence on liberty and democracy for the workers in industry and in the unions.

"The most fallacious application of the principle of liberty" [says Russell] "has been in international affairs. While it has been generally realized that liberty for the individual depends upon law, it has been thought that liberty for nations depended on the absence of law." Substantially the same may be said of the application of the principle of freedom in the world of organized labor. While there is a firm conviction that democratic unionism requires rules and laws to assure freedom for the workers in their organizations and in their places of employment, there is the equally strong belief that each national union must be a law unto itself, must be autonomous, sovereign. Just as "it was thought that, when once national boundaries and parliamentary institutions had been established, . . . the democracies would cooperate freely," so it has been assumed that free and independent unions, each with its own representative government and its jurisdiction de-

[25] James T. Shotwell, "Freedom, Its History and Meaning," in *Freedom,* edited by Ruth Nanda Anshen (Harcourt, Brace, 1940), pp. 15 & 16. In same volume, Bertrand Russell, "Freedom and Government," p. 285.

fined, would naturally cooperate. Like nations, the unions do co-operate to some extent, but they also raid each others' jurisdiction, engage in cold and hot wars against each other as well as against employers.

If Professor Shotwell is correct in concluding that "The chief enemy of liberty is nationalism, the very thing which liberty itself created when it rescued nations from feudal tyranny or the over-lordship of kings," can we rule out the possibility that unionism which liberty created to rescue labor from the tyranny or over-lordship of industrial kings and corporation managements may also become the chief enemy of freedom for the workers?

IT IS IMPORTANT to know in what direction American unionism is heading. A free country cannot suppress labor unions. The or-ganized labor community in the United States has become too large a portion of the voting population to make effective legislation directed against it which it persists in opposing. It fights and gains strength to force modification of the laws. The federal and state statutes outlawing closed shops are flagrantly violated, while the 1947–51 provision for union-shop elections worked for that time to promote compulsory unionism. Union membership has con-tinued to increase despite the Taft-Hartley Act and the repressive laws. In spite of setbacks, labor influence in industry and govern-ment continues to grow.

In a sense we are betting on the democracy of American labor organizations. The assumption is general that democratic political institutions can hardly be maintained without free trade unions. Their primary objective, collective bargaining—now established by law as the national labor policy—is considered essential to democracy in industrial relations. If, however, the unions are not the inherently democratic organizations we assume them to be, if industrial democracy must indeed be a one-party system of democ-racy, then organized labor may be leading to a society marked by more authoritarianism than liberty, while it is being protected and supported as a movement essential to a fuller democracy.

Security, discipline, and administrative efficiency are essential to labor unions if they are to perform their necessary functions in an industrial society. But, how are American unions coping with the problems of combining these with popular control of their governments and individual freedom for the workers? Are they maintaining governments of the people, by the people, and for the people as the Webbs found, or are they finding popular control unworkable as Hoxie thought, and moving toward less government by the people and more domination by official hierarchies of the organizations?

We have seen that the basic problem of security has not been solved. Judging by the pronouncements of union officials one may doubt if any progress is being made toward solving it. Whether the dangers come from opposition by employers, from interunion strife, unfavorable legislation, or are merely whipped up by leaders, the feeling of insecurity persists after the unions have become strong enough to force the largest corporations and whole industries to share the government of the employees with them, and after they have won substantial influence in the government of the country. Insecurity of nations, we are told, makes them less tolerant of liberties and democratic rights. Can we expect freedom and democracy to flourish in national labor organizations while they feel themselves insecure?

The insistence of American unions on the traditional union shop policy seems to indicate that they can find no other way of maintaining unity and discipline except by compulsory membership. Fears for the safety of the organizations seem to make necessary sacrifices of rights of individual workers, limitations on their freedom to choose the organizations to which they want to belong, and the shift in authority from the membership to governing officials that many observers have noted. This same psychology is apparently also responsible for the belief that one-party government is essential to effective collective bargaining or industrial democracy. The emergence of political action as an integral part of trade union activity, with the resulting pressures on members to vote as a class, arouses public sentiment in support of employers' proposals for curbing the powers of labor, and the resulting restrictive legislation makes the unions feel more insecure; which in turn leads to greater pressure on the membership for greater sacrifices of rights and liberties in the face of the greater dangers.

But this is not the whole picture. Democratic traditions are strong in American labor unions, and their strivings for subjecting management to rules of law embodied in working agreements made jointly with representatives of employees are certainly in line with these traditions. Basic democratic rights, such as equal application of laws, equality of opportunity, and individual freedom make it necessary that those who have economic or other power to oppress shall be restrained to enlarge the liberties of those who are disadvantaged. When employers are free to run their industries as they please, employees are not free in their workplaces. Forcing managements to bargain with unions chosen by employees places limits on their freedom in order that workers shall have freedom to a voice in making the shop rules that govern them. Thus is liberty enlarged and balanced. It may well be that the restrictions which union governments impose on the liberties of their members and on nonunionists will work out to provide greater freedom for all employees.

Moreover, it must not be forgotten that organized labor is still in the process of building a labor community that will encompass the whole country. Less than two decades have elapsed since unionism began to get a foothold in our mass production industries and more than a small percentage of wage earners became subject to its rules and its industrial governments. To date union members still constitute less than a third of the wage and salaried workers in the United States. On a nation-wide basis organized labor may still be said to be in that early stage when, as Bagehot put it:

The quantity of government is much more important than its quality. What you want is a comprehensive rule binding men together, making them do much the same things, telling them what to expect of each other—fashioning them alike and keeping them so. What this rule is does not matter so much. A good rule is better than a bad one, but any rule is better than none. . . . But to gain that rule what may be called the impressive elements of a polity are incomparably more important than its useful elements. . . . Nothing is very like those old communities now, but perhaps a "trade's union" is as near as most things.[26]

[26] Walter Bagehot, *Physics and Politics*, (New York, Knopf, 1948), pp. 28–29.

Bagehot wrote when labor in England was organized about to the extent that our unions achieved in the mid-years of the 1930s. He mentioned a union leader named Broadhead who apparently was the John L. Lewis of the time. In the decades that followed, however, organized labor in Britain developed the outstanding example of democratic union governments with individual freedoms for the workers. Whether this can be maintained in Britain with its higher degree of nationalization is now being questioned just as the democracy of our own labor organizations is being questioned as they become more political in character.

The influence of the rank and file, and of the leaders too, is not in one direction. As awareness of common interests develops for which the unions are ever striving, and as workers through organization raise their living standards, social status and political influence to approach those of ordinary business and professional people, sentiment is growing among them, much more so than among the office holders, for a unified labor confederation strong enough industrially and politically to defend their organizations against attack from any source. Impatience with jurisdictional and other interunion strife is also increasing inside the labor movement as it is outside. The attempt of the federal government in the Labor-Mananagement Relations Act of 1947 to decide such disputes has also stimulated efforts of unions to agree on rules for preventing conflicts and settling differences peacefully. These beginnings and the tendency already noted to exercise control over affiliated unions may well lead a unified labor confederation to develop a system of laws governing interunion relations.

In some such way the fervent feeling of insecurity that prevades the unions may be dispelled and lessen the need for keeping them psychologically and otherwise on a war basis. Union security thus established would free the energies of the organizations for the more constructive tasks of developing the institutions of democracy and liberty in industry and in the unions in accordance with their avowed ideals. There are observable trends in this direction in the American organized labor, as well as those of an anti-democratic character that have been emphasized above.

This emphasis has been deliberate—to challenge common assumptions about union democracy, to show that the undemocratic aspects of unionism may not be as exceptional as they are regarded by the friends and supporters of organized labor, but may rather be expressions of a trend away from American democratic principles. Doubtless the points have been overstressed; but the purpose of this chapter has been not to answer, but only to raise questions about unionism and democracy, about the kind of industrial and political democracy a laboristic society led by organized labor is likely to want in place of what is called capitalistic democracy.

The labor movement in the United States is marked by conflicting trends; and it will have to make choices, which to further and which to suppress. The contributions organized labor has made and is making toward democratizing industrial management and developing a fuller life for the wage earners of the country are continuing factors making for more freedom for more people. The evidence of undemocratic tendencies in union governments has been stressed to make plain that there is a threat to freedom, either in national union leaders' assertions of *de facto* sovereignty, or claims of legal autonomy to reject voluntary, self-imposed, or compulsory public controls. During the nineteenth and early twentieth century, most of those who were in favor of freedom favored the removal of legal restrictions upon union activity, in spite of the fact that these restrictions were defended in the name of freedom of employers who wished to retain their monopoly of economic power. Nevertheless, it has always been clear that the power of trade unions *might* become a genuine menace to freedom.

No one knows enough about American union governments to give a definitive answer to the question whether organized labor is actually becoming a menace to freedom, or whether despite serious lapses among the organizations into autocratic patterns, its overall movement is toward more democracy and enlarged freedom. Clues to the answers may perhaps be found if we examine in some detail the governments that labor organizations have developed for their internal rule, for the handling of interunion affairs, and for joint rule of their relations with industrial managements. The rest of this volume is therefore devoted to a study of the basic institutions of labor unionism in the United States, the constitutional principles and machinery of its complex of union governments, their politics and administration, judicial processes, operating methods, and the forces that spur and guide the organized labor movement.

PART TWO

UNION GOVERNMENTS
IN OPERATION

V

THE NATIONAL UNION:
BASIC GOVERNMENTAL UNIT

ASK A UNION MAN to what organization he belongs, and he may answer: AFL, CIO, or he may name an organization like the Machinists, Autoworkers, Teamsters, Carpenters, Steelworkers, Railway Carmen. Again he may say he belongs to Local 3 or 600 or some other numbered local union or lodge. These typical responses may reflect pride in being associated with an organization that is powerful and well known, or loyalty to a subdivision of a union which looks after the member's interests in dealing with the management of the shop in which he works. They do not ordinarily indicate his status as a citizen, so to speak, under the union government which is the source of his rights, privileges, and immunities as an organized worker, and whose laws he is bound to obey.

There are no individual members of the AFL-CIO. Only unions are members of this labor confederation, as only nations are members of the United Nations. In the manner of any alliance of nations, the confederations deal with and act through the governments of the member unions. Unlike our own federal government, they do not have direct authority over the subjects or the citizens of the various union governments. They may not tax individual union members, adopt laws or working rules for them, try them for offenses, discipline or expel them. These are prerogatives of the separate member unions. With certain exceptions comparable to the territories and possessions of the United States, each affiliated union is a national organization, self-governing like a sovereign state.

A union worker is normally a member of one of these national unions. Its government is the highest authority over him in American organized labor. He ordinarily holds this membership in a subdivision of the national union for the locality or plant in which he works, but when he moves to another place he must transfer to another such local union. As the constitution of the Ladies' Garment Workers Union puts it: "The membership of the ILGWU shall consist of individual workers organized in local unions in the manner provided in this constitution."

A new member is usually initiated in a local where he pledges allegiance to the constitution and laws of the national union, sometimes without mentioning the local constitution, which must conform to the national and be approved by a national officer. Applicants are ordinarily prohibited from applying or being admitted to membership in any local other than the one designated for his place of work. Many unions also provide for holding membership directly in the national organization, and for initiation by national officers. The qualifications for membership are prescribed by the national constitution, and the obligation the member takes when initiated is essentially to the union as a national organization. Typical is the statement he must repeat and sign to become a member of the International Brotherhood of Electrical Workers: "I . . . do sincerely promise and agree to conform to and abide by the Constitution and laws of the IBEW and its Local Unions. I will faithfully further, by every means in my power, the purposes for which the IBEW is instituted."

Thus the basic unit of union government is the national union, and not the local as is often supposed. It commonly calls itself "international" because it has members and branches in Canada and sometimes in other North American countries. Some of the older unions, in the fashion of fraternal organizations, name their national or international union the Grand Lodge to distinguish it from subordinate governmental units. We shall continue to refer to them as national unions since their membership outside the United States is a small fraction of the total.[1]

[1] In 1949 less than 5 percent of the members of American unions were located in Canada, but a majority of Canadian organized workers are included in this membership.

All sovereign powers are in these national unions. Their governments are supreme over all members, local unions, and other subordinate governing bodies. The AFL-CIO derives its powers from them. They decide to form, join or not join, any such association of unions. Some belong to the "National Independent Union Council" on the "Confederated Unions of America," which are small and relatively unknown. Many remain independent.

In terms of citizenship a union member is a citizen under the government of his national or international union. The location of his work determines the branch or local to which he must belong, just as a citizen of one of our states must vote in the locality where he resides. But he does not have dual citizenship as an American is a citizen of one of the forty-eight states as well as of the United States. He is a citizen of his union only, not of the confederation of labor with which it may be affiliated.

Local unions are mere subdivisions of the national organizations whose constitutions provide for their government as a state does for its counties, cities, towns, and villages. The amount of home rule they enjoy is determined by the national, and they are bound by the laws of their national governments. They are authorized to adopt local constitutions and by-laws and the national constitution usually prescribes the form of local government. National laws provide for the suspension, merging, and abolition of local unions. Local officers may be removed by the national executives who may appoint administrators to manage their affairs, sometimes without the consent of the local members.

The national union has other subordinate governmental units—district and regional councils, joint boards, trade or craft councils, and often also state councils. These are delegate bodies composed of representatives from local unions, and their powers and duties are defined by the national constitution. Some of them are given extensive supervisory powers over the locals. They are subject to the authority of national union officials, and the locals are usually required to join such councils.

Historically national unions were built by local trade unions joining to form a national organization to govern their particular trades, related occupations, or industries. But once they joined they became subject to the laws of the new national governments they created. The local unions did not merely delegate certain limited powers and reserve others to themselves, although sometimes they insisted on and were granted a certain amount of home rule. There are examples, also, of two or more national unions forming a single organization with each retaining autonomous rights over its own trade. But usually the national union has a centralized government ruling all members and all subordinate organizations.

AS EVERY political state has some definite territory, so every national union has what it calls its jurisdiction—the kind of work and workers it claims the exclusive right to organize and govern. The feeling of inviolability of its jurisdiction is not less strong in a union than is the sacredness of its territory to a national state. Woodruff Randolph, President of the International Typographical Union, expressed it this way: "The ITU is a craft union exercising jurisdiction over all composing room work. Our jobs are dependent on that work. The life of our trade is dependent upon that jurisdiction. Whatever weakens or destroys our jurisdiction destroys our union."

Industrial unions feel much the same way about the industries they stake out as their domains. Some unions, like the Pacific Coast Marine Firemen's Association, are sectional, and do not claim jurisdiction outside the areas in which they operate. Nor do the international unions which extend beyond the boundaries of the United States vigorously pursue exclusive jurisdictional claims in the foreign countries.

Although few unions succeed in enrolling within their ranks all workers in their asserted jurisdiction even in the home country, they nevertheless are intolerant of any trespassing on their exclusive domains; and one union will often demand that workers organized by another in what it considers its territory shall be turned over to it. Thus, like nations, unions have their boundary disputes and irredentist movements which at times break out in interunion wars—jurisdictional strikes, picketing and boycotts, not infrequently accompanied by violence. Like nations also, national unions form or join alliances to deal with such problems of conflicting interests as well as common defense against employers, and promotion of common interests. The AFL and the CIO (and now the AFL-CIO) are merely the most comprehensive of these. The railroad unions have a Railway Labor Executives Association, and there are other alliances, comparable to the Benelux combination and the North Atlantic Alliance.

Being alliances or leagues rather than super-governments, the AFL and CIO had as little success in preventing conflicts among the national unions or settling them peacefully as the League of Nations did among the national states, or as the United Nations has thus far been able to achieve. Perhaps in the American world of labor, an overall government of organized workers will be needed to assure peace among the national unions as many think World Government is the answer to wars among the nations. For the present, however, relinquishment of any of its sovereignty is as abhorrent to a national union as it is to a national state.

Industrial unionism has reduced jurisdictional disputes among the organizations—CIO unions were not as plagued with them as the AFL unions—but it has not abolished them. On the other hand the existence of two competing confederations created new conflicts of jurisdiction between the unions affiliated with one against those of the other, and the independent United Mine Workers through its so-called District 50 extended its jurisdictional claims over workers in many industries. Failure of organized labor to develop its own governmental machinery for settling interunion controversies makes it most likely that the United States government will supply this lack. A beginning has been made in the Taft-Hartley Act of 1947, which authorized the National Labor Relations Board to decide such controversies.

In dealing with the problems of organizing nonunion workers and establishing new national unions, the leagues or confederations have been more successful because national unions have been more willing to delegate to them adequate powers for these purposes, at least in recent years. Both the AFL and the CIO were authorized to organize local unions, known respectively as "federal labor unions" and "local industrial unions," and to charter and govern them in the same manner that a national union does with its own locals. The merged AFL-CIO has similar powers. Until the members of such local unions are assigned to affiliated national organizations which claim jurisdiction over them, or until the locals can be combined to form a new national union, the federation in effect acts like a national union in relation to them. The workers in such locals may perhaps be considered exceptions to the rule that there are no individual members in the AFL-CIO.

Prior to the organization of the CIO, the jurisdictional claims of the craft unions made it almost impossible for the AFL to organize the mass production industries. Joint committees of a score or more craft unions were established to do the organizing, and each wanted the skilled mechanics that came within its jurisdiction rather than the establishment of a new industrial union. After 1934 when the AFL convention adopted a resolution authorizing the organization of industrial unions in specific mass production industries, it was less hampered in this respect. The merged federation may still labor under difficulties, because a union is not ordinarily admitted to membership if any organization that is a member objects. Thus jurisdictional claims of the crafts may still prevent an industrial union from affiliating with the federation on equal terms with the other organizations; but the objections are more easily overcome, and adjustments are usually made permitting the craft unions to retain jurisdiction over workers in the industry who are covered by their agreements with employers.

In establishing new national unions, the old AFL joined existing federal labor unions of the same craft or industry under a national council which governs them under its supervision until they are considered ready for self-government and affiliation as autonomous national unions. The CIO likewise was empowered to combine its local industrial unions into national unions, but it more generally reversed the process by creating national organizing committees for particular industries which functioned like national unions from the beginning. They carried on active organizing campaigns and set up their own locals. A national organizing committee remained a subordinate organization until in the judgment of the CIO, it was ready for self-government, when it was admitted as an autonomous member union equal in status with the other affiliated national organizations.

Thus the local unions attached directly to the AFL and the CIO were governed like the dependencies of the United States such as Guam and Puerto Rico, while the national councils and organizing committees are similar to territorial governments of Alaska or Hawaii. The affiliated national unions, however, did not occupy the subordinate position of the states in the federal government of the United States. They had all the sovereign powers that wholly independent unions have which are not affiliated with any confederations. But it is significant that in practice the CIO exercised a measure of authority over its affiliated national unions that the AFL organizations ordinarily would not permit. Whether this was due to so many of them having grown out of organizing committees which the CIO created or whether this is the beginning of a trend toward a federal union government superior to those of the national unions, only the future can tell.[2]

Establishment of national unions as the supreme governmental units of organized labor was a slow development. A full century had elapsed from the time when trade unions first appeared before these independent labor states emerged as survivors in the struggle of different forms of government with which workers experimented as they strove to meet new conditions and new problems.

In labor circles today, independence and equality of the government of each separate union is accepted as normal and permanent regardless of whether the workers are organized by trades, crafts, industries, or any combinations or divisions of these. When the CIO was formed to promote industrial unionism, it did not question the desirability of national government of the unions which the craft organizations of the AFL had worked out. Sixty years earlier, when the AFL was battling with the Knights of Labor the main issues between them did involve differences as to how unions should be governed. The Knights attempted to set up a centralized

---

[2] In general, the merger of the AFL and CIO has not changed these structural relationships between the national unions and the federation. A more detailed discussion of these matters will be found in Chapter XIV.

government over all American labor with the national unions subordinated to it.

The earliest unions had town meeting governments subject to no higher authority, except as all unions then and now have been subject to the general public law. They were local unions, but self-formed and autonomous. Each union, or trade society as it was known, was governed by the meeting of its members. Its officers had few duties and little power. When anything was to be done the meeting appointed a committee for the purpose. The members governed directly, not through representatives. Internally, these first trade unions were popular democracies.

The beginnings of representative government came when the separate trade organizations in a city leagued together in a joint movement against employers. Then each society elected delegates to a local assembly which became known as a "trades' union." This union of trades, however, did not combine the memberships under a single government. Each society continued to rule its own affairs, and retained authority over its members. The trades' union could act only through the separate organizations, and it got its funds from them, not from individual members.

Through the trades' union, the organizations helped each other in strikes, and dealt with problems common to all the trades. Representing all organized labor in the city, it concerned itself largely with promoting legislation in behalf of the wage earners, and from the first political action rather than trade union activity became its sphere. Direct bargaining with employers and regulation of employment by working rules were matters that each trade society handled for itself. Union laws were local laws; today a local union gets permission from its national organization to adopt local laws.

As these local delegate bodies spread through the country, they in turn set up a national representative body on the same model. The first of these was established in 1834 when at a convention of delegates from city trades' unions the National Trades' Union was formed. The local trade organizations were only indirectly represented in this. It was an association of city associations of unions.

Reflecting the general disillusionment with the workingmen's parties with which the city unions became identified during the last years of the previous decade, it adopted a resolution that "no party, political or religious questions shall be agitated or acted upon in the Union." But it did not condemn lobbying for legislation in the interest of working people, and concerned itself a good deal with agitation and pressure for such legislation.

Prior to this time several attempts had been made to combine local societies of the same trade in different cities under a national government of the trade, but no such national trade organizations succeeded in establishing themselves. Thus a pattern of union government was set quite different from that which prevails today. The basic governmental unit was an autonomous local craft organization which alone had authority to make rules binding on the individual members, to tax and judge them, to bargain and make agreements with employers for them. Beyond this there was no higher authority over the memberships. The meeting of this organization was the final judge as to whether it would go along with any action taken by a city trades' union or the National Trades' Union.

This pattern prevailed down to the last quarter of the nineteenth century. During the long depression that followed the Panic of 1837 what labor organizations there were took the form of mutual benefit societies, producers and consumers' cooperatives, and political and social reform associations, although their memberships were by no means confined to wage workers. Delegates from such organizations met several times in national industrial congresses, but these concerned themselves with politics and social reform.

When trade-unionism revived in the 1850s and 1860s, it followed the pattern set in the earlier years. Again a multitude of local trade organizations sprang up, and these joined in forming city representative bodies which they called "trade assemblies." The term "trade union" had become the customary name for the local trade societies. In 1864 an attempt was made to set up an "international industrial assembly" modeled on the former National

Trades' Union, but the effort went to naught. In the thirty years that had elapsed, a new method of governing unions nationally had developed which departed from the old pattern.

While the local unions still found the city trade assemblies useful for common local purposes, a national association of such city assemblies no longer met the needs of some of the trades. As national markets developed, more and more of the local unions found that a wider governing unit than a local community was needed for effective union regulation of wages and working conditions. Competition of employers of the same trade in distant cities threatened the standards of the local union, and when the members struck to maintain or better conditions, they often found their work transferred to an employer in another city. This led unions of the same trade in different cities to give up some of their autonomy, and combine under the government of a single national union of their trade, of which they eventually became subordinate local divisions.

In the 1850s a few such nationally governed unions had established themselves, but the following decade saw a rapid growth of national trade unions. Some well-known existing national unions date from this period.[3] The main body of organized labor, however, still followed the old pattern. Rising living costs during the Civil War brought new crops of local unions, and these formed or joined city trade assemblies. This movement culminated in the organization of the National Labor Union in 1866 which also was an assembly of unions on the model of the old National Trades' Union.

Although the nationally governed craft organizations participated in its formation, its delegates represented mainly city trade assemblies and local unions. It also accepted delegates from various kinds of social reform organizations.[4] Despite its title, it was not a higher organ of authority among labor unions, and was not con-

[3] International Typographical Union (1850), International Molders Union (1859), Brotherhood of Locomotive Engineers (1863), National Union of Cigar Makers (1864), Order of Railway Conductors (1868). Four of the building trade unions, Carpenters, Bricklayers, Painters and Plasterers were organized in 1865.

[4] Susan Anthony appeared as a representative of the women suffragists, and an attempt was made to exclude her, but after a debate she was seated.

cerned with integrating local unions in wider governmental units. It was a political rather than a labor organization. Its main objective when first established was the eight-hour workdây, to be secured by legislation rather than by union bargaining or strikes, and it soon turned itself into a "national labor and reform party." [5]

The national trade unions began to withdraw earlier, dissatisfied with the concentration on politics. Thereafter they twice attempted to set up a "national labor congress" that would confine itself to trade union problems, but without success. Nevertheless the nationally governed unions won the day. Most of them survived the Panic of 1873 and the depression that followed, while other workers' organizations went to pieces. With the upturn of business in the late seventies, country-wide organizations by crafts or trades spread and gained strength, and by the end of the century, the pattern of nationally governed union organizations had become dominant.

But this was not achieved without a bitter struggle for survival lasting almost two decades with another type of union organization and government which sought to unify all labor organizations under a single supreme authority. The Noble Order of the Knights of Labor met in open convention for the first time in 1878. It had been formed as a secret society with vague idealistic aims by a group of tailors in Philadelphia led by Uriah Stevens. At the convention it adopted a constitution designed to embrace

[5] At the 1871 convention of the Typographical Union the following report was received: "The undersigned, delegates from your body in the Labor Congress held in Cincinnati, August, 1870, report that we attended said Labor Congress from the opening to the close of the session, and failed to discover anything in the proceedings, with the exception of the report of the committee on obnoxious laws, that would entitle the congress to representation from a purely trade organization. The congress was made up of delegates, with few exceptions, who openly avowed the object to be the formation of a political party. Played-out politicians, lobbyists, woman-suffragans, preachers without flocks, representatives of associations in which politics are made a qualification for membership, and declaimers on the outrages perpetrated on poor Lo, formed the major part of the congress. The session was one of continuous confusion, in which personalities abounded, and charges and counter-charges were made of attempts to run it in the interest of both the old political parties. The only thing accomplished was the formation of the Labor Reform party and the adoption of a platform announcing its principles." John Collins, Harry P. Temple, delegates. (George A. Tracy, *History of the Typographical Union* [Indianapolis, International Typographical Union, 1913], p. 256.)

"all toilers" in one organization governed by a centralized authority at the top. It aimed at establishing an empire of labor including not only wage workers, but "all the producing classes." The central government would have direct authority over individual members however they might be distributed among subordinate organizations. Its motto, "An injury to one is an injury to all," expressed its ideal.

At the top was a national assembly composed of elected representatives in which was lodged all powers—"constitutional, legislative, judicial, and executive." "It alone possesses the power and authority to make, amend or repeal the fundamental laws and regulations of the Order; to finally decide all controversies arising in the Order; to issue all charters (to subordinate organizations). . . . It can also tax the members of the Order for its maintenance." Between sessions of the assembly, a national executive board exercised its powers, presided over by a Grand Master Workman. Beneath the national assembly were district assemblies, and at the bottom local assemblies which any ten or more workers could form upon receipt of a charter from the national executive board.

The jurisdiction of the Order covered all work and workers excepting only lawyers, bankers, stockbrokers, professional gamblers, and saloon keepers. Its governmental subdivisions were based on geographical units rather than on craft or industry. Although three-fourths of the members of local assemblies were required to be wage earners, these did not have to be of the same trade or occupation, or even related employments. The membership of the locals could be mixed or of the same trade depending on the kind of "toilers" that wanted to join them. A majority were mixed, but many local trade unions joined in a body, became local assemblies, and continued to function as they had before joining.

As the Knights of Labor grew in numbers and prestige after it shed its secrecy, it also absorbed some existing national trade unions and it organized some new ones. For these it made a place under its all-inclusive government by establishing them as trade districts or trade assemblies on a par with its territorial district assemblies. At one time it had as many as twenty-two national trade assemblies. The national governments of these unions were thus made subordinate divisions of the Order, subject to its general laws and to the authority of its executive board.

Although the Knights rose to great power for a brief period, the plan never did work out in practice. Many of the subordinate assemblies went pretty much their own way, disregarding the central authority. Diverse interests among the heterogeneous membership—farmers, tradesmen, professional people, wage workers, and political reformers—caused constant conflict within the organization, and led to early disintegration.

For some years, however, it looked as if the centralized empire of labor about which the Knights dreamed would become a reality. Between 1880 and 1886 the membership of the Knights of Labor increased from 28,000 to more than 700,000. It absorbed many national unions and established them as subordinate trade districts, while numerous locals of the craft unions went over to it en masse. Even the most prominent leaders of the national unions, men like Samuel Gompers of the Cigar Makers and P. J. McGuire of the Carpenters, who sponsored and led the American Federation of Labor, had been members of the Knights of Labor. At the same time, it was attracting every variety of reformist group to its ranks.

But even while it was having its spectacular growth and success, the trade unions feared they were being submerged in the conglomerate organization, and fought to establish their autonomy while the various reform groups struggled to have their pet programs adopted as the official platform of the Order. The most important opposition came from the national unions, however. In 1881 they launched the Federation of Trades and Labor Unions as a rival to the Knights of Labor to promote the cause of self-governing national craft or trade organizations. The drift of skilled as well as unskilled workers to the all-inclusive organization was too strong, however, and by 1885 this alliance of unions was little more than a name.

Then the trade unions started a movement for the eight-hour day to be secured directly from employers by bargaining or strikes which the Knights of Labor condemned, though it was not averse to legislation to secure the same end. This movement made great headway the following year, and the national unions profited by their sponsorship, while the Knights began to lose members. The same year a committee of trade unionists issued a call for a convention to form an "American federation or alliance of all national and international trade unions," to which representatives from twenty-five organizations responded. "Moved by a common feeling of the menace of the Knights, these delegates agreed to form themselves into an American Federation of Labor for mutual aid and assistance." [6]

This absorbed the defunct Federation of Trades, and under its leadership, the national unions succeeded in establishing their supremacy. By this time the Knights of Labor had already passed the crest of its power; and further weakened by struggles with socialist and anarchist groups among its members, it disintegrated as rapidly as it had grown. By the end of the next decade nationally ruled trade organizations were firmly established as the dominant form of union government.

In the early years of the present century, the national unions perfected their internal government and administration, established adequate revenue systems, developed methods of making joint agreements with groups of employers, and extended their working rules into national laws. To safeguard the stability of the organizations and the collective relations with employers established by the agreements, they gave national officers more control over locals and disciplining of members, required national authorization or approval of strikes, and established strike benefit funds as a means of enforcing the controls.

This process had begun earlier. The Molders' Union pioneered in the 1860s in developing techniques for integrating local unions into the national union governments, and the Cigar Makers some years later carried its methods further. In fighting the Knights of Labor the national unions found it necessary to restrict autonomy of their locals, and to exercise more direct control over their members. Building on this experience, most unions lodged more and more power in their national governments and officers, with little in the way of checks on their authority.

[6] Lewis L. Lorwin, *The American Federation of Labor* (Washington, Brookings Institution, 1933), p. 22.

Later, the adoption by many unions of the referendum and recall of officers marked a reversion to popular government, and this was reflected also in restrictions on the appointive power of union executives. More recent years have witnessed a resumption of growth of appointive and other powers of union officials, and development of new agencies and techniques for mass organization from the top down, with less reliance on self-organization of the workers. New administrative departments have sprouted—for research, labor education, political activity, and community service, as the unions began to make their strength felt in national, state, and local community affairs.

While the national unions were strengthening their internal governments, the American Federation of Labor was developing organs for interunion cooperation among them all along the line on local, state, regional, and national levels, and on an industry basis where different crafts unions operated within the same industry.

For these purposes it made use of the old machinery of trade or labor assemblies, but it established these representative bodies as subordinate governmental divisions of the Federation. In every city where there were local branches of national unions affiliated with the AFL, it issued a charter to a city central body which was variously known as Central Labor Union, Trades and Labor Assembly, or City Federation of Labor and was composed of delegates from the locals within the city or urban area. Similarly, state federations of labor were formed and chartered to include representatives from the subordinate organizations of the affiliated national unions located within their boundaries.

But for common action along industrial lines, the interunion agencies were established at the national level by creating "departments subordinate to the American Federation of Labor" at the headquarters in Washington. The national unions in the building industry were joined in the Building and Construction Trades Department, railway unions in the Railway Employees Department, metal workers' organizations in the Metal Trades Department. Affiliated with these were local, regional, and state trade councils. There was also formed the Union Label Trades Department composed of organizations which have labels or similar devices to advertise the insignia among consumers and otherwise promote the use of goods made by union labor.

The CIO paralleled the AFL with local, district, and state interunion organizations known as industrial councils, but because it rarely had more than one national union for each industry, it did not need and made no provision for departments like those of the AFL.

Despite the establishment of these interunion agencies as subordinate divisions of the AFL and the CIO, the national unions did not lose, and under the merged AFL-CIO have not lost, control over their locals and other branches that were joined in the various councils. Although the Federation insists that locals of affiliated national organizations must join city and state federations or industrial councils, some refuse to join, or having joined they not infrequently withdraw. The national unions decide for themselves whether they will or will not participate in such interunion organizations. Moreover they may enter into cooperative arrangements with other unions which are not affiliated with the confederations to which they belong. In the railroad industry, for example, the Railway Labor Executives Association includes officers of independent unions and AFL-CIO unions.

Thus, though the AFL-CIO has the main responsibility for interunion relations, participation in these subordinate agencies remains essentially voluntary, and each national union reserves its autonomous or sovereign rights.

This devotion of each union to its independent governing authority is a constant source of criticism in and outside of organized labor. The jealousies and jurisdictional conflicts which it engenders are apparent contradictions of the ideal of labor unity. But the struggle between the Knights of Labor and the national unions led by the AFL taught the lesson that one big union embracing all workers is not the way to real unity. The Knights, despite their solidified government, were more torn by dissension in their ranks than are the self-governing national unions in the AFL-CIO. Workers learned that the basis of labor organization must be their specific interests in their jobs, wages and working conditions, not the general interests that all wage earners have in common and together with other disadvantaged groups.

Nevertheless the vision of all workers joined in a single organization has remained a strong motivating force in American labor movements. In 1905 the IWW (Industrial Workers of the World) revived the idea of a centralized empire of labor. It assumed leadership of many strikes, conducted them in a spectacular manner, and won much publicity, creating the impression of a powerful organization which its meager membership belied. Being made up mainly of unskilled, seasonal, and migratory workers, and opposed to making contracts with employers, its organizations proved ephemeral. It disintegrated during World War I. After that war another movement for "One Big Union" received a good deal of publicity, but nothing came of it. More recently there has been the successful effort in 1955 to unite the AFL and the CIO in a single confederation. Even before the merger, the AFL, CIO, and independent Railroad Brotherhoods formed the United Labor Political Committee for the purpose of planning and pursuing common action in national election campaigns, in lobbying, and in dealing with government departments and agencies. In all these developments, the autonomy or sovereignty of each national labor union has been acknowledged, but the tendencies in these unifying movements toward subjecting the autonomous national unions to the rule of an overall government of labor organizations are not to be underestimated.

VI

THE UNION CONSTITUTION

THERE ARE APPROXIMATELY two hundred national unions in the United States, each with a constitution of its own devising which is the supreme law for its members. The government set up by each union constitution is normally independent of legal control by any other union government and free to determine the nature of its relations with other unions. There is no one fundamental union law that governs all organized labor as all the states and their inhabitants are subject to the Constitution of the United States. The constitution of the old AFL provided that affiliation shall be "based upon strict recognition of the autonomy of each trade." In practice this meant autonomy for each union since multi-trade and industrial unions are among its member organizations. The old CIO constitution contained no such express guarantee of autonomy, but it avowed the same principle. The constitution of its largest affiliate, the United Automobile Workers, stated as one of its objectives: "To work as an autonomous International Union with the CIO together with other international unions." The principle of national union autonomy survived the merger of the AFL and CIO. Thus there is no essential difference between the governments of the organizations leagued in the confederations and the unaffiliated or "independent unions." They are alike independent, autonomous, except as all unions are subject to the general laws of the country.

Like sovereign states every national union claims equal recognition and standing for its government regardless of how small its membership or how limited its jurisdiction. Some restrict eligibility to craftsmen whose total number in the country is but a few hundred. Others are open to employees of a variety of occupations in many industries so that their potential membership may be several million. In 1950 twenty-two national unions had less than 1,000 members apiece, and the membership of thirty others ranged from 1,000 to 5,000. More than a third of all unions each had less than 10,000 members. At the other extreme were two unions (AFL Teamsters and CIO Auto Workers) which have claimed around a million members, and four others had 500,000 or more. About thirty had between 100,000 and 500,000 members, and almost half the unions fell in the groups between 10,000 and 100,000. Many of the smaller organizations have fewer members than are to be found in a single local of other unions; but whatever the size, normally each national union asserts its right to autonomy.

Most union constitutions are not submitted to the members for approval. They are adopted and amended by conventions of elected representatives. Only about twenty require ratification of constitutional changes by popular vote. More than half do make a plebiscite possible if a sufficient number of local unions or members invoke referendum provisions contained in the constitutions, and frequently conventions and executive boards have discretion to refer constitutional amendments to a referendum. In such cases clauses adopted at conventions may be rejected, or new clauses inserted by vote of the membership. But the prevailing practice is to make convention action final on all matters relating to the rights of the members and the government of the union. In this respect union governments resemble parliamentary states whose legislative bodies also have authority to make constitutional changes.

Indeed the typical union constitution identifies the national union with the representative convention rather than with the body of its membership. "All sovereign powers, including the legislative, executive, administrative and judicial of the International Union of Operative Engineers, shall be vested in its General Convention when in session." [1] In one way or another most union constitutions say much the same thing.

[1] Constitution (1938 as amended in 1944), Art. III, p. 8.

Like the Operating Engineers, the Rubber Workers provides in its constitution: "Supreme governing powers shall be vested in the (Union) in Convention assembled." [2] And typical of the railroad brotherhoods is this from the Railway Clerks' constitution: "The sovereign body of the Brotherhood shall be called the Grand Lodge (composed of convention delegates and elected officials) and will have absolute and exclusive jurisdiction over all matters pertaining to the Brotherhood; it is the true and legitimate source of all authority, the final resort of appeal, and there is no power vested in any officer, committee or body of members to repeal, alter or change its laws and decisions, except by referendum vote as hereinafter provided." [3]

The constitution of the United Mine Workers which is now "independent," puts it this way: "The International Union shall have supreme legislative, executive, and judicial authority over all members and subordinate branches, and shall be the ultimate tribunal to which all matters of importance to the welfare of the membership and subordinate branches shall be referred for adjustment." [4] That "The International Union" as here used means "the Convention" is made plain by a further provision that "between International Conventions the supreme executive and judicial powers shall be vested in the Executive officers and Executive Board . . ." It is significant, also, that the Miners' constitution and some others including the Steelworkers, which provide for election of national officers by referendum vote of the members, neither require nor permit a referendum on constitutional changes.

The national convention is the basic governing body provided for by practically all union constitutions. This assembly of elected delegates was substituted by the national organizations for the general membership meeting which governed unions when they were small and locally autonomous. The constitutions of a few unions of professional employees still provide for such meetings of the members rather than for a representative body (e.g., actors and artists). Like the general meeting, the national convention

---

[2] Constitution (1946), Art. IV, p. 5.   [3] Constitution (1947), Art. II, p. 3.
[4] Constitution, 1944, Art. III, pp. 5–6.

is not an occasional assembly for the limited purpose of revising fundamental laws, but an active, continual organ of union government; it is at once a legislature, a constitutional convention, and a supreme judicial court.

With few exceptions, the constitution requires the convention to meet regularly as the legislative body of the union, and the power to legislate includes authority to amend or revise the constitution. Rarely is a greater majority specified for changing the constitution than for adopting laws or ressolutions. In addition the convention is authorized to decide, on appeal, any controversy arising within the union, including questions of constitutional interpretation. Intervals between convention sessions are short for most unions. Annual or biennial meetings are fixed by two-thirds of the constitutions. The rest set meetings every three, four, or five years, except a few that specify no time, but leave the frequency of sessions to be determined by vote of the members. At least one (Die Sinkers') requires three meetings every year, and all constitutions provide for special sessions on call of executive officers or petition by certain percentages of the membership and local unions.

By lodging all governmental powers in the representative assemblies and requiring regularly recurring sessions, the constitutions establish a form of rule for the unions which is in effect government by constitutional convention. There is no separation of powers and no checks and balances. Between conventions executive, judicial, and to some extent legislative authority is delegated to the president of the union, to the executive board and to other agencies. But these are not coordinate branches of government with independent powers; they are rather parts of a graded order of authority. Thus administrative and judicial decisions of local unions are subject to appeal to the president. His acts and decisions usually require approval by the executive board, while its determinations are appealable to the convention which alone has final authority.

The theory that dividing the powers of government among more or less independent departments adds safeguards to individual rights and liberties finds no favor among union constitution-makers. They are more concerned with building governments for effective action, and to that end concentrate powers in a single agency to which all governing officials and departments are responsible. There are no bicameral legislatures so that one may block laws desired by the other; and normally no executive has authority to veto legislation. There is no independent judiciary authorized to set aside laws that contravene the constitution or that infringe on liberties reserved to the members.

The single chamber representative assembly enacts laws, determines policies, amends or revises the constitution, and acts as a supreme court. It assigns duties and responsibilities to governing officials, and usually it also elects the national officers. In most cases popular control is considered sufficiently assured by the power in the membership to elect the convention delegates. Only about a fourth of the constitutions provide for direct election of executive officers by the members, and though many make provision for a referendum to be taken on petition of a specified portion of the membership, these often contain restrictions that discourage its use.

The wording of the constitution is rarely precise and clear. Much of its meaning depends on knowledge of prevailing practices in the trade or industry to which it applies. Normally, however, it organizes the powers of government as indicated, though it may not formally describe the successive levels in the hierarchy of authority. From those constitutions that do contain such a description, the underlying pattern of all of them is easily recognized. No matter how the constitution may be worded or its parts arranged, its organization of authority will be found in some such order as the following:

1. The union "shall be composed of workers eligible for membership . . . and may be divided into local unions and district (and other subordinate) organizations . . ."

2. This union "shall have supreme legislative, executive and judicial authority over all members and all subordinate bodies" . . . "To it shall belong the power to determine the customs and usages in regard to all matters relating to the craft (or the trade or fellowship)."

3. All powers of the union "shall be vested in its convention."

4. "When the convention is not in session, they shall be vested in the Executive Council (or Board)."

5. "When the Executive Council is not in session, they shall be vested in the International officers (or the president)."

DESPITE THE UNIFORMITY of their governmental frame, union constitutions vary widely in their detailed provisions. The range of variation may be gathered from the length of the written documents. Some are complete in less than 3,000 words, others run to more than 75,000 words. The shorter constitutions are most frequently those of industrial unions. Craft unions usually write theirs at much greater length. One reason for this is that craft organizations customarily include working rules, standard conditions of employment, and regulations of apprenticeship in their fundamental laws, as well as provisions for insurance or beneficial departments. Industrial unions generally rely on their collective bargaining agreements with employers to provide such regulations, and often make but scant references to them in their constitutions.

Another reason is that the constitutions grow in size as the unions grow older, and most industrial unions are relatively new. But just as the line between craft and industrial unionism is being blurred by technological developments, so the constitutions of the two kinds of organizations are becoming more alike. A marked trend is evident in the constitutional revisions of industrial unions to add provisions dealing with standardizing working conditions, regulating collective bargaining, handling grievances, and providing beneficial features or welfare plans in the manner of craft organizations.

However brief or extended the constitutions may be, and much as they may vary in content, they normally include the following:

1. Statement of Objectives of the union and Description of its jurisdiction. These clauses usually repeat in more specific terms what is generally proclaimed in the preamble attached to most constitutions. Sometimes this contains the objects of the union, but more often the preamble declares principles and broad purposes while specific objectives are listed in the constitution. (Occasionally there is also a platform.)

2. Governmental Structure: (a) Definition of powers of national

union and its authority over local organizations and other subordinate bodies, including power to grant and withdraw charters. (b) Executive Organization. Titles, qualifications, and duties of national officers; method of nomination and election; term of office, salary provisions; national executive and administrative board or council and trustees, how constituted, functions including publication of official organ or journal. (c) Convention. Election and qualifications of delegates, basis of representation, frequency of meetings; functions including amending constitution, convention officers and committees and their duties (often includes order of business and rules of order).

3. Statutory Enactments. Provisions dealing with strikes, collective bargaining, and methods of handling grievances. Practically all constitutions have these. Many contain more extensive laws governing also wages, hours, employment, relations with employers, shop chairmen, stewards, and committees. Sometimes these are grouped as separate parts of constitution and titled statutes, by-laws, general laws, standing rules, and resolutions.

4. By-Laws for government of local unions, district councils and other subordinate organizations. Frame of local government, names of executive officers, how and when elected, their duties and responsibilities; frequency of membership meetings and order of business; power to adopt local laws and working rules; extent of jurisdiction and autonomy of locals, limitations.

5. Membership Provisions. Eligibility, initiation, suspension, expulsion, disqualifications; obligations of members, minimum number to form and maintain local unions, transfers between locals.

6. Revenues and Expenditures. Dues, assessments (conditions of levying), fees; apportionment of funds, audits, control of disbursements, and finances of locals.

7. Disciplinary Provisions. Violations of constitution and laws; charges against members and national and local officers; trials, appeals, penalties.

Plainly this subject matter covers a good deal more than what is ordinarily contained in a written political constitution. Statutes, by-laws, rules, and work and strike regulations are interwoven with constitutional provisions. Often policy resolutions and rituals are included. The union constitution is in fact a compilation of all its laws, though some unions attempt to distinguish between a fundamental instrument and other kinds of laws. Most commonly, however, the laws appear as articles and sections of the constitution and this usually bears a double title such as Constitution and Laws, Constitution and By-Laws, or Constitution and Rules (or Statutes).

The laws of the International Typographical Union, according to its constitution, "shall be comprised in: (a) The constitution. . . . (b) The by-laws. . . . (c) The general laws. . . . (d) The convention laws . . ." and these are bound together in its "Book of Laws." But the Printing Pressmen's Union embodies all such laws in one document, its "Constitution and Laws." Similarly the Railway Clerks classify separately the "Constitution of the Grand Lodge, Statutes for the Government of Lodges, and Protective Laws," while the Locomotive Firemen and Enginemen incorporate all enactments in their constitution, as do the Trainmen. The Conductors, however, differentiate statutes from the constitution, but unlike the Clerks, they make no distinction between protective laws and statutes for subordinate lodges. The "Laws of the Pattern Makers League" make no mention of a constitution at all, but classify separately laws of the national organization, laws for the government of subordinate "Associations," and "Rules for Shop Committees." On the other hand the "International and Local Laws Governing the Metal Polishers . . . Union" are all embodied in the forty-three articles of its "Constitution."

Industrial unions rarely attempt classification of their laws, but merge them all in a constitution or constitution and by-laws. Attached to the Steelworkers constitution, however, is a "Manual" for local unions and "Instructions . . . [for] Trial, Discipline, and Expulsion of Members." The American Newspaper Guild similarly appends a "Collective Bargaining Program" and "Model Local By-Laws." (This organization, though one of its objectives is "to promote industrial unionism in the newspaper industry, is primarily a union of professional workers.) The "Constitution and Laws" of the Bakers and Confectionary Workers also form one document, but appended to it are "Rules for Local Unions" and togther they are covered in the Union's "Book of Laws."

Thus there is no common recognition among labor organizations of an essential difference between their constitutions and other laws. Those that group statutes, rules, or by-laws separately invariably print them together with their constitutions. There is little uniformity in classifying matter under such headings, and most unions incorporate all laws in one instrument. Union members do not revere their constitutions above their laws, doubtless because they see little distinction between the two.

The union constitution departs in another respect from the traditions of American political constitution making. It normally contains no bill of rights. Duties and obligations to the union are emphasized, but there is no general practice of guaranteeing to individual members basic freedoms which are beyond the reach of union legislation. A few unions have a constitutional provision like that of the Bricklayers: "Every member . . . shall stand equal before the law in his rights and privileges, and shall be entitled to all benefits and protection, providing he conforms to the rules and form of procedure." [5] And a rare provision in the Machinists' constitution provides that "All authority and power not specifically delegated to the officers in this constitution is reserved to the membership." [6]

But these limit only acts of officials, and the officers interpret the laws. The constitutions do not guarantee individual rights against legislation enacted by a convention or of the union government as a whole. The legislative power is not restricted to prohibit adoption of laws that invade specified liberties which are considered inviolate. All matters are subject to majority rule either of convention delegates or members participating in a referendum, and usually a simple majority is sufficient. Only about a third of the unions require more than a simple majority for constitutional amendments, and the same majority is generally fixed for changing the constitution as for enacting statutes.

With few exceptions, however, the constitutions do provide

[5] Constitution and Rules of Order (1944), Art. XII, Sec. 2, p. 51.
[6] Constitution (1946), Art. XXVI, p. 55.

that members and officers accused of offenses against union laws shall have trials. Written charges are required, as are opportunity to answer, due notice of hearings, appeals, review of decisions by higher tribunals, etc. The right to be represented by counsel is usually specified, though the counsel must be a member of the organization. But no provision is made for specialized judges and courts to guard these procedural rights. For each case the executive of the local or the national union appoints a committee to conduct the trial or may itself act as court.

In so far as there is any jury it is the members present at the local union meeting. They must approve or disapprove the findings and judgments of the trial committees. On appeal this decision is reviewable by the national president or executive board, and final appeal is to the convention whose delegates by majority vote determine guilt or innocence. Accompanying these provisions is commonly a strict rule that members must exhaust all procedures and remedies within the union before resorting to any court of law or equity. But at least one constitution (Printing Pressmen) requires every member to pledge in addition: "I will not apply to the courts from decisions of the majority of the union." [7] This provision, if tested in the courts, would probably be set aside as judges have often reversed disciplinary action by unions because procedures did not assure a fair trial. Such rulings by the courts are largely responsible for the careful spelling out of trial procedures in union constitutions.

SOME CONSTITUTIONS contain clauses forbidding commitment of the union to any religious creed or organization, and prohibiting "partisan" politics or endorsement of any political party. But while the references to religion are unequivocal, the political clauses are enigmatic, and may not square with other provisions in the same documents. For example: "The Brotherhood of Locomotive Firemen and Enginemen [according to its constitution] is a nonsectarian and nonpartisan organization, and no person shall be barred from membership on account of religion or political affiliation." Yet it provides severe penalties for "any

[7] Constitution (1940), Art. VII, p. 23.

member interfering with legislative matters . . . , or who engages in any political campaign against any candidate for political office, after such candidate has received the endorsement of the organization . . ." [8]

A less direct though no less important contradiction between specific provisions and the general assurance of political freedom may be seen in the constitution of the United Mine Workers. This ordains that the union "as an organization shall not be committed to or favor any particular religious creed; neither shall affiliation herewith interfere with the religious or political freedom of individual members." But other clauses make it a punishable offense to circulate or cause to be circulated "false statements about any member . . . , or wrongfully condemning any decision rendered by an officer of the organization . . . , [and] the above shall be construed as applying to any local officer or member reading such circulars to the members of a local union, or who in any way gives publicity to such." [9] This hardly seems compatible with free political campaigning, particularly as the national officers are the judges of what is false or wrongful.

And more direct control or censorship of communication among members and local unions may be found in the same constitutions that apparently guarantee individual freedom in politics. The Railway Clerks' constitution, which pledges that "The influence of the Brotherhood as a body shall never be enlisted or used in favor of any religious organization . . . or partisan politics or any political party," also provides that: "Except in the case of subordinate units addressing their own members, no circulars or petitions shall be issued without approval of the Grand President. His approval must be shown on the petition or circular when authorized." Such approval is also required when a referendum vote is pending within the union: "No member or subordinate unit shall issue any communication whatsoever for the purpose of influencing such [referendum] vote . . . until copies have been filed . . . and approved." Further, any member sending letters or circulars to any member or lodge or in any way circulating

[8] Constitution (1948), Art. XX, p. 261; Art. XVII, p. 231.
[9] Constitution (1944), Art. XXI, Sec. 3, p. 79.

reports liable to cause trouble or injure the Brotherhood or its members shall be expelled." [10]

The by-laws of the Typographical Union provide that "No subordinate union shall assess its members for partisan political purposes," though expressly authorizing it to "take political action when the interests of organized labor as a whole and the craft in particular may be benefited thereby." [11] Similarly the Bricklayers' constitution prohibits its national secretary-treasurer from approving any expenditures for partisan political purposes. Such provisions in union constitutions are not common, however.

Such conflicting provisions are more or less inevitable where unions attempt to guarantee individual freedom in politics and at the same time promote programs for labor and social legislation, indorse political candidates, and engage in other political activities. Perhaps the difficulties of reconciling the individual's rights in such matters with his duty to support organization policies explain why most constitutions contain no proscription against union interference with the individual member's political activities and beliefs. Neither do most constitutions attempt to guarantee freedom from interference with religious beliefs. Although the same difficulties are not present as in dealing with politics, the organizations apparently prefer to leave matters of creed to the good sense of the membership.

Absence of a bill of rights does not mean of course that basic liberties are entirely unprotected. As governments of democratic states which lack such a bill guard freedoms by legislation, so do unions, by custom, practice, and law. But the legislative authority is usually unrestricted in its discretion as to rights it will or will not protect. Thus the laws of some unions guarantee freedoms that others deny. The initiation rules of the United Steelworkers and some other unions direct presidents of local unions to say to all candidates for membership before obligating them: "Let me assure you that in this obligation there is nothing contrary to your civil or religious duties." [12] On the other hand every worker ad-

[10] Constitution (1947), Art. XVI, pp. 63–64.
[11] Book of Laws (1945), Art. XX, p. 84.
[12] Constitution and Manual (1944), p. 68.

mitted to the Typographical Union must "solemnly and sincerely swear (or affirm) . . . that my fidelity to the union and my duty to the members thereof shall in no sense be interfered with by any allegiance that I may now or hereafter owe to any other organization, social, political or religious, secret or otherwise." [13] The ritual of the Painters, Decorators and Paperhangers' Union contains a similar provision.

Equal treatment for all members under the laws of the union, though rarely specified as a guaranteed right is usually considered required by the general statement of purpose contained in most constitutions: "To unite in one organization all workers eligible to membership." Many add the phrase, "regardless of race, creed, color, nationality, or political affiliation," and some, like the Rub ber Workers, pledge themselves also "to secure equal pay for equal work regardless of age or sex." But other constitutions and laws distinguish different classes of membership, and do not grant the same privileges and protection to all classes. The classifications do not necessarily involve unjustifiable discrimination, but sometimes the discriminatory intent is clear and avowed.

Organizations of professional employees may not grant full membership rights to beginners in the profession or those who engage in it only intermittently. Thus the Screen Actors Guild has a Junior Membership for those who have not acted in at least two motion pictures in parts receiving screen credits, and a Class B membership for those who have served only as "extras." The Airline Pilots Association until recently allowed to copilots only half the voting strength in its conventions that pilots enjoyed, and a copilot could not be president of the organization. Its 1948 convention removed these distinctions.

Craft unions too do not give full membership rights to apprentices, and where they admit helpers and miscellaneous workers not skilled in the trade, they may group them as a separate class of members with limited privileges. The Brotherhood of Electrical Workers, for example, authorizes the establishment of Class B local unions, admitting to membership employees engaged in the miscellaneous branches of the electrical industry. The mem-

[13] Book of Laws (1945), Art. XII, Sec. 1, p. 17.

bers of these locals do not participate in the insurance benefits paid by the union and they are exempted from paying premiums. A large proportion of them are women, and they pay lower dues than the journeymen electricians. Other unions provide for non-participants in insurance funds without establishing a special class of membership for them.

Such "nonbeneficiary" members suffer no discrimination in so far as insurance benefits are concerned; they draw no benefits because they make no contributions to the insurance funds. Some pay smaller premiums and get smaller benefits. They may enjoy the same protection of the union as fully insured members in collective bargaining, in handling grievances, and in other dealings with employers. In internal government of the union itself, however, some constitutions still restrict rights of less-skilled members as compared with those of the craftsmen. Thus Class B locals of the Brotherhood of Electrical Workers are allowed one delegate to the union's conventions for each 500 members whereas the craft locals get a delegate for each 100 members. And when the full voting strength of the membership is registered, a craft delegate casts a vote for every member he represents, while a Class B delegate has one vote for every 50 members.

Similarly "non-craft" locals of the Flint Glass Workers Union are represented in its conventions on the basis of twice as many members per delegate as are allotted to the craft locals. The constitution of this union provides further: "When voting on important questions in convention by division vote, . . . the voting power shall be equal between the seated delegates representing (non-craft) local unions and the (craft) local unions." [14] Wall Paper Craftsmen and "workers" having joined in one union allow a delegate for each 50 craftsmen, but "workers'" locals get a delegate for each 200 members; and "the number of delegates representing craftsmen shall equal the number of delegates representing workers."

The Glass Bottle Blowers base their representation in conventions both on the number of members and the amount of dues paid. Craftsmen paying $2.50 per month get one delegate

[14] Constitution (1950), Art. IX, pp. 23–24.

for each 50 members, and miscellaneous locals (paying $1.50 or less) one delegate for each 100 members. On the other hand, the National Brotherhood of Operative Potters provides for equal representation of all members in conventions, and all enjoy the same rights, privileges, and benefits. There is no separation of craftsmen from less-skilled or unskilled laborers. All belong to the same local unions. Most building trade and metal trades craft unions which formerly restricted the representation rights of helpers now allow them full and equal membership rights.

Unlike the Flint Workers, the Glass Bottle Blowers' Association does not equalize the voting power of its craft and non-craft local unions. Hence, despite the weighted representation in favor of the craftsmen, the less-skilled workers dominate its conventions. But according to its president the national executive board is balanced between the crafts and the unskilled workers. "Our union has established separate local unions for the skilled and unskilled. In some localities, at the request of the workers, we permit one local union . . . we have no iron clad rule as to the separation. . . . Our so-called craft locals are small in number and run in size from 35 to 200 members. Our other locals run in size from 150 to 900 members. . . . Craft locals are permitted one delegate for each 50 members. Miscellaneous locals, one delegate for each 100 members. This may sound unfair but our conventions are dominated by the miscellaneous locals with the voting strength three to one over the crafts. In other words, the miscellaneous locals control our International Union. I might add in passing that as International President, I came from the miscellaneous department. In view of this fact, my Executive Board is balanced as between the crafts and the miscellaneous departments." [15]

The Potters' Brotherhood by including miscellaneous employees in the same locals with the craftsmen and making no distinctions between them has, in effect, become an industrial union, and because the less-skilled operatives and laborers are a majority in practically all such unions, they are in a position to subordinate the interests of the crafts to their own. Skilled mechanics in industrial unions complain no less of domination by the unskilled

[15] L. W. Minton, International President, letter to the author dated March 16, 1950.

than do factory operatives and machine hands in the unions that are controlled by the skilled craft workers. Thus the constitutions and laws of all manner of unions are concerned with maintaining a balance between the skilled groups and the others, but the general trend is toward equalizing the rights of individual members with consequent greater weight and influence of the unskilled in the government and politics of the organizations.

As IMPORTANT as equal treatment of members within the union is equal application of union laws to potential members. The trend of constitutional changes in this respect has also been generally in the direction of admitting eligible applicants without discrimination. Many unions have discarded the old custom borrowed from fraternal organizations and clubs of requiring workers to be "proposed for admission" by a number of members, and have substituted a simple application by one who wants to join. Union rules which barred women and the foreign-born from membership have quite generally disappeared, and much progress has been made during the last decade in eliminating discrimination on account of race or color. This trend was quickened by a presidential Fair Employment Practice Commission established during World War II, and by statutes enacted in a number of states providing for similar commissions. It is continued under pressure of court decisions interpreting labor relations laws and of the public agitation for a federal FEPC law.

The constitutions of seven railroad brotherhoods still (1950) restrict membership to "white born" persons, and some of them exclude not only Negroes, but also "Mexicans and those of Spanish-Mexican extraction." These organizations are composed of employees in engine and train service or in other work directly connected with the movement of trains, and among their other qualifications for membership are U.S. or Canadian citizenship and ability to read and write English. They are known as "operating employees." [16] The unions of "nonoperating" employees which represent about three-fourths of all railway workers no longer have

---

[16] They are the engineers, firemen, brakemen or trainmen, switchmen, and train dispatchers. The Order of Railroad Telegraphers, though classified as "nonoperating" also excludes Negroes.

constitutional bars against admission of Negroes. A few of these, however, segregate colored members in separate local unions which are required to be represented in national conventions by white delegates. Such provisions are not confined to the railroad locals of these unions; most of the nonoperating railway organizations normally function in other industries as well, and similar segregation is practiced in those industries too.

But in and outside the railroad industry the discriminatory provisions are rapidly disappearing from union constitutions. Since 1945 the Blacksmiths, Boilermakers, Sheet Metal Workers, Railway Carmen, Maintenance of Way Employees, and the Railway Clerks have dropped clauses requiring segregation of colored members and representation by white delegates. The Clerks' Brotherhood had previously eliminated the restriction of membership to white persons, the Switchmen's Union did the same in 1946, and the Machinists have recently removed the bar against Negroes from their ritual. The number of constitutions containing clauses discriminating against colored and Mexican workers has been reduced to less than a dozen, and these are definitely on their way out, although the "white men's" transportation organizations are still strongly resistant.

Absence of constitutional discrimination, however, does not mean that race prejudice among the members has been wiped out. Discriminatory practices persist in local unions and on the national level. Applications for membership in the Air Line Pilots Association, for example, "must be accompanied by a photograph of the applicant"—a device often used in industry generally for barring Negroes. The Boilermakers require an applicant for membership to be "a citizen of some civilized country"!

When the U.S. Supreme Court upheld decisions of lower courts finding the Brotherhood of Locomotive Firemen guilty of unlawfully discriminating against Negro workers covered by its collective bargaining contracts,[17] this union did not eliminate from its constitution the white-born qualifications for membership. It merely added a sentence stating that "if these provisions conflict with any

---

[17] Steele v. L. & N. Ry. Co., 323 U.S. 192; Tunstald v. Locomotive Firemen & Enginemen, 323 U.S. 210 (1944).

federal, state, or Canadian laws, the provisions of such laws shall supersede these provisions to the extent required to bring about conformation . . . and to remove the violation or conflict."

Some national constitutions provide that qualifications for membership shall be determined by the local unions, and doubtless because of continued abuses, some of them have added clauses specifically prohibiting discrimination and imposing penalties. Thus the Hotel and Restaurant Union declares: "Any local law prohibiting the admission of any competent person, male or female, because of race, religion, or color is contrary to our laws, and is therefore null and void." Two building trade organizations (Plasterers and Bricklayers) prescribe a penalty of $100 for "members who refuse to work with any member on account of his race, color, or nationality." The Newspaper Guild's constitution prescribes that "no eligible person shall be barred from membership or penalized by reason of sex, race, or religion, or political convictions, or because of anything he writes for publication." And as already mentioned, some industrial unions have found it necessary to appoint fair employment practice committees to enforce their provisions against discrimination not only by employers, but by their own members as well.

In one respect there is an increasing tendency to deny equal protection of union laws to eligible workers and to members. More and more unions are disqualifying adherents of Communism and other totalitarian doctrines from membership, requiring the expulsion of any found within the ranks. In 1950 about sixty constitutions contained such provisions. The clauses are variously worded. Most commonly anyone is declared ineligible who is a Communist, Nazi, or Fascist, or belongs to such a party or to an organization which advocates overthrowing the government by force, or to a "subversive group seeking to advance the interests of totalitarianism." Sometimes merely advocating such causes is ground for exclusion, or belonging to an organization "hostile to the American form of government," or that "expounds principles inimical to our constitutional government." A few constitutions also bar members of the Ku Klux Klan.

Communists, of course, denounce the interdictions against them as attempts at thought-control inspired by political motives, but they see nothing wrong in excluding Nazis or Fascists. Little attention needs to be paid to their argumentation. More disinterested critics, however, condemn all the exclusions as discriminating among union members and applicants for membership because of political affiliations or beliefs. Fearing the effects on freedom of opinion, they question the justice and wisdom of closing the unions, and thus denying equal employment opportunities to workers otherwise eligible who espouse unpopular causes or who adhere to groups advocating repugnant doctrines. From these quarters have come proposals for remedial legislation to prohibit this kind of discrimination as well as other discriminatory practices of labor organizations.

Discussing these proposals two able lawyers argue:

Those favoring the exclusion of Communists from labor unions do not explain why it is that we are justified in prohibiting the exercise of arbitrary power by unions to exclude people from equal work opportunities on the basis of race, creed or color, while permitting exclusion because of political belief. It may be doubted whether such justification exists, at least so long as adherence to these unpopular political beliefs and support of the party which advances them are not themselves unlawful.[18]

This hardly states the problem in realistic terms. It assumes that opinions or beliefs are the basis of the exclusions rather than overt acts or a course of conduct. True, loose wording of the discriminatory clauses lends itself to this interpretation; but the fact that the same constitutions which exclude Communists and other "subversives" sometimes also prohibit commitment of the union to any political party, or require admission of eligible workers regardless of political affiliations or beliefs, should raise doubts that the proscriptions are directed against mere beliefs or political allegiance.

The assumption that Communists are excluded "because of political belief" has little basis in fact. Unlike socialists, single taxers, and other political and social propagandists who strive to commit labor to their doctrines, they rarely explain their beliefs or

[18] Benjamin Aaron and Michael I. Komaroff, "Statutory Regulations of Internal Union Affairs," in *Illinois Law Review*, Vol. 44, Nos. 4 and 5 (1949), p. 652.

attempt to justify them in open union meetings. Instead they vaunt their devotion to trade-union objectives, and surreptitiously seek control of the organizations through "cells" made up of small groups of disciplined infiltrators. These plan strategy and tactics to further Communist ends.

VII

THE UNION CONVENTION

THE NATIONAL UNION "in convention assembled" is in many respects a unique political institution deserving more attention and study than political scientists have given it. Though a representative body, the typical convention is identified with the union itself as if it were a general meeting of all the members. On roll call votes the full membership of each local union is voted by its representatives in some conventions. In most, the same plebiscite effect is achieved by the delegates from each local casting a fixed number of votes proportionate to its membership. Often the elected delegates are instructed by their locals how they shall vote on certain issues.

The convention is the big meeting where the union as a whole acts, in contrast with the numerous smaller meetings of shop units, local unions, district councils, joint boards, trade divisions, territorial conferences, and committees through which the every day business of the union is done. It is the most formal and most authoritative meeting. "All sovereign powers," as many constitutions say, are in the convention, or, as the 1951 convention notice of one union put it: "It is during conventions that the Grand Lodge [national union] is the governing body of the Die Sinkers [Union]."

Combining within itself the functions of a constitutional assembly, a legislature, and a supreme court, it is also a nominating convention with many of the spectacular features of the quadrennial political conventions that nominate candidates for President and Vice-President of the United States. In most conventions the delegates are also the electors of the president and other chief union officers, and all national officials are responsible to the convention. Theoretically, if not actually in practice, the convention controls administration. In addition, it serves fraternal, educational, and social purposes which have come to be regarded as of almost equal importance.

Besides the accredited delegates and officers who constitute the convention proper, alternates are elected and ex-delegates are often honored guests. Rank and file union members and staff employees come as visitors: "All members of the Order [Railway Conductors] who are in good standing shall be honorary members of the Grand Division [convention], entitled to admission during any of its sessions unless excluded by a majority vote." Many bring their wives, and often a ladies' auxiliary association sponsored by the union meets concurrently. There are fraternal delegates from other unions at home and abroad. The Die Sinkers, a small union with 150 delegates at its 1947 assembly, reported 450 visitors in attendance.

The convention is more than a meeting of a legislative body; it is a general convocation, a big social event. Leaders and followers from all sections of the country get reasonably acquainted, new friendships are made, local officers and members from distant places compare notes, varying conditions under which members work become commonly known, unity is promoted. Speeches, debates, and group meetings indoctrinate in "union principles," fraternal delegates and public figures in and outside the labor movement deliver addresses, and not least appreciated are the entertainment features—a banquet, a ball, dinners, music, a show —often at the expense of the union though not without some misgiving.

At the 1944 meeting of the Amalgamated Clothing Workers, an earnest delegate urging the importance of political action remarked: "It is all right to be at a convention, it is all right to have a good time, and God knows a good time has been shown to us so far. Some of our delegates have said to me: 'I do not know what to do with my expense money. We have dinners every night.' " The same year the Steelworkers at their convention banquet witnessed a one-act play by professional actors dramatizing the life of the union president, while the United Electrical Workers meeting in Manhattan distributed tickets to plays and movies. James J. Walker, showman, song writer, and sometime Mayor of Greater New York, told the Ladies' Garment Workers that year: "Today I did witness the convention and the pride I anticipated was enhanced by the performance. I have never seen more delightful showmanship, coupled with substantial purpose, such splendid decor, so effective, so touching in spots."

Not all conventions organize their entertainment with professional skill and decor, but the unions that manage to have little controversy on the convention floor tend to be the more lavish in their entertainment. Practically all conventions, however, combine entertainment with the serious business of enacting laws, adjudicating internal disputes, and policy making. In all its functions the convention serves to train union leaders and to enlarge the knowledge of the membership both as to union and public affairs. Whatever it does, whether it legislates with deliberation or echoes the executive while those in attendance are charmed by entertainment, delegates and members see it happen, and their reports to local union meetings pass on what they have learned to the rank and file.

A veteran delegate to Glass Bottle Blowers' conventions expressing reluctance to change from annual to biennial meetings, observes: "It is a great educational force and I delight in attending." A novice agrees: "New delegates like myself can learn a whole lot and it is well worth while." At an Electrical Workers convention a delegate explained the purpose of a proposal to increase the size of local delegations in these words: "Its main purpose [is] to give to our membership the opportunity to send to this convention more members in order that they may receive the education and the things that are so necessary for the rank and file members back in the locals to know, in order to become leaders and to carry out the policies that are adopted in these conventions." A glass worker told the 1929 convention of his union: "It is well for us to come in contact with each other and exchange ideas both in the business and trade union way, to say nothing of the enjoyable social side.

It all helps, and it instills life into our organization and brings about effective cooperation in many ways."

Two visitors to a Railway Signalmen's convention summed up their impressions in the September 1946 issue of the union's *Journal:*

A Retired Signalman—I'm broke, just back from the best convention I ever attended. Everybody was congenial, but boy did they hit the floor and argue on everything that came up, not a resolution was railroaded through, standing and roll call votes were common. The convention reelected all our present officers with very little opposition; no need of it. They are doing a very able job and getting better all the time.

Per-cap [dues to national] had to be upped a little to take care of extra expense, but this would not have been necessary if it had not been for the cheap, free riding nons [nonmembers]. If you get them in there will be no need of any further raises. Don't forget, this is everybody's job, not just the secretary or griever. . . .

The banquet Thursday night was a real success and wound up with everybody singing. . . .

This convention also decided to go back to the American Federation, provided we live under our own tent. [About twenty years earlier a jurisdictional dispute with the Electrical Workers brought a break with AFL.] It is time all labor got into one big family of American craftsmen and kicked out these foreign isms.

A Signalman's Wife—Since wives have been along to the convention, I would like to invade the men's territory just one more time. I think I can speak for most of the wives . . . in saying that we enjoyed the convention and that we appreciate the fact that our husbands were either willing for us to go or wanted us as the case may be. Anyway we were there.

This was my first convention and I was highly impressed by the friendliness of every one there and by the ability and pleasure to mingle and mix. It was like one big happy family. . . . It was like I heard one woman say. 'This is swell here. You can meet people and know they have no more than I have and I have no more than they have.' But honestly, I have never seen such a group of people with so much genuine friendliness as was at the convention. . . . Wouldn't it be a grand world if our nations could all have the same spirit that was at our convention!

Despite their common functions, union conventions are by no means all alike. The friendliness and apparent unanimity noted by the two visitors are by no means universal. Bitter factional conflicts are not uncommon, and some break out in violence. From union to union, and within the same organization at different times, conventions vary widely in character. Some are models of self-government, others mirror the powers of a dominating executive. There are conventions in which the delegate body is not much more than an audience registering approval of programs presented by the officers while it is being entertained. Others are truly deliberative bodies with wide participation by delegates in formulating, discussing, and adopting laws and policies. Some conventions are placid routine affairs, others are turbulent, riotous contests for power. A first convention forming a new national union differs markedly from its later periodic meetings, its delegates are more earnest spirits devoting themselves to the serious business of building a new government and social features are minimized.

Such differences are due not only to the age and experience of the union, but in part also to the variations in size of conventions. Some are small with half a hundred delegates or less, others range up to as many as two thousand and more. Like American legislatures generally, union conventions are reluctant to reduce the number of elected representatives as membership in the organizations increases, and the tendency is to enlarge the delegate body. As the assemblies grow larger, delegates find it more difficult to express themselves, and the greater is the likelihood that the conventions will be controlled by the officers or an organized faction. But there are outstanding exceptions, and small conventions may be autocratically ruled.

The physical surroundings of the union convention today are very different from those at the beginning of the century when nationally governed unions came to prevail. The typical convention no longer meets in a dingy union hall, in the lodge rooms of fraternal organizations, or in the "labor temples" of city central labor bodies, as used to be the custom. Ball rooms of large city hotels, public auditoriums, and assembly halls in resort towns like Miami and Atlantic City are common meeting places. Delegates are usually seated at long tables arranged in rows at right angles to the stage, and surrounding them at the sides and on the balcony is the visiting audience. At the front is a press table for newspaper reporters; union conventions have become news. The stage where officers and guests sit is flag-bedecked and decorated with flowers. Back of them a huge picture of the union president is sometimes displayed, and there may be other pictures of revered labor leaders or a popular President of the United States. Banners hang from the balcony and loud speakers are suspended from the ceiling. There is a microphone on the stage and one or several on the floor at which delegates line up when they want to speak. At the Ladies' Garment Workers 1917 convention in Cleveland's municipal auditorium, each delegate was furnished with a wooden block for pounding the table and sparing the hands in applauding. In its outward aspects the national convention of a labor union is as modern and efficient as business men's and political party conventions.

How important unions regard their conventions may be gathered from an editorial in *The Advance,* organ of the Men's Clothing Workers (May 15, 1948): "The Parliament of our sister organization, the Textile Workers Union of America, has adjourned almost on the eve of our own parliament meeting in the same place [Atlantic City]. Both of these parliaments legislate to further the interests of over a million men and women, and contrasted with what the Congress sitting in Washington is *not* now doing in the interests of this same army of workers, their proceedings are of much more importance."

ENTITLED TO REPRESENTATION in the convention are the officialdom of the union, the local unions, and the membership. National officers are generally delegates by virtue of the positions they hold, though some constitutions limit the privilege to certain chief officers or to the president alone. Others give officials a voice in the convention without the right to vote, except as they may be elected delegates from the local unions to which they belong. The practice of making officers "delegates at large" as the Commercial Telegraphers call them, is not universal, however; some unions require them to seek elections as representatives of the local unions in which they hold membership. On the other hand there are examples of nonofficers whose positions entitle them to be delegates. The Teamsters include ex-officio delegates. Some railroad unions give the same right to each general chairman who heads the bargaining and grievance committee on a railroad system.

Every local union however small its membership is entitled to at least one convention delegate just as in our state legislatures each county, or in New England each town no matter how meager its population, has at least one representative. Beyond the first delegate, representation of local unions is usually in some proportion to their memberships, except for a few unions which have a flat rule of one delegate and one vote per local. Often also, a maximum number of delegates is fixed that no local may exceed, or a maximum number of votes per delegate. The membership represented is determined by the per capita taxes each local has paid to the national organization during a fixed period prior to the convention.

Subordinate organizations other than local unions do not ordinarily have the right to be represented in the convention; but some unions permit their district councils, joint boards, or similar bodies each to send one delegate. Nor are branches of local unions or sub-locals given separate representation. The members of these are normally treated as belonging to the locals of which they are subdivisions, and their members are counted together with the main local's members in electing the representatives. Some of the larger industrial unions, however, have what they call "amalgamated locals" with sub-locals in various plants known as "units," and these sometimes have separate representation in proportion to their memberships. The constitution of the United Auto Workers so provides. Most unions also permit small locals which cannot afford the expenses of a convention delegate to join with others in sending one to represent their combined memberships.

Both the right of local unions to be represented in a convention and the right of delegates to represent the members are qualified by a requirement that they must be in "good standing." No member may be elected or serve as a delegate unless he has paid his dues and assessments regularly for a year or longer, and none of the local's representatives may be seated by a convention if the local has not paid to the national organization the per capita taxes and other required charges. Nor may local unions suspended for violation of union laws or other misconduct be represented at a convention. Typical is the provision in the Bricklayers' constitution that a local union shall not be entitled to representation which owes three months tax to the International Union. The law of the United Mine Workers is more specific: "No local union shall be entitled to representation that is in arrears for per capita tax or assessments for two months . . . and which has not in every particular complied with the constitutions of the International Union and of the district and sub-district to which it is attached." [1] An additional common qualification for delegates is that they must have attended at least half of the regular meetings of their locals for a period (usually six months or a year) prior to their election.

Though seemingly routine matters, these qualifications sometimes become important subjects of controversy in conventions. Supporting a proposal requiring regular attendance at local meetings as a condition for serving as a delegate, a representative at the 1944 Miners' convention said: "These guys come in three months before the election and bring their moonshine whiskey and everything else in. They don't know what the local is doing and they get elected." The United Electrical Workers' convention was informed by a delegate: "I happen to know that at the membership meeting of the local union that elected 10 delegates with at least 70 votes on this floor only 92 members participated in that election out of about 7,000." By way of remedy, some constitutions provide that delegates must be elected at specially called meetings by secret ballot or by referendum, and others require that they shall be chosen at the same time when members vote for officers. But the problem of delegates and officers elected by too few participants to be truly representative of the entire membership remains as serious in the unions as it does in elections for members of Congress and the President of the United States.

Except in the few unions where locals are entitled to but one

[1] Constitution (1944), Art. XII, Sec. 6, p. 40.

delegate with one vote, the number of votes in a convention is always greater than the number of delegates. Although proxy voting is generally prohibited (Longshoremen and Blacksmiths are exceptions), every convention delegate casts not only his own vote, but a share of the voting strength of the local union he represents as well. This voting strength varies with the size of the locals, and the total vote of a local union may be divided among its delegates or one of them may cast all its votes. The basis of representation and the methods of basing voting strength on size of local memberships differ among the unions, but three main types are recognizable in the constitutions.

The first is the most common. This bases both the number of delegates and the number of votes on the same specified number of members, so that both increase roughly in proportion to membership increases. An example is the Steelworkers' rule: "Each delegate shall have one vote for the first 100 members or less in the local union he represents and an additional vote for each additional 100 members or majority fraction thereof, but no delegate shall have more than 10 votes." [2] This maximum is an incentive to add delegates as membership rises above a thousand. The quotas for each vote vary in different unions, some fix it at 25 or 50, others at 200 or 300; and the maximum on votes per delegate is usually less than 10. Related to this plan of proportionate representation and voting are those like the Teamsters which authorize a delegate for every 300 members and one vote per delegate.

The second type holds down the number of delegates but grants additional votes in direct proportion to membership. Thus the Brotherhood of Maintenance of Way Employes limits the delegates to one per local, but gives him as many votes as the local has members in good standing. The International Brotherhood of Electrical Workers provide that each local union is entitled to one vote for each member in good standing but a delegate for each 100 members. Class B locals (non-craftsmen) have a vote for each 100 members and a delegate for each 500. The Woodworkers have a provision similar to that of the electrical workers for their skilled

[2] Constitution (1944), Art. VI, Sec. 2, p. 30.

men. The Auto Workers' constitution allows one delegate for 200 members, a second for 300, and additional delegates at the rate of one for 800 members, but grants a vote for every 100 members. Others (e.g., Machinists) base the representation in the convention on twice the number of members required for each vote. Usually when the number of representatives is restricted the votes are divided equally among them, but the Auto Workers limits each delegate to a maximum of 8 votes.

The third type increases both the number of delegates and votes at a lessening rate as the membership increases. This has many formulas, but the principle is the same—the larger the local union the smaller its proportion of representatives and votes. Usually each delegate is limited to one vote, but for additional delegates above the first one the required number of members per delegate is increased. In the Typographical Union's convention each delegate has only one vote, but the smallest locals with less than 100 members are entitled to a delegate, while those with 1,000 members are limited to four delegates, and one additional delegate is allowed for every 2,000 members. The Carpenters have a similar schedule but allow no more than four delegates for 1,000 or any greater number of members. The Newspaper Guild has one delegate for 7 members or less, two for 26 to 50, and thereafter one for each 100 members, no delegates having more than one vote. There are many other variations. In this group also belong those few organizations which allow but one delegate to a local regardless of the number of its members.

All three types attempt to balance in some measure the representation of local government units and size of memberships, i.e., of small and large locals. In all three every unit usually has the right to be represented, but in the first, voting is directly proportionate to membership, even to the extent of registering the votes of every member in some cases, thus giving the larger units greater influence. In the second this is also largely true, though modified by the limitations on number of delegates and votes per delegate. The third clearly gives greater representation to small locals than to large ones, and relatively greater weight is given to representation of governing units than numbers of members. The various formulas reflect compromises made to settle controversies about over-representation and under-representation.

Lacking bicameral legislatures where one house may represent governing units while the other represents numbers, growth in the size of the legislative body is a more serious problem in union governments than it is in most parliamentary or congressional governments. In organizations confined to craftsmen, it is not difficult to keep the number of delegates small enough to maintain the convention as a deliberative body, and to allow wide participation in debate. The Pattern Makers, for example, had only about 100 delegates at their most recent convention while in 1926 it had 75. Even a much larger craft union like the Typographical Union with a century of continuous existence did not exceed 300 delegates until about ten years ago, and in 1950 it had 368.

Much larger are the conventions of those craft organizations which have admitted semiskilled workers, operatives, and laborers. Thus the Machinists' convention usually seats more than 900 delegates, the Brotherhood of Electrical Workers more than 1,600, and the Railroad Brotherhoods run to 1,000 or more representatives. The Teamsters' Brotherhood which refers to itself as a craft union seats about 1,500. Unions of professional people are commonly small, but the Musicians had close to 1,000 delegates at their 1950 convention.

Industrial unions have the biggest conventions. The Rubber Workers, a relatively small organization with only about 250 local unions have between 500 and 600 delegates, and the CIO Electrical Workers' Union before the 1950 split had close to 800. The Men's Clothing Workers' delegate body and that of the Ladies' Garment Workers each number about 1,000. The Hotel and Restaurant Employees send nearly 1,200 delegates to their conventions, the Textile Workers more than 1,600. At the top with the largest representative bodies are three unions—Auto Workers, Miners, and Steelworkers—each with more than 2,000 delegates, the Miners

The conventions grow larger and little thought is given to the close to 3,000.

effect of their size on democratic procedures. Not infrequently a delegate rises to complain that important matters are being pushed through without consideration, but there is scant sentiment for reducing the number of representatives. Nothing like the strong feeling for smaller assemblies is evident today that existed in the Miners' Union four decades ago when its convention was half its present size. In 1912 a delegate supporting a constitutional amendment to cut drastically the number of representatives argued:

Anyone who has attended our international conventions must realize that they have reached a size where delegates can no longer take intelligent action on the questions that come before them. . . . This convention is so large that at least one-half the delegates are paying no attention . . . because it is impossible for them to hear the debates that are going on. And if the mining industry is ever thoroughly organized in this country, imagine the conventions we will have! They will be mobs and nothing else . . . mob rule would prevail more than intelligence. . . . A large body is more easily swayed by men who want to use political methods than a smaller body in which each member can hear everything that is going on.

The amendment was defeated, but two years later upon urging by the president of the union, the convention submitted the same proposal (one delegate per 1,000 members) to a referendum of the members with a statement that the convention was becoming too large and too expensive. Only about a third of the membership participated in the voting, and the proposal was again rejected. The president in his annual report to the 1916 convention pointed out that in many locals the entire membership "was credited adversely when in reality only a few participated in the vote." He recommended another referendum: "The scenes at last convention afford ample proof that the basis of representation should be changed. I am sure that the disorder that prevailed is an argument in favor of the constitutional amendment . . . 1,511 delegates attended the last convention." But though a committee reported favorably stating that 1,200–1,500 delegates cannot operate and that 400 were enough, the proposal was defeated.

Those who opposed the change contended that under the new plan delegates would have to be chosen by districts rather than by local unions, the large locals would dominate the elections, and they held that big conventions were desirable because attendance was educational. At the 1941 Woodworkers' convention a proposal to allow fewer representatives from the larger locals was defended because their greater voting strength would be maintained, but this was rejected on the ground that it would put them at a disadvantage unless they forced roll call votes. National officers generally have not been averse to reducing the size of the legislative bodies. It is the delegates who prevent such action, and in this respect they accurately reflect the will of the memberships. Sentiment is strong in the local unions for wide opportunities for members to attend conventions as official representatives.

Typical of more recent attempts to reduce the huge delegate bodies was what happened at the 1946 Steelworkers' convention. The constitution committee had received no proposal for reducing the number of representatives, but it did get five resolutions from local unions "limiting the number of votes of all International officers and district directors at the convention." The committee reported nonconcurrence with these, and recommended instead that existing representation (roughly one delegate for each 100 members) be changed to one for each 500 members, no local to have more than 10 delegates, and no delegate more than 10 votes.

Many delegates rose to oppose the amendment. "It seems to me," said one, "the committee must have been out somewhere last night when they thought that thing up . . . this is a violation of democracy for ourselves and our children and [so] vicious it will take away every single iota of democracy for our Union." Another complained: "You talk about democracy and things like that and I don't understand it. I am representing 2,000 members and there are some people that never have a chance, you don't know anything about them in their struggles." One argued the amendment would discriminate against large local unions, another that the small ones would be most hurt. Several emphasized that staff representatives appointed by the president would continue to vote in the convention. "You would have the same number of staff representatives and district directors here, but you would not have the rank and file here."

Only President Murray spoke for the proposal. He argued:

Conventions should be parliamentary bodies without destroying the fundamental system of true democratic representation, and should necessarily be compact bodies. You get a convention of 2,700 delegates and it is not—[apparently he was going to say it was not a parliamentary body, but he continued] I am speaking frankly now—it is a parliamentary body in the sense that it is enormous, it is big and it is extremely difficult to yield the proper amount of time to each of the delegates that wants to be heard. . . .

As your organization is constituted today, there are only three cities in the United States that have halls large enough to accommodate the delegates. The change suggested does not deprive [any] member of proper democratic representation, because no matter how small a local union may be, that local union can elect a delegate. . . .

Now I appreciate the feeling [for widest delegate representation], and when I saw that army rise on the floor here a few minutes ago, I expected it, because it was a very natural thing to do. . . . [He was careful to add] You are absolutely free if you want to vote this down, you won't offend me, it will be perfectly all right.

The amendment was rejected, the only one of about eighty constitutional committee recommendations not adopted.

Since the Miners settled their controversy in favor of big conventions, greater emphasis has been placed on the importance of large assemblies in making a show of union strength than on the need for deliberative and orderly procedures. "I ask the public at large to look upon this delegation assembled in this convention today as an answer to the charge that the Mine Workers' Union is weak, that it is about to crumble, and that we are about to be torn asunder by the common enemy—the coal operator." Thus spoke a leader of the union to the delegates in 1927, and a veteran organizer told the Automobile Workers' Union at its first giant convention in 1937: "Us old-timers, who have gone along and served the workers of this nation and who have had for many years the opportunity to witness similar gatherings, find assembled here in this hall today, the largest delegation of labor excepting only one, the Miners' Union, in the history of the labor movement." At its 1939 convention a speaker made plain the advantage of size when he emphasized: "Your presence here, this great convention . . . is a symbol and fact of strength." So also a vice-president of the United Electrical Workers connected the achievements of his union with the size of its 1944 convention when he said: "The fact that there are so many delegates here attests to the fact that we did well."

Small conventions are not necessarily more orderly and democratic than large ones, nor are their legislation and policies certain to be more carefully considered. The Locomotive Firemen with 1,000 delegates met for a month in 1945 and transacted much business in a deliberative manner, while the Marine Engineers with only 40 delegates at their 1944 convention was more disorderly than the huge Auto Workers' assembly. With microphones, public address systems, and other modern facilities, the physical difficulties stressed in the Miners' controversy is no longer a serious problem for big delegate bodies. But the fact is that the schemes of representation popular in the unions are leading their conventions to become great mass meetings. Useful purposes are served by large attendance of members and visitors, but bigger and bigger legislative bodies are not aids to more effective democratic government. From this point of view the emphasis now placed on exhibiting union strength at conventions and the declining interest in their lawmaking procedures take on added significance.

NOT ALL local unions exercise their right to representation. Inability or neglect to send delegates to conventions is an old problem in some unions. A secretary of the Typographical Union reported in 1885: "Nearly one-half of our total membership of over 18,000 are practically disfranchised in the way of representation in the international body, owing to the poverty of small [local] unions and the great expense necessarily incurred in sending representatives long distances. . . . As an illustration of this disfranchisement, it may be mentioned that at the last annual session of this body less than one-third of the enrolled unions were represented at all. . . . Such a condition of affairs is so manifestly unjust as to demand immediate redress." His suggested remedy was not adopted, and also rejected was a proposal at the 1891 convention to fine any local with more than 100 members for failure to send a delegate. By 1950 this union had about 900 locals, but only

368 delegates attended. Less than a third of the Machinists' 1,700 local lodges were represented at that organization's convention in 1945, and those that sent no delegates accounted for almost half the union's membership.

This condition has been chronic in many unions, especially in those having numerous locals with small membership and which require the locals to bear the expenses of their representatives. The Glass Bottle Blowers changed from annual to biennial conventions to reduce delegates' expenses, but their small branches, which may have as few as 7 or 10 members, still are generally unrepresented at the meetings. Some constitutions provide fines for locals which send no delegates, unless they have been excused (Miners, $25 for each 100 members, Bottle Blowers, $100 per local) but the penalties are often not collected. More effective has been the policy, increasingly being adopted, by which the national unions share with the locals the expense of being represented in conventions.

Among the unions which hold annual conventions the American Federation of Musicians is unique in paying all costs of the meetings out of its national treasury, including compensation for the delegates' services, their transportation, and other expenses. Normally, the organizations with meetings every year require local unions to defray the expenses of their representatives. This delegate expense is the greater part of the cost of a convention, and the total cost in the case of the Musicians runs to almost 20 percent of the annual income of the union. In 1949 it spent $293,000 on its convention, and its general revenues were $1,532,000. The typical national union with annual sessions keeps its cost down to around 1 percent of its operating income by making no payments to delegates. Rarely does a union with annual assemblies spend more than 2 percent, and to some the cost is less than half of 1 percent.

About a third of all the organizations (the largest group) have biennial conventions, and most of these also require their local unions to bear the delegate expense. But costs to the national are hardly changed by meeting in alternate years. A greater proportion of the income during the convention year is spent, but on annual basis the percentage is about the same as for the unions which meet every year. Exceptional in the group with biennial conventions is the Brotherhood of Electrical Workers. It pays each delegate 15¢ a mile, one way, for transportation and living expenses, plus $40 to those remaining until the close of the convention. Its 1948 assembly cost about 8 percent of the year's receipts (exclusive of benefit assessments), 4 percent for the 1946–48 biennium.

The national organizations which assume the delegate expense in whole or in part are mostly those whose conventions meet less frequently than every two years. Each quadrennial convention of the Railway Clerks' Brotherhood fixes the compensation delegates shall receive for their services, and the expense and mileage allowances both ways. Its total convention expense in 1939 was $151,400 which spread over the years between conventions amounted to about 5 percent of the union's annual income. Its San Francisco convention in 1951 cost more than $650,000, the most expensive to date. This union not only pays delegates for time spent at the convention but also for working time lost enroute to and from conventions. It sets aside a portion of its per capita tax receipts in a convention fund, and for the next quadrennium this will be close to 7 percent of the receipts.

The Machinists, also meeting quadrenially and with about the same number of locals as the Railway Clerks, but paying only transportation for one delegate from each local, keep convention costs to the national union down to about 3 percent of receipts in the year of the meeting, less than 1 percent when spread over the four years between conventions. The Ladies Garment Workers Union spends the same proportion of its revenues on its triennial conventions, though it has but a fourth the number of locals the Machinists have, and may defray expenses of a delegate only from those that "are financially unable to pay."

The Brotherhood of Railroad Trainmen seems to be the most generous of the organizations in the payments it makes to convention representatives. "Delegates shall receive pay for their services at the rate of not to exceed seventeen dollars ($17) per day. . . . Pay shall be allowed at the rate of time and a half for night sessions and overtime, six hours or less to constitute a day." [3] In addition delegates receive mileage allowances and a per diem to cover other expenses which is fixed by each quadrennial convention. This seems to be the only instance of a national union paying delegates a premium rate for overtime.

Taking the unions as a whole, the main burden of convention expense is borne by the locals rather than the national organizations. Even some unions with the longest periods between conventions assume only the general administrative expenses. Thus the delegates to the Operating Engineers and the Teamsters whose assemblies convene every fourth and fifth year, respectively, make the delegate expense a charge against local treasuries. Comparatively few unions pay all convention costs out of national funds; more relieve the locals of part of the expense of sending delegates; most make it a responsibility of the subordinate organizations to finance their own representation.

High costs are usually given as the reason for lengthening periods between conventions; but to the national unions with annual or biennial meetings, the cost is quite small—generally not much more than 1 percent of receipts. Theirs is the least part of the expense. Much greater are outlays of the local unions for their elected representatives, and the membership, of course, bears the total expense. The problem is not so much the amount of the expenditures as the way the cost shall be distributed among the governing units. When the secretary-treasurer of the UAW-CIO at its 1942 convention argued for less frequent meetings and urged that delegates bear in mind the cost of annual conventions, one replied:

We cannot expect to hold our conventions without an enormous expense.

On the other hand, I always put my money into the dues window, not to build banks, but to defray the legitimate expenses of this International Union, one of which is conventions where the membership also put their dollars into that dues window to send us here and take care of their problems in the shops. We certainly can't do it in the shops. That is why we have conventions.

[3] Constitution, 1954, Sec. 66, p. 45.

But the fact that many unions whose conventions meet but once in four years pay all convention costs including compensation for the delegates' services, and spend a greater portion of their incomes than those with annual or biennial sessions, suggests that other reasons than high costs may lead national officers to urge longer periods between meetings. One is the amount of work involved in preparing for the conventions. Another is suggested by a union president who referred to his convention duties as "feeding the animals." Union executives must give an account of their steward-ship at each assembly, and to do this less frequently is not an un-natural feeling. Compensating delegates for their services as well as paying their expenses may also make the representatives more amenable to doing the bidding of the national executives. At any rate, as national unions get older and their presidents are repeat-edly reelected, they tend to lengthen the periods between conven-tions and to assume a larger part or all of the costs of the meetings.

But the conventions of a majority of the unions still meet in annual or biennial sessions, and require the locals to bear their delegate costs. As their membership has increased, the locals have grown in size with ample treasuries that are not strained by paying the expenses of convention representation. Also, there has been a tendency in recent years to combine smaller locals into larger units and thus to strengthen them financially. Nevertheless it cannot be said that the unions with more frequent conventions are freer of control by national officers than those which meet at longer in-tervals and pay all costs of the assemblies. Local unions with large memberships are as apt to be dominated by officers or a controlling group as large conventions, and the chances are that the local's top job holders will be part of any power group that may dominate the national union.

DESPITE constitutional requirements that the convention shall meet regularly at specified times, it does not assemble automatically like the ordinary political legislature. Every union convention, whether regular or special, is called into session by the national executive. An "official call" is usually issued by the chief officers or by the secretary-treasurer, notifying local unions of the exact time and place of the meeting, directing attention to laws governing convention matters, and furnishing other information. Some constitutions prescribe such a call, others merely require that notice of convention meetings be given to all locals; but the call is customary though it may not be expressly authorized. Similarly the general practice is for "all the arrangements for the convention to be made by and at the expense of the International," as the Typographical Union provides, though most constitutions contain no such specific provision.

The call is published sixty to ninety days prior to the convention, and must be read to the members at local meetings. Two general types of call may be distinguished. One contains mainly instructions regarding the basis of representation, election of delegates, certification of credentials, introduction of resolutions, and similar matters. The other minimizes these, and emphasizes important matters of business to be brought before the convention, describes the economic and political climate in which the meeting is to be held, points with pride to gains made by the union in the preceding years, and warns of dangers ahead. Something of the flavor of each may be gathered from the following excerpts:

To All Local Unions And Joint Boards   Feb. 25, 1948
    Amalgamated Clothing Workers of America
Greeting:
    The Sixteenth Biennial Convention will convene in Atlantic City at Convention Hall on Monday, May 10, 1948, and will continue for that week.
    The . . . convention will meet in a critical period in American history. Our standards of living are being impaired by ever-rising prices. While prices are at an all-time high, many people of America are without adequate homes, and necessities of life in many instances, are beyond their reach. The infamous Taft-Hartley Law and its counterpart in many states have curtailed labor's rights to organize and to bargain collectively and have reintroduced an era of government by injunction. . . .
    The fight to protect our economic security at home must be accompanied by the building of a lasting peace. . . .
    The Amalgamated has continued to meet the needs of its members. Wage increases, greater holiday and vacation benefits, and other improvements in working conditions in all industries under our jurisdiction. A landmark was reached in our insurance program on January

1, 1947, with the inception of payments of old age retirement benefits . . . while achieving all these gains through collective bargaining, . . . the Amalgamated has continued to organize the unorganized with unremitting zeal . . . and it now enjoys an all-time peak membership.

With the security and welfare of its members reinforced by these substantial gains, the convention may face with confidence the tasks that lie ahead.

July 1, 1944

To The Local Unions Of The United Mine Workers of America
Greeting:

You are hereby notified that the Thirty-Eighth Consecutive Constitutional Convention will be held in the . . . Music Hall, Cincinnati, Ohio, beginning September 12, 1949, . . . and adjourning not later than Thursday, September 21, at noon.

This change in date and place of meeting was approved by the International Executive Board, . . . under authority granted it in Section 1 of Article 12 of the International Constitution.

Article 12 . . . provides the basis of representation, the procedure of electing delegates, and the basis on which transportation will be paid. . . .

Please see inside pages of this call for further instructions and explanations.

The call sets in motion the procedures for selecting convention delegates, special meetings normally being required for the elections. In almost all unions representatives are chosen after the call is issued, and their service is limited to the regular or special session designated therein. The only exceptions are some unions with the Grand Lodge form of organization whose constitutions require subordinate lodges to elect delegates for a term of years which includes one regular convention. Should a special session be convened during this term, the same delegates are allowed to represent their lodges in such a session.

Pursuant to the call, other business, too, devolves upon the local unions in preparation for the convention. Local officers must bring their books up to date and square accounts with the national union, for voting power of the locals is based on paid-up memberships. Resolutions and proposed constitutional amendments to be submitted to the convention must be drafted, discussed, and adopted. The issues may be circulated among the locals and entail much correspondence. Many unions require locals to send their resolutions to the national office some time before the convention assembles if they want them considered. Membership meetings decide whether delegates shall be instructed to vote as a unit for or against certain questions at the convention, or whether they shall be free to use their own judgment. Credentials have to be filled out and certified with the local union's seal on forms supplied by the national union to which copies must be sent. Delegates' expenses may have to be advanced and many other details attended to.

For the national officers and their staffs, the issuance of the call marks the beginning of a period of still more intensive preconvention activities. They must get the organization ready for the convention, and the convention ready for the organization. The secretary-treasurer's office straightens out accounts with the local unions, auditing committees and outside accountants go over the books, department heads and staffs are busily engaged in preparing the president's and other officers' reports to the convention. The chief executive reviews the reports, makes sure that "the State of the Union" is properly pictured, that actions taken to carry out instructions of the last convention are fully set forth, and that recommendations to the coming convention are persuasively explained. Some of these reports have grown to great length. The 1944 report of the general executive board to the Ladies Garment Workers' convention ran to more than 200 printed pages, the Railway Clerks' Grand President's report in 1951 to 470 pages, with an appendix of almost equal length.

The president consults with executive board members, field representatives, and district leaders on major issues to come before the convention, on appointments to be made to various convention committees, on matters of strategy for guiding the meetings. Where there are factions or strong opposition to the incumbent administration, he may try to adjust differences, offer inducements to secure unity, or arrange for answering criticisms and overcoming recalcitrant elements. He makes up the list of speakers who will address the convention—some to spur morale among the delegates, some to fill in the places where the convention will mark time while waiting for committees to be ready with their reports. He has his own speech or speeches to prepare, special guests to invite, and he must attend to many other details. In the convention city, representatives of the national union work with the host local on the physical arrangements for the convention, with hotel or auditorium managers, city officials, and railroad lines.

Out of all this activity, there emerges an unofficial key committee of the executive group—the convention managers. Sometimes the whole executive board may serve in this capacity, if the union is small and there are no factions. More often the managing group is made up of the president's confidential staff, his personal aides, his closest associates among the elected officers and staff members, though others may be called in and given special assignments. As the convention date draws near, the group meets more and more by itself as a planning and strategy committee. It whips the agenda into shape, prepares the action that it feels certain a majority of the delegates will approve, and takes measures to meet what may be presented by locals or factions known to be opposed to the administration or about whose voting the committee is uncertain. Meanwhile the opposition groups, where they exist, are busy in much the same way, circulating their proposals among the locals, working for the election of delegates of their persuasion, and drumming up support for their candidates for national offices.

The preconvention activities reach their peak during the week before the assembly is to meet. The officers and the managing group come to the convention city, and hold almost constant sessions. Often unions make preconvention week the occasion for formal meetings of their executive boards. The convention agenda is drawn up in its final form, and last minute changes are made in the list of speakers. The membership of convention committees is finally determined, subject only to approval of the delegate body. Certain committees, such as those on credentials or on laws and the constitution, are already meeting to get their reports or resolutions completed, having been appointed earlier by the president as many constitutions require. Sometimes the executive board acts as the credentials committee, and prepares the preliminary list of accredited delegates so that the convention can get started without delay. Often the resolutions previously sent to the national union by the locals must be collated and printed for distribution to the delegates on the opening day. Preconvention week is a sort of a rehearsal period for the convention; every one takes a last minute view, checks his position, attends to matters that he may have overlooked, or goes over his lines.

By the day before the convention meets most of the delegates have arrived, and hotel lobbies are full of them. They greet each other, go off to social gatherings, to drink or eat or play cards in someone's room, or they sit chatting in the lobbies. There are secret sessions of groups discussing strategy and making deals. The air is heavy with union talk, full of rumors and the vague declarations by which men try to size up a situation. Few are willing to disclose what is really on their minds; there are many strangers and conversation is guarded until who is who is known or liquor loosens tongues. If one is part of the opposition, he wants to know whether he can speak freely to the delegates he meets, for they may be administration men. If one is part of the administration, he wants to be sure he is not tipping off carefully planned moves to an opposition delegate. The big meeting will not convene to the next day, but the talking has already begun, quietly or loudly, here and there occasionally breaking out in violence.

EARLIER in this chapter a distinction was indicated between the convention that founds a new union and the regular sessions of a well established organization. Before describing the normal convention at work, therefore, it is well to examine briefly some of the initial meetings that give birth to national union governments.

VIII

FOUNDING CONVENTIONS

A NATIONAL UNION is born at a convention and is then presumed to have a continuous existence, its periodic sessions being successively numbered from this first meeting. The earliest meetings are naturally concerned with constitutional questions and with organization to build the new union's strength. Later the assemblies become more legislative in character, and increasing attention is given to developing policies and settling disputes within the organization. The founding convention is made up of delegates from existing self-governing local unions much as subsequent sessions are gatherings of representatives from local subdivisions of the national union. But since the 1930s when the big industrial unions burst into existence, there has come about a far-reaching change in the character of founding conventions.

The oldest union in the United States, the National Typographical Union, had its birth on May 5, 1852 after the efforts of three successive conventions of journeymen printers, and two more meetings, were needed to put it on its feet.[1] The first of these conventions met in 1850 in response to a circular issued by printers' unions in Boston, New York, and Philadelphia, and delegates came from five states. This meeting did not attempt to establish a nationally governed union but laid the basis for such a government. It resolved: "That a standing national executive committee of three from each state be appointed to enforce the

[1] George A. Tracy, *History of the Typographical Union*, pp. 137 ff. The 1869 convention "changed the name from 'National' to 'International' Typographical Union, the jurisdiction of the organization having been extended to include the seven provinces of Canada."

execution of all resolutions of this convention . . . , to gather information on all matters of interest to the trade; to report the same quarterly to the different [local] unions and to the next convention . . . , and to make arrangements for the assembling of the next convention." Then the group proceeded to "recommend to our brethren throughout the country the formation of [printers'] unions on the basis of a set of principles" which it listed:

1. Regulation and adjustment of the different scales of prices [wages] so as not to conflict with each other.
2. Giving traveling certificates to their members . . . which shall recommend the holders thereof to assistance and traveling expenses from the union in any city where they can not obtain, work. . . .
3. Keeping a registry of the names of "rate," and sending copies to the other unions.
4. Receiving no stranger as a member . . . who shall not produce a legal certificate of membership from a society or union of the place to which he belongs.
5. Levying a monthly contribution on each member . . . to accumulate a defense fund.
6. Establishing the right of any sister union to call upon them for pecuniary assistance, if necessary, to the amount of $1 from each member. . . .
7. Granting certificates from one union to enable members thereof [to join] any other, without paying an entrance fee.

A separate resolution recommended limiting the number of apprentices.

The convention condemned "the system so universally adopted by the legislatures of giving out the printing by contract to the lowest bidder, declared itself opposed to the establishment of a government printing office." Possibility of the unions establishing a cooperative to do the government printing was discussed and referred to the next convention. An "Address to the Journeymen Printers of the United States" was issued which summarized the session's work, explained the principles recommended to the local unions, and urged them to send a full representation to the next convention.

At the second meeting in 1851, delegates were in attendance from eight states as compared with five the previous year. The matter of government printing was referred to a special committee which reported, and the convention adopted, a "Memorial to the Congress of the United States" urging that the public printer be chosen from among those who have served an apprenticeship and had practical experience, and that legislation be enacted to this effect. It reiterated opposition to letting work to the lowest bidder, "whereby a system of auctioneering has been carried on," and proposed that rates of pay on public work be fixed by a joint committee of three practical printers and three Congressmen.

Another committee had been appointed to draft "a constitution for the permanent organization and government of a national printers' union," and the rest of the session was devoted to considering and revising its draft. The constitution "seemed to be regarded by all as highly satisfactory. It was signed by the members of the convention, and forwarded to the different typographical unions for their satisfaction." An attached schedule provided that upon approval by the local unions of five states, the executive committee should announce that the National Typographical Union has been formed, and should issue a call for election of representatives to an assembly of the national organization. In May, 1852, the necessary approval having been received, the third convention met in Cincinnati with delegates from fourteen cities attending; the national union was declared organized, and the constitution declared formally in effect.

The supremacy of the national government thus established, the subjection of the independently governed local unions to its authority, and the identification of the union with the national convention was made plain and emphasized in the first two articles of the new constitution:

ARTICLE I

This body shall be known by the name of "The National Typographical Union" and shall be acknowledged, respected, and obeyed as such by each subordinate union in the country. It shall possess original and exclusive jurisdiction in all matters pertaining to the fellowship of the craft in the United States. All subordinate unions shall assemble under its warrant, and derive their authority from it, enabling them to make all necessary local laws for their own government. It shall be the ultimate tribunal to which all matters of general importance to the welfare of the members of the different unions shall be referred, and its decisions thereon shall be final and conclusive. To it shall belong the power to regulate, fix, and determine the customs and usages in regard to all matters appertaining to the craft. It shall possess inherent power to establish subordinate unions, who shall always act by virtue of a warrant granted by authority of this body.

ARTICLE II

The members of this National Union shall be composed of its elective officers and representatives from subordinate unions, acting under legal, unreclaimed warrants granted by this National Union.

Thus was the pattern of national union governments set just a century ago by the Typographical Union, the oldest continuous labor organization in the United States. It originated the wording which has since become standardized, and is now repeated with slight variations in the constitutions of most American labor unions.

THE FIRST CONVENTION of the Bricklayers' Union was a two-day meeting of ten delegates in Philadelphia in October, 1865. Only two local unions were represented (Baltimore and Philadelphia), but according to the minutes the delegates acted with all the formalities of a large assembly founding a new government. They examined credentials, framed a constitution, adopted a seal and a password, and made provision for another convention to be held early the following year. They also elected officers from among the delegates. "The secretary was instructed to correspond with all Bricklayers' Unions in the United States that are known to exist requesting them to send delegates to the next international convention."

At the 1866 meeting in Baltimore four national officers and 13 delegates attended, but six additional locals were represented besides the original two. The following year 29 delegates represented eighteen locals, and six others were unrepresented. The president told them: "The entire trade throughout the country is looking forward to the action of this convention." By 1869 the union was apparently well established; 69 delegates met in Washington representing forty-seven locals, while membership had grown to more than 5,000. At this convention the president refused to run for office again, saying: "There are other gentlemen in our national body who are equally if not more capable of carrying on this organization."

The total receipts of the national union during the first year were $31.25; it spent $36.85. "Economy must rule," the secretary reported, "when an officer has to help furnish the means to carry on the organization and wait until the next convention to be repaid." A 13-cent tax was levied on each member to meet expenses. The secretary received a small stipend, but the other officers served without pay; there were no paid organizers. The convention authorized the president to appoint deputies from among the delegates to supervise and help organize local unions, but the locals lacked funds to pay organizing expenses. Spread of the union depended largely on correspondence and a few trips by the president and the secretary, and on itinerant members who acted as voluntary organizers.

The main activity of the Bricklayers' National Union in its early days was to help collect funds for locals on strike "for keeping their members and also in sending strangers back to their homes." At first this was done by circulating appeals to local unions. Then the president, in his second annual report, emphasized the importance of taxation, "especially the tax in reference to strikes," and he recommended that the convention define what strikes were entitled to support and the amount of benefits to be paid. The 1868 meeting prescribed conditions for securing strike aid, and the following year the convention rejected a claim of $7 per week for members of the New York local on the ground that the strike was "not lawful." This result was reached only after heated debate, but the Bricklayers held on to their law. In a similar manner these early conventions adopted laws directed toward establishing standard wage rates and providing for discipline of local unions and members.

The second convention resolved that the union "discountenances party politics and partisan politicians," though it favored national and state legislation to establish an eight-hour workday. At the fourth meeting in 1868 a proposed union rule to limit working hours of all members to eight per day was discussed, but not adopted. The convention did approve local strikes for the eight-hour day, and it defeated a proposal that financial aid should be given to locals only when at least one third of the employers refused a demand for the shorter workday. One of the main objectives of the "nonpartisan" political policy was to secure repeal of the conspiracy laws as they applied to labor unions, and the 1869 convention voted support for local members arrested for conspiracy. The convention also dealt with what was apparently an important matter of internal politics. It adopted a resolution that "no member of this body be assailed outside of this hall for remarks made on the floor."

As in the case of the printers, it took five conventions to weld together the autonomous Bricklayers' local unions in a national organization and establish its authority to tax and discipline them and their members. This was quite typical of the founding of the older craft unions, and down through the first quarter of the present century national organizations, including multi-craft and semi-industrial unions, were still being established by gradual stages in a series of conventions. Fifty years after the printers, the Ladies Garment Workers Union was founded in much the same way.

In March, 1900, the Cloak Makers Union of New York published a call for a convention of a women's garment workers, and invited "all workers in the trade in the United States and Canada, those who have unions and those who have none, to join us in our effort." It had "come to the conclusion," the call said, "that in order to improve our condition we must have not only local unions, but also a well-organized national union." Three months later eleven delegates, representing seven local unions in four cities, met in New York and voted in favor of organizing a national union. Each local represented was assessed $10 to create a fund to begin the work of organization. The new union, to be known as the International Ladies Garment Workers, was authorized to issue charters to local unions, and to levy a per capita tax on the membership of the locals, which was fixed at one cent a week per member. The session lasted one day, officers were elected from among the delegates, and after a banquet arranged by the New York local in honor of the delegates, "the convention adjourned amidst great enthusiasm." [2]

But of the seven locals represented, only four joined the "International." When the second convention met a year later, nine had been chartered and the per capita tax was raised to 1¼¢ a week. The third showed twenty-one locals represented, and the fourth fifty-one. The original four locals were in cities located in three eastern states, but by the fifth convention in 1904, the union had spread to twenty-seven cities in fifteen states and in Canada, and the number of locals under charter was sixty-six. Membership had grown to almost 9,000, and with the per capita tax raised to 5¢ per month, the national union's income was in excess of $5,000. It had rented a headquarters the previous year and felt itself rich enough to pay its general secretary a salary of $15 a week, on condition that he devote full time to his duties. To this convention, Samuel Gompers, President of the AFL with which the union was affiliated, sent a telegram offering "congratulations upon the development and success of your grand organization."

The delegates to the early conventions of these older unions were usually a selected few, earnestly intent upon uniting all workers in their trades under a national government, and their watchword was "harmony." "Meeting together as we do almost entire strangers to each other," said a Bricklayers' report, "we must cultivate a feeling of friendship that will lead us to bear with each other and to submit to the will of the majority with becoming decorum."

QUITE DIFFERENT have been the circumstances surrounding the establishment of new national unions since the advent of industrial unionism in the mass production industries. The Automobile Workers Union may be taken as an example, though in some respects this is a unique labor organization. It does typify, however, the stresses and strains and the atmosphere of present-day found-

[2] Louis Levine, *The Women's Garment Workers* (New York, Huebsch, 1924), pp. 102–4.

ing conventions. When its first convention assembled in 1936, a mass union of auto workers was already in existence and under constant internal and external tensions. A year earlier it had met as a "Council of Federal Labor Unions" authorized by the American Federation of Labor which had previously chartered each of the locals separately. Its president was appointed by the Federation, and he had authority to veto decisions of the council's elected officers. After bitter rows between the appointee and the other officers, the AFL granted the union autonomy, and the 1936 convention was called to establish an independent government.

There were 216 delegates at this convention, and William Green, President of the AFL, came to bless them. He designated an elderly organizer as his personal representative when he left, but CIO agents were working behind the scenes. The convention framed a new constitution, and in electing a president, secretary-treasurer, and three vice-presidents, attempted to ease internal conflicts by distributing the offices among the three main regions of the country from which the delegates came. The supporters of the former appointed president pledged their loyalty to the new officers. Said one: "Then as delegates to this convention who have only one purpose in mind, . . . to organize the automobile workers, let us uphold our officers. . . . We must support the officers we elect or our International Union will perish." Another came to the platform to say: "I want to go out of here united . . . , and pledge my unswerving loyalty and support so long as they build and work for the best interests of this International Union."

It is worth noting that the longed-for unity common to all unions was here sought in loyalty to the officers, whereas the founders of the Bricklayers' organization looked for it in "submit[ting] to the will of the majority." At any rate the delegates did not "go out united." They were divided not only by the leadership quarrels and the efforts of the CIO and AFL to secure their adherence, but also by differences about national political issues. At an early session of the convention a resolution to support Franklin Roosevelt for a second term was defeated, but toward the end of the convention this action was reversed. The first resolution followed the AFL's nonpartisan political policy, the second the CIO's policy which had not yet crystallized into nonpartisan support of candidates favoring labor, as it later did.

When the second UAW convention met a year later, 1,175 delegates answered the roll, more than five times as many as at the first. During the year that had elapsed the union swallowed in one gulp 300,000 members from Michigan plants, and its adherence to the CIO was apparently pledged. At the opening session of the convention, a CIO agent, an old confidant of John L. Lewis who then headed the CIO, sat on the platform advising on procedure. William Green appeared and urged the authority of the AFL convention decisions. He was formally answered by the Secretary of the CIO, and then the delegates were welcomed by its leaders (John Lewis, Sidney Hillman, Philip Murray) to "the ideals and traditions of industrial unionism."

Despite the strong sentiment favoring the CIO, the delegates were divided in their views on the internal government of the union, and the factional feuds continued. These prevented the convention from getting down to the business of devising a constitution adjusted to the needs of a greatly increased membership and new geographical centers represented in the delegate body. The major factions took the form of caucuses, the "Unity" caucus and the "Progressive." Each was well organized, holding regular meetings, and delegates wore badges denoting their allegiance. A motion to outlaw the badges was ruled out of order by President Martin. Said he: "I don't think the wearing of insignia of any kind is going to destroy our organization. . . . I think that by holding differences of opinion, by debate, and by taking our position as automobile workers, we strengthen and build our organization rather than destroy it."

After a week of bickering, delay, and deadlocked committees, however, he changed his mind. "I would like to say there has been, in my opinion, a lot of deliberate interference with the work of the constitution committee. If necessary, I will expose those parties to this convention. Your committee has been working day and night and there has been one interference after another. I don't want to have to say any more about that, but I can tell this convention a rather sordid story if these parties do not desist from their activities." Meanwhile John Lewis and other CIO officers were meeting off the convention floor with faction leaders, and arranging compromises. Understandings were finally reached which provided for two additional vice-presidents and 17 regional members of the union's executive board to reconcile factional and regional contests for power; and it was agreed that the constitution would vest broad governmental powers in the national president.

The agreements were announced to the delegates by a CIO spokesman who concluded: "I hope . . . there will be unanimous approval, unanimous decisions, unanimous action, and a uanimous spirit at this convention." Whereupon a spokesman for each faction rose to declare that his group was ready "to abide by the wishes of J. L. Lewis." The veteran miners' leader then spoke, stressing the leaders' role:

> Your leaders were trying to find a way out, so that you may give joy and happiness to the friends of our cause, . . . and disappoint all those who are expecting a permanent internal fight in this organization. . . .
> I shall now ask the convention, since we have all found each other Brothers in the Mystic Knights of the Sea, if we are ready to proceed with the election of the president.

The convention agreed, and without a hitch all officers (president, secretary-treasurer, and five vice-presidents) were elected by unanimous ballots for single nominees. The delegates insisted, however, on secret ballots to settle contests for regional members.

With the elections out of the way, the convention had little difficulty in finishing the business of adopting a constitution, all differences as to specific provisions being settled by caucus agreements. President Martin summed up the work of the convention when he explained that the auto workers must take the United Mine Workers and John Lewis as their models, and he concluded: "We want you to understand in standing unalterably for the principle of a responsible, authoritative International Union, we are standing for it and by it because we know it is the only kind of a union that can possibly succeed."

This formula for success proved to be illusory; a few months after the 1937 convention adjourned, the union split in two. The majority group remained loyal to the CIO and formed the United Automobile, Aircraft, and Agricultural Implement Workers. The minority, led by President Martin, established a separate organization affiliated with the AFL which called itself the United Automobile Workers, but remained an ineffective competitor. In 1939 a convention of the CIO adherents had to found their union anew. Only 325 delegates were present—about a third of the number at the previous meeting two years earlier. The split was only partly responsible for the smaller assembly; in part it was due to the unemployment brought on by the business recession of 1937–38.

Again at this convention, the evils of factionalism were denounced, and the importance of unity emphasized. The opening session heard an off-the-record speech by Philip Murray which was described as "giving them hell," telling them to stop their bickering, "a calling down." George Addes, Secretary-Treasurer of the union, tried to explain the disunity. "In August 1937, the UAW was split, it was split badly. Now we know the real reason today. It is because at that time we had at the head of our organization a man who was driving a wedge deeper and deeper into our ranks." Then he went on to describe the divisions at the previous convention, and ascribed the factionalism to the evil leader.

That convention was everything a convention ought not to be. On that convention floor, there were two groups arrayed against each other, fighting each other to the knife. But there the real convention was not in the convention hall . . . it was on the outside with power groups assembling and outlining tricks of strategy.

We are assembled here today in an entirely different atmosphere. . . . This convention sees the auto workers welded into a powerful unified union, and we are going to see to it that it remains unified and becomes more powerful. We must wipe out the last vestige of that destructive factionalism which the ex-president and his eastern advisor introduced into our union.

But the factions were as evident in this convention as in the previous one, and another union leader told the delegates: "Let's don't swallow hard here and then go out and cuss one another in the beer gardens." He thought that groups with different opinions were bound to exist in the union, and it was better to recognize them.

The main quarrel between the factions again centered on the vice-presidencies and the powers of the president, and again CIO advisers arranged the compromises. This time, it was agreed that there should be no vice-presidents at all, and that the president's powers should be drastically reduced. The faction leaders publicly announced their acceptance and pledged loyalty to the CIO. Said one: "We have called upon the CIO every time this union became sick. . . . So let us forget our opinion as individuals and once more accept the advice of the organization that made possible this convention." Another agreed: "This convention came together with two distinct opinions as to the proper structure of this union, which different opinions were honest points of view . . . This is a recommendation for the whole union. It is a victory for the whole union."

The president was selected from two candidates each of whom claimed he belonged to no faction, and the new constitution transferred some of the former powers of his office to the executive board which was authorized by majority vote to determine policies and settle internal disputes between sessions of the convention. When this assembled in 1940, the number of delegates had almost doubled as compared with the previous year; and when it ended, it was plain that the UAW-CIO had established itself as the union of automobile workers. Nevertheless, the convention saw the older CIO advisers who had preached unity quarreling among themselves about indorsing Franklin Roosevelt for a third term and the preparation for war. The factions picked up the quarrel, those who were against Roosevelt speaking in the name of Lewis, those for him speaking in the names of Hillman and Murray.

This division was sharpened by a resolution condemning totalitarianism, including Russia. The leftist opponents charged that its sponsors intended to create factionalism "so that they can make political capital out of it for grabbing off positions of power within this organization." Whereupon an officer rose to lament: "It is unfortunate that the trade union movement when confronted with a resolution which carries a difference of opinion immediately divides the ranks of the workers." Philip Murray had warned: "I want the people of the United States, through the medium of this convention, to know there is no disunity within the CIO"; but as debates continued, delegates referred to the "power caucuses" as normal things. The union was firmly established and the factions no longer threatened its existence.

The founding conventions of other large industrial unions lacked the exaggerated conflicts and the spectacularism of the UAW-CIO. Otherwise they differed little from the auto workers' early meetings. Most of them were faced with the same problems of mass unions already formed when they were trying to establish autonomous national governments. Either a CIO national organizing committee had organized and combined local industrial unions in a temporary national organization governed by its appointed officers, or the AFL had established a national council of federal labor unions and appointed a president to rule it like a proconsul. Usually there were factions favoring affiliation with the competing confederation or desiring to maintain an independent union. Often such disputes were settled in bitterly contested local elections conducted by the National Labor Relations Board, as was done also among the auto workers. The same contests for power and control by leaders and regional groups appeared in most of the conventions, political questions divided the delegates in much the same way, and there were the same conflicts over concentrating authority in the national officers against allowing more home rule to the subordinate organizations.[3]

[3] The youngest of the large national industrial unions—the Communication Workers of America—epitomized the experience of its elders. It was officially born at a convention of Miami, Florida, in June of that year as an independent union, claiming at its birth 161,000 dues-paying members. A temporary organization had been set up some weeks earlier by various local, regional, craft, and departmental unions which had participated in a disastrous strike earlier that year. These had been part of a loose network of organizations formed ten years earlier, known as the National Federation of Telephone Workers. When this disintegrated following the strike, the CIO created a Telephone Workers Organizing Committee for the purpose of enlisting in its ranks all workers in the telephone industry. The Brotherhood of Electrical Workers (AFL) also had contracts with some of the Bell companies, and this union was simultaneously bidding for the membership of the conglomerate unions in the Federation of Telephone Workers.

A few days before the Miami convention the temporary president issued a state-

The founding of the United Steelworkers of America, though similar to the other industrial unions, differed enough from them to merit description of its exceptional features.

The political system that governs the Steelworkers Union is of more than ordinary importance. Modeled on the United Mine Workers, it has itself become a model. The powerful organization its leaders have built in the relatively short period of its existence, the stability of its government, and the absence of open factional fighting in its ranks are admired and envied for the strength and "successes" it has achieved. It is looked upon as an outstanding example of that unity and democracy for which modern, progressive unions are striving. Its influence, therefore, extends beyond the limits of its own jurisdiction.

The Steelworkers Union was a mature and disciplined organization when in 1942 it held its first constitutional convention. The new national union was brought into existence with nothing like the birth pangs of the other constitutional assemblies. It needed only one four-day convention to fully establish itself as an autonomous body politic, and through all the sessions it succeeded in maintaining that "unity" for which the others were longing and could not achieve until after many conventions. Continuing factional struggles and bitter election contests in other unions were often pointed to as evidence of their democracy; in the Steelworkers' convention democracy was identified with its unity.

Six years earlier the CIO had appointed a Steel Workers Organizing Committee which in the intervening period recruited 600,000 members and welded them together in a stable organization with local unions grouped together in district and regional organizations shaped to the model of the United Mine Workers. By the time the founding convention met, the committee had already established a strong government national in scope which, though

___

ment charging the CIO with trying to "raid" the Communication Workers Union: "We intend to combat all attempts to divide us, whether these attempts come from the AFL, the CIO, or the Company." But the convention voted to put the question to the membership whether the new organization shall join the AFL, the CIO, or remain independent. The Federation was dissolved, the AFL Electrical Workers refused to participate in the referendum, and a majority voted for the CIO. At the third convention of the Communication Workers in 1949, it officially affiliated with the CIO and absorbed the Telephone Workers Organizing Committee.

nominally still a dependency of the CIO, was actually controlled by its appointed officers and administrators. All that remained to be done by the 1,700 delegates from 1,100 local unions who gathered in Cleveland was to confirm the actualities: adopt a constitution spelling out the principles of government and administration as they existed, declare the union autonomous in its own right, and voice their confidence in the appointed officers by electing them to administer the new sovereign organization. That, in substance, was what the convention did.

"How many of you steelworkers in this convention dreamed years ago of the day when you would have a steelworkers organization with a constitution, a democratic organization?" asked Philip Murray, chairman of the S.W.O.C. and of the convention, in his opening address. He went on to say: "Two years ago in the city of Chicago the officers of your organization said that we must meet somewhere in the United States two years from now for the purpose of electing officers and creating for the first time . . . a constitution set up and providing for democratic control. Well, here we are today, . . . meeting in this great hall, ready to do that job." Later in the address he emphasized: "I do not want internal strife within this union or in the CIO. . . . I do not want this convention to waste a single solitary minute of its time discussing, by resolution or otherwise, internal differences of any description within unions in America," and he linked disunity in the ranks of labor with "promotion of national discontent and national confusion" in the face of the enemy with which we were then at war.

There was no disunity in the convention. There was tumult, disorder, protests, and pointed questioning by some delegates, but nothing that could be called factional strife. The questions made plain that there was a Communist element among the delegates and another group that opposed concentration of power in the national officials and wanted more home rule for the local and district organizations. But all outward evidence of factionalism was suppressed. Every clause of the constitution was adopted by the delegate body without changing a word in the printed draft submitted by a committee. Each of the national officers was elected by unanimous ballot. They were the same men who had previously served as officers of the Steel Workers Organizing Committee by appointment of the CIO.

The reverence in which Philip Murray was held was evident from the beginning to the end of the convention, and he took note of it at the first session: "I should hate if anyone should promote the idea that the successes brought into the life of this organization are attributable to any one man or any particular group of officers. I want this organization to be builded upon the basis of love for the union rather than for the man." But repeatedly when he answered delegates' questions, they said "Thank you Mr. Murray," and there were many references to "our great president." Typical were the remarks of a delegate after Murray had discussed at some length a section of the officers' reports about which there had been some questioning: "I just want to say how very, very grateful we are to President Murray. He just made one of the most wonderful speeches I ever heard, and I stand behind it." Nevertheless, as we shall see, Murray had a few embarrassing moments.

Steel Labor, the official monthly paper of the union and of its predecessor the S.W.O.C., reported: "Within a few minutes after [the opening address] the convention unanimously adopted Article I of the constitution which gave the union the name: United Steelworkers of America." [4] All the other articles of the constitution were approved later almost as unanimously, though some delegates were "hesitant about doing the right thing for your union," as Murray told them. The Organizing Committee had held two "Wage and Policy Conventions" prior to 1942, and the order of business developed by these meetings was carried over into the convention that framed the government of the new union. Adopting the constitution took little more than one of the four days of the meeting. Otherwise the convention functioned like one of the periodic sessions of an old union. After the singing of the national anthem, the invocation, and the preliminary speeches, the composition of convention committees previously appointed were announced by the chairman and unanimously approved by the

[4] *Steel Labor,* Vol. VII, No. 5, 1942. "You will notice how the word 'steelworkers' is spelled—as one word. Thus the abbreviation of this great steel union becomes: USA."

delegates. The reports of the committee on rules and of the credentials committee were similarly adopted. There was no contest regarding the seating of any delegate.

The next order of business was the report of the committee on officers' reports. "We regret," said the committee, "that the Steel Workers Organizing Committee is about to come to an end, but we know that the great union which will be established will be on the policies and principles of the Committee." The report was presented in sections, each dealing with one of the subjects covered in the officers' reports, printed copies of which had been distributed to the delegates. The committee concurred in all the actions of the officers, praised their work and policies, and as each section was read it moved that the convention approve. All the sections were adopted without modification of any kind. On a few of them there were questions, and some objections, but for the most part the motions carried without discussion, except as officers explained and emphasized matters in their reports they considered important.

At one point Chairman Murray asked: "Might the Chair with your permission, precipitate a little discussion." His speech took five pages of the printed proceedings, but no discussion followed. The objections delegates raised were directed against employment of "learners" and restrictions on "premium pay" for overtime and holidays to which the officers agreed with the U.S. Government as a necessary policy for the period of World War II. The chairman answered the critics at some length, and concluded: "There is nothing in this report that we ask you to do other than support the position taken by the CIO and the President of the United States." To a delegate who asked if he could offer an amendment, he replied: "It would not be in order. The rules of the convention provide that the report of the committee must be given prior consideration. The convention must vote up or down the report of the committee, [then] substitute amendments or new resolutions will be in order."

The officers' reports disposed of, the resolutions committee reported that several hundred resolutions had been submitted to the convention, many of which dealt with the same subject. The committee had classified them by subjects, and offered twenty-five resolutions as substitutes for all that had been submitted. These were read aloud by the secretary of the committee. There were some questions and explanations, some comment from a few delegates, usually favorable, but no debate, though occasionally a delegate asked that a resolution submitted by his local be read. This was done in a few cases, and all the committee's resolutions were approved by the convention. A number of others, in accordance with its recommendations, were referred to the incoming executive board for appropriate action.[5]

A little side play showing Communist tactics in unions is worth noting. In the midst of considering the resolutions, Joseph Curran, President of the National Maritime Union, was introduced as a guest speaker, as from time to time other presidents of CIO unions were presented to the convention. Curran was then working with the Communists, though he later broke with them and became their bitter enemy. He brought to the stage with him two sailors whom he introduced as war heroes, and they made some patriotic remarks. Then a delegate rose, asked that "resolutions [be] brought on the floor dealing with a second front, and I think the body will go down the line with me." Several such resolutions had been submitted by local unions, but had not been reported out by the committee, and Murray suppressed the Communist move by saying it was not in order.

THE CONVENTION had been in session for two and a half days when consideration of resolutions was completed, and it was scheduled to adjourn at the end of the fourth day. In the afternoon of the third day the committee on constitution submitted its report in a pamphlet on twenty-four printed pages containing the text of the fundamental document. The committee chairman explained to the delegates that for some time before the convention, members of the staff of the S.W.O.C. and the legal department had been working on a draft. The announcement two years earlier that a

[5] The full text of all resolutions submitted by local unions was later printed as Volume Two of the proceedings: *Resolutions Presented to the First Constitutional Convention.* There were 368 assigned to the resolutions committee, 115 to the wage scale committee, and 354 to the committee on the constitution.

convention would be held to adopt a constitution, he said, was notice to the local unions of opportunity to express their ideas concerning the nature of the instrument; but he did not mention any of the controversial problems raised in the 354 resolutions submitted by the locals. He went on to explain that a day or two prior to the opening of the convention the prepared draft was presented to the constitution committee composed of 40 members, "and the document now in your hands represents the unanimous thoughts and approval of the committee."

Article I had been previously adopted. The secretary of the committee read Article II, and after he had finished a delegate rose to speak. He emphasized that this was the most important part of the convention and the delegates were not familiar with what is proposed. "Don't you think [he asked] it would be legitimate to allow us to study this over for some time, so we can discuss intelligently as it is read over?" Murray, presiding, answered:

I think you can follow the committee as it reads this report. They will only read what you have in your hand, and I imagine you will be able to follow it as speedily as I can. . . . You don't need any recess here to go back home and read your copy and then come back and talk about it. You will have plenty of time to follow . . . , to discuss every phase of it. . . . If you want additional information, the committee will explain the meaning.

Another delegate wasn't satisfied: "I apologize for my mental capacity which is not as brilliant as that of some people here. I can't assimilate as quickly as some. . . . I would like a little time to study it." Murray told him: "The convention has decided to continue with the committee's report. We are doing the best we know how." Several others wanted time, but a motion for a recess "to give the delegates an opportunity to read this book" was defeated. Then a delegate asked: "I would like to know if each section can be amended?" The answer was: "No, it can not according to the rules passed." The questioner continued: "Then we can vote down the report?" To which the reply was: "You can vote down the report [and] make a motion to recommit in the event the report is voted down."

Obviously nettled, Murray made a little speech:

Now let me say this. . . . I think there is just a little confusion in your minds and some misunderstanding here, and I shouldn't like to have the delegates getting the impression that it is the intent of the Chair to push something down their throats. There isn't a single, solitary line in this constitution that this chairman is going to push down your throat in this convention. Now, please get this and get that to begin with. . . . Let's forget this bickering and this noise making, and cease whistling, and all that stuff. You are in a convention . . . a parliamentary body. . . . Demonstrate your ability to do this job [of] representing the steelworkers of America. Let's have none of this bickering.

This brought a mollifying response from one delegate who said: "I think our very able chairman explained the point there. . . . The delegates are trying to do a good job in order to bring a good report back to their locals, a job that all will be proud of. . . . It is possible that members who are not delegates might be able to shout louder than some who are delegates." He suggested that in voting on the motions, "the delegates be given the privilege of a standing vote rather than a voice vote." Murray agreed and asked all on the main floor who were not delegates to go to the gallery. But one delegate still had something on his mind.

Now I would like to give my reason for asking that [a recess be taken]. I think this constitution paper we have here is going to build our rights for years to come, and we have got to establish them. . . . Now we have got a paper in our hands which we received just before we started to work on the voting of the sections of the constitution. We have not had time to study it; however the body has seen fit to vote down a request for a recess. But I have this to say at this convention: I don't want to be here and see people holler and boo and comment up in the balcony and down on the floor here in regards to raising of a question on these points. It's been done here before, this morning.

Now we have only come here for a period of four days. . . . We have entertained speakers. . . . We have entertained the presentation of gifts and so forth. I think we have our constitution here which means much more to us, and more time should be given to it than any of the other items, and I want to see every man entitled to his rights on this floor to speak on that point.

The chairman's comment was: "I wonder when the delegates are going to start talking on the point," and a delegate concurred, saying: "We have had discussion here, but we have had no discussion on the point." Thereupon the previous question was raised, and a motion "to cease debate" carried. The first section of Article II declaring the objects of the union was then approved by a standing vote. But before the remaining sections could be read (they were adopted without debate) a delegate had still another question. He wanted to know if it was possible for the committee to refrain from making a motion to accept each section as it is read, and he asked if the motion to accept or reject could not be made from the floor. Chairman Murray's answer was: "Well, that is a form of totalitarianism"!

Article III, Eligibility of Members, brought objections from a number of delegates apparently following the Communist line, because it did not provide for "freedom of political affiliation." In the sentence which made eligible "All working men and women employed [in the industry] regardless of race, creed, color, or nationality," they wanted to include the words "or political beliefs." At the same time other delegates were asking for explanations of a provision which excluded from membership any "person having the power . . . to hire and fire." In replying, Chairman Murray explained, according to the convention *Minutes*,[6] "that it was not possible to make a board ruling on all these points without necessarily creating conflict within the organization in a great many places." He ignored the questioners about political affiliation and said that "eligibility of supervisors could best be left to the determination of the local union and the International Executive Board."

A delegate then asked whether local union by-laws which contain the additional term, "or political affiliation" would be in violation of the national constitution. To which the reply was: "I should not say that it would. There is nothing in the constitution [on] the question of political affiliation at all." But when a woman delegate "said she believed local unions should have some right of determining whom they did or did not want to

---

[6] In addition to the *Proceedings of the First Constitutional Convention,* the daily minutes of the convention were bound and published separately. The text of the *Minutes* is abbreviated, though it contains matter omitted from the *Proceedings.*

admit to membership," he added that it would have the power in the first instance, but upon appeal "the International Executive Board, as governing body between conventions, would exercise the right to pass upon the judgment of the local union."

No one questioned, and there was no discussion of another clause which read: "Officers, staff representatives, or employees of the International Union or of the Steel Workers Organizing Committee are eligible to membership." This seemed necessary since the officers and many of the staff representatives had not been employed in the industry, but as a permanent part of the constitution it would open the gates of the union to non-steelworkers by virtue of appointment as staff representatives or employees by the national president. Communists favor such clauses as a means of getting their agents into the organizations, and so do socialists and "intellectuals" of various persuasions in order to make it possible for organized labor to get "better" leaders.[7]

NEXT TO BE CONSIDERED were the provisions for national officers and definition of their duties and powers (Article IV). Several sections of this article and two of Article XIV dealing with division of dues between the national and the local unions were the only things in the constitution that aroused serious opposition. These, and the effort already described to get a recess so that delegates might read and study the draft constitution, occasioned practically all there was of debate about the union's basic law.

Discussion of the first section relating to officers began with some questions as to the reasons for providing two assistants-to-the-president and no vice-presidents, with no one designated to assume the president's duties if something happened to him. Chairman Murray tried to explain:

[7] Noteworthy, also, is the wording of the eligibility provision requiring that a worker be "employed" in the industry before he can become a member. This is common in industrial unions, whereas craft unions generally require that he must be a member prior to being employed. The latter is referred to as the "closed shop," which has been outlawed by the Taft-Hartley Act. But when industrial unions require employees to become members within thirty days after they are hired, this is dubbed a "union shop" and that law specifically recognized it as legal. Both make union membership a condition of employment. Why compulsory unionism should be lawful when an employer hires workers directly and illegal when they are sent to him by a union is something of a mystery.

The officers . . . who are acquainted with all the factors having to do with the operation of this great, huge organization should know what they are doing, they should understand what they are doing. No one, by the farthest stretch of his imagination, can construe in this provision . . . anything designed to take advantage of the membership. That is not in our minds. . . . I think it is perfectly proper, and it is wholly based on the experiences I have had. I have been required during the past four years to take . . . a number of trouble shooters, and shoot them straight across this country, crisscrossing the country, and going into others' jurisdiction, to adjust internal difficulties arising within the union, and difficulties arising out of collective bargaining conferences with companies. . . . So, this problem of the two assistants . . . can best be solved by accepting the recommendation of your committee on constitution.

The recommendation of the committee was adopted as read. But at the 1946 convention an amendment was approved providing for a first and second vice-president in place of the assistants.

With only an occasional query for clarification, the next five sections were approved as drafted. Then Section 7 was read: "The International President shall have the authority to appoint, direct, suspend, or remove such organizers, representatives, agents, and employees as he may deem necessary. He shall fix their compensation subject to the approval of the International Executive Board." The first three delegates to rise spoke in opposition. Said one: "In our little steel valley, . . . when complaints about organizers not doing their duties came on the floor [of the local union] the answer always was, 'Boys, be patient, in just two years we will become of age and we will have the say-so of who will have control of us!' No one realizes more than I the need for strict executive authority. . . . But are you going back to our locals and say, 'Boys you can elect your local officers'? The man who is more or less over you carries a lot of weight and you will have no say-so about it." He admitted that field representatives for organizing work in "virgin territory" should be appointed and disciplined by the national office, and he did not think "our president would appoint anybody unworthy. But in a place like ours which is fully organized, an organizer means he is more on the lines of a business agent of other unions. The local should have some control over him. This is one thing the president has the power to veto over anybody. . . . I do feel the only way we can get something a little more democratic is by defeating this resolution."

The second said he believed "this gentleman speaks the sentiments of the house here, and I am really sincere. . . . We all say, 'Yes, yes,' when the president asks for a vote, but that does not necessarily say that is the majority of the people voting in this house." He thought there ought to be a roll call vote on the question, so that the full voting strength of the local unions would be registered. (No such vote was taken at the convention.) The third talked in the same vein: "I joined this organization because I thought we would have a little bit more to say than we did in the American Federation of Labor. I surely am surprised to see this paragraph. Why, in most AFL locals the business representatives are elected by the rank and file, and now we turn around and give this power to our president. . . . We are laying the groundwork for a bureaucratic setup. Brothers, that is very serious."

A storm seemed to be brewing, and the Secretary of the Constitution Committee moved to allay it. He assured the delegates that "in so far as it is practical," the committee gave "recognition to the thoughts that prevail in the individual localities with reference to preferential representatives. But it considered that the union "must continue for quite a period to be a mobile organization, one in which the representatives can be moved from section to section. The task of organizing . . . the United Steelworkers . . . has not been completed." He pointed out that the constitution provides for election of national officers, and an executive board with "a veto power even over the president on appointments, the membership is well protected. [The section as worded makes only the compensation subject to the board's approval.] There is no such thing as not having the right to protest against some action of an organizer that does not meet with approval of the membership." He was inclined to think that the delegates were "getting into a frame of mind that the International Officers or the constitution committee has in mind putting something over. That is not the case. This is your union. . . . I plead with you to exercise good judgment if you expect this union to continue to carry out the program you have set for yourselves."

At this point another delegate injected an additional bone of contention: "I believe," he said, "that this paragraph in our constitution does not protect the present staff members or those who may later come to the staff, with the very benefits which we are trying to bring to the workers in whose welfare we are working." Murray then threw his weight into the controversy. Main points of his address were:

Might the Chair try to enlighten the convention as to what the intent of this section is?

You are changing from an organizing committee to a constitutional organization. . . . The work of the past six years has been a work of organizing. The work of the next two years, in addition to the ordinary administrative duties that will naturally devolve on your new officers, will also be a work of organizing. I should not like the delegates in discussing this question, to create the impression that we are an old union, that the functions of your organization have been so stabilized that we can run the gamut of every known kind of democratic procedure, even to the point of license. . . .

I don't mind telling you in this convention that your interests still need some safe-guarding in this man's country . . . and I say that [as an officer and member] who believes just as much in the true spirit of democracy as any delegate attending this convention. . . .

I am not talking to you as a politician looking for a job. I am talking to you as a servant of labor, anxious to serve labor. . . . I am trying to give this convention, as best I know how, a constitution that I think . . . the best kind of a constitution possible under [existing] circumstances.

When I give you the benefit of my judgment . . . it isn't for the purpose of imposing my will upon you, because in the end you can do as you please. This happens to be your organization; but as an officer, I know more about your problems than most of you do. I should not want you to believe that there is any member of the committee on constitution anxious to impose a dictatorship upon the membership of this union. That is not true, it must not be true; it will not be true.

Your incoming president, whoever he may be, should be given the power to remove for justifiable cause any man who does not carry out the policies of this organization. If you have an elected field worker responsible only to the group that elects him in the given district, often times that individual does not feel responsible to the president or to the Executive Board. He takes a certain kind of license unto himself, and he may very well defy even the president, creating internal strife, and causing internal political friction.

You are taking your first step in a democratic setup, and you are perfecting the instrument . . . and no officer or staff member that participated in the preparation of this report had any thought of playing politics with the United Steelworkers. If you recommit this matter, I tell you that you will build a hornet's nest within your union. . . . I am now addressing myself to a few of the delegates who are evidently anxious to have their organizers elected. I do not think, as good as your intentions may be, that you should assume the hazard of placing your union in jeopardy. . . .

It runs to this—that the labor union and its membership either have confidence in their elected officers or they do not, and if they don't have confidence in them they should not elect them.

A delegate who apparently had been or was a staff representative, then protested: "This Section 7 . . . has teeth in it and it bites. You have to leave out personalities [it] applies to any President you might elect. . . . I ask you why in the Lord's name you want to impose a dictatorship upon the men you intend to employ?" Murray interrupted him. "I think I should correct the delegate right here because he is making a very bad record. First you are not telling the truth when you say that this provision imposes a dictatorship; and second, you are not telling the truth when you say the individual does not have recourse to the courts of this organization because he does." The delegate continued, however, insisting that his "interpretation of the English language so far as this section is concerned" was correct. But the tide was now turning and a delegate attending his first convention spoke up: "I am just a little disappointed. I've seen a lot of you fellows waving banners, talking about your confidence in Phil Murray. Well where is it? . . . Up there is the best chairman you ever had," and he appealed to the delegates "to show some respect to him, the kind of respect that you expect from the rank and file."

Clinton Golden, Assistant to the President and Chairman of the Constitution Committee, took up this theme. But first he corrected several delegates who had talked against appointment of district directors by the president; the draft constitution provided that they were to be elected. He then continued: "If most of you feel that Phil Murray has not led you astray, it would seem to me consistent to think that he isn't trying at this late date to lead you astray. . . . I should hate to think that there were many delegates here, after six years of association, who think that something has happened to question the honesty and integrity of the man who has had so much to do with bringing this union into being."

Someone moved the previous question, but Murray permitted three others to speak against the committee's recommendation. To an objection, he replied: "Well, the chairman was a little fearful that some of the boys might think that this was not a democratic convention so I ignored the motion for the time being." The final speaker was Van A. Bittner, an old associate of Murray in the Miners' Union, and, like Golden, an Assistant to the President. He summed up with a warning about democracy and an appeal for confidence in Murray:

When we talk about democracy, my friends, we must talk about democracy as it affects the welfare of the United Steelworkers of America. You know none of us can live without air, but when we get too much air we get a cyclone. . . . We can't live without water, but too much water makes a flood, which again is destructive.

As far as the organizers are concerned, the best interests of your union will be preserved by electing officers that you have confidence in, and placing the responsibility for directing the affairs of your union squarely on their shoulders and backing them up . . . one hundred percent.

I know you have confidence in your chairman. I know you have said in this convention time and again that you are going to back him to the last degree. If you are going to support Philip Murray, if you are going to appreciate the work he has done for the steelworkers, their wives, and little children, then you will adopt this report of your constitution committee.

The officers' advice was followed, their exhortations had quieted the brewing rebellion. After a standing vote, the Chair declared the recommendation of the committee adopted "by the overwhelming majority of the delegates attending this convention."

THE REMAINING sections of Article IV and all the rest of the nineteen articles, except one, were approved in a routine manner with occasional requests for explanation of the meaning of a clause.

The exception was Article XIV dealing with finances. There was some questioning of a provision requiring the full amount of all dues and initiation fees collected by each local to be sent to the national secretary-treasurer who would retain what was due to the national union and return what was left to the locals. But the main controversy was about apportionment of the receipts from members between the national and the local unions. Minimum dues were fixed at $1.00 per month, but with the permission of the national executive board these could be raised to $1.50 per month. All locals were required to charge an initiation fee of $3.00 for each member admitted, of which one-third was to go to the national treasury. Dues in most locals at that time were at the minimum, though some were charging $1.25 and a few $1.50 per month. Regardless of the amount collected, however, the draft constitution provided that the national union's share shall be 75¢ per member each month.

Discussion began mildly when a delegate said: "I don't see why all the money collected should be sent in instead of just what is due to International secretary-treasurer. I think we should change this paragraph. . . . Also, on this question we have to send it in within fifteen days to Pittsburgh, but it does not say when Pittsburgh will send it back to us. I know of some occasions where locals haven't got their per capita tax returned for one or two months." The secretary-treasurer denied that there was any delay except perhaps over week-ends. He was supported by two delegates and the provision was approved. Since it is the policy of the union to get its members to authorize their employers to deduct dues from their earnings and transmit the amounts directly to the national organization, there was little reason for quarreling with the recommended section. But the "check off" of dues was not mentioned in the constitution, and no one questioned the policy of having employers collect dues for the union.

When the paragraph providing for the monthly per capita tax of 75¢ and one-third of the initiation fee was read, however, "several delegates jumped to their feet and asked for the floor." They were not recognized, and Chairman Murray spoke in part as follows:

I am going to indulge in one of those little blitzkriegs myself. I understand there has been a little job going on in town here for a day or two. It hasn't lacked leadership and evidently it hasn't lacked organization.

Now I want to [give] you the benefit of my own opinion about this situation. You have adopted a constitution here, virtually a whole constitution. What you have adopted forms the basis for the expenditures of fixed sums to administer the affairs of this organization. This morning I attempted to explain that the approximate cost [is] $300,000 per month.[8] If the national office's collection is $400,000 and it retains $300,000, it just leaves enough to operate fairly, barely fairly. Now, if it is your purpose to take away from the national office that portion of those funds, you might as well start with page 1 again . . . discard every bit of work this convention has done. . . .

I am just appealing to your sober judgment. We are either going to be a group of wise men or a band of fools; one or the other. I wish that some of the objectors to these policies would come up here and take this job. I would be delighted. . . .

Now, let's be reasonable. I know a lot of you had a meeting last night, crossed your heart and swore to God that they would step over your dead body before you would pay 75¢ to your national union. That's what I call bad business. Before you caucus you ought to get this side of the story. . . .

So I don't mind telling you that I want to build up the most powerful union in the world in steel for you people; and I don't think it is going to be possible until you give them the money to do it.

I am conscious of the fact that a number of local unions here have their problems. We suggested that those problems be met by adding 25¢ per month to [local dues]. There are a number of you hesitant about doing the right thing for your union. I am willing to give you the benefit of the doubt. But will you believe me as your leader . . . you are making a mistake.

So let us not quarrel about this. You don't have to adopt the committee's report because Phil Murray is asking you to do it. You get up on your feet and try to vote the report down, which I know you are not going to do. But if you try, your position will be understood, because the officers have told you that they need this income to administer the constitution. I am not going to make any appeal to you at all. I am giving you a factual statement. If you want to cripple your union, destroy its efficiency, undermine its administrative forces, then vote to reduce the tax coming to your national office.

[8] At that time he had said: "You have five hundred employees working for this national union from coast to coast and over in Canada. That is a mighty big institution."

After this admonition the first delegate to speak explained that many delegates were instructed by their locals to vote for a larger share of the dues. He judged from the "uprising" when the committee's proposal was read, that "sixteen hundred delegates must have been pledged at home." After expressing "great admiration for our worthy chairman," he concluded: "One thing I am not going to try to do is to debate against Brother Murray. But I will appeal to him to intercede for us in softening just a little bit this thing in our behalf, because these delegates are pledged, and there is only one thing they can do, and that is to live up to their pledges."

A delegate from Alabama said locals in the South "are unable to return to the national office 75 percent of [dues], but we must do it in self-defense, the national office can't operate without funds." Another stated that his local in Indianapolis adopted a resolution "providing for 60-40 percent—60 percent back to the local and 40 percent to the International [but] we are backing [the officers] 100 percent. We were not instructed to back up anything that is not right. Let's not be selfish about the whole thing." Three more delegates spoke before the vote was taken. Two, uninstructed, urged support of what was recommended. "We are all behind our executive officers," said one, but the other thought some delegates do not have the confidence that they profess, and he argued: "If these men were trusted by the United Mine Workers with $600,000 [loan to S.W.O.C.] why can't we trust them with 75¢ a month per member to carry on this work that they have so honestly and fairly done." But the third speaker put his position bluntly: "We are all back of Phil Murray, but we have to retain our local in Buffalo, too, and we can't do it on the per capita [share of dues] we are getting. We had a meeting and I came up here with a pledge to vote for a bigger per capita tax, and I intend to do it."

When the constitution as a whole was adopted with each of the sections intact as originally presented to the delegates, a total of less than ten hours had been devoted to its consideration. It was completed in the afternoon of the fourth and last day of the convention. The officers were then elected: Murray, President; David

McDonald, Secretary-Treasurer; Golden and Van Bittner, Assistants to the President—each by a motion that the secretary cast a unanimous ballot. The convention then recessed to meet again in a night session, at which the 39 district directors were chosen by caucuses of the delegates from each district. Beginning with 1945, the constitution provided, both the Officers and the directors were to be elected by referendum vote of the members. The most important business of the night session was the report of the Wage Scale Committee which recommends the policies as to wages and collective bargaining the officers are instructed to follow until the next convention. The report was submitted to the delegates in fifteen parts, and each was adopted without discussion.

In his closing address President Murray said, among other things:

> It has been a remarkable convention in every sense. The delegates have displayed a rare tolerance and splendid statesmanship in the discussion of the many important matters brought to the convention.
>
> You came here from almost 1,200 local unions throughout this country and Canada. It is extremely difficult . . . to visualize the bigness, the magnitude of this movement. Most of you, strangers to each other, came into this convention last Tuesday with a singleness of purpose to do the job that you have done. . . .
>
> There was no friction in this convention, there was no predetermination of the course that should be charted by you. There was no buying of anybody. You did your job, you did it well, squarely and openly, right here on top of the table where America could see you doing it. That is a remarkable thing in itself for which you should be commended.

Steel Labor, describing the accomplishments of the convention (May 29, 1942), wrote that it "adopted a constitution which now completes the trilogy: *For* the steelworkers; *Of* the steelworkers and *By* the steelworkers. Autonomy, too rare in many other organizations, is now the property of the steelworkers in the short period of six years."

Was it accidental that *For* the workers was mentioned first, or was it suggested by the proceedings? In Lincoln's phrase, "for the people" was placed last. Much that happened at the convention suggests that the plan was to give the steelworkers a government considered good for them, rather than to permit their representatives to frame one more to their liking. The leaders themselves seemed to imply this when in answering criticisms they argued that only a "first step in the direction of a democratic setup" could be taken, that "centralization of authority and direction" would be needed for some time to come because the union was young and there was still much organizing work to do, and that it was "not sufficiently stabilized to run the gamut of every known kind of democratic procedure."

It is significant, however, that ten years after the founding convention—with the union's membership grown to almost a million—the sections of the constitution that were attacked as smacking of dictatorship had not yet been changed, though minor amendments had been adopted at each of the biennial sessions since 1942. Noteworthy too is the fact that neither the original constitution nor the amendments had been submitted to a vote of the membership for ratification, as the laws of the more democratic American unions require.

The size and prestige of the Steelworkers Union gives added importance to the question whether the founding fathers of the Steelworkers Union actually did take steps toward "a democratic setup," as they repeatedly assured the delegates. However sincere and actuated by high purpose they may have been, the instrument of government they brought forth and their method of handling the first constitutional convention suggest that the steps taken were rather in another direction. To an objective observer it might well seem that the design was to establish a government for the union that would be free of external control and in large measure also of popular control by the members. Perhaps the convention leaders were unaware of it, but their "setup" was reminiscent of those governments that have freed nations without freeing their people. History is not lacking in examples of the rulers of such nations being elected by the people. The thought seems farfetched, but the fact remains that the Steel Union's constitution makers provided for election of national officers by referendum vote of the members (beginning three years after its adoption) but made no provision for such popular ratification of the fundamental instrument of government or any of its provisions or future amendments.

IX

THE NORMAL CONVENTION
IN OPERATION

THE UNION CONVENTION, as it normally operates, begins with certain ceremonies that have become traditional. As delegates stream into the meeting hall, there is usually a band or an organ playing. In small conventions seat places may be marked for each delegate; in larger ones table placards indicate localities or areas. But some delegates "like to spread around the hall," and it is customary for a delegate to keep the seat he first takes. The stage where the officers, speakers, and invited guests sit is the last to fill, the president often delaying his arrival to enter with a leading guest celebrity.

The first opening move is made by a local leader of the union who steps forward to the lectern and calls the assembly to order. He usually introduces a professional to sing the national anthem and asks the audience to rise and join in the singing. Where there are substantial delegations from Canada, he calls also for the Canadian anthem. In some conventions he leads in reciting the salute to the American flag. This done he presents a local clergyman who offers the invocation. Representatives of different denominations are invited to invoke divine blessings at each day's session, and in some of the smaller conventions lay preachers or delegates perform this service. After the invocation the vocalist is usually recalled for a few songs, and there may be other music.

The temporary chairman then introduces in succession a number of speakers each of whom welcomes the delegates and visitors to the city. The speakers are mainly representatives of local and state labor movements and of the city government. The mayor comes in person to a large convention, he sends a representative to a small one. The chief of police may offer the delegates freedom of the city with intimations of leniency in enforcing local ordinances. Occasionally a local community leader, a chamber of commerce official, a governor, or his representative are among the welcomers. The speeches are invariably complimentary. It is always a great convention, a historic event. The city or state is proud of the honor. A young union has made a great beginning; it has a great future ahead of it. An old union has great traditions and great accomplishments. The union's president is always a great leader.

The last act of the temporary chairman is to introduce the constitutional presiding officer of the convention—the union's national president. This is done with some fanfare; the audience rises, there is loud applause, and often a demonstration. In larger conventions, local members may parade through the hall led by a fife-and-drum corps or a band, carrying banners of their local unions. Sometimes they bring floral sets, or a huge picture of the president or other revered leader which are placed on the stage.

The president acknowledges the greetings, thanks the welcoming speakers, the local arrangements committee, the delegates, visitors, and the union; then proceeds to deliver his "opening address." He reviews the progress of the union, emphasizes the accomplishments since the preceding convention. He calls attention to the officers' reports, summarizes portions of them, reiterates major recommendations. He discusses critical problems facing the union, and stresses the serious work ahead for the delegates. His speech sounds a keynote for the convention, and sometimes it foretells what the assembly will do. The president of the CIO Electrical Workers' Union told its 1944 convention that it was going to endorse Franklin Roosevelt for a fourth term, condemn the War Labor Board, and reiterate its no-strike pledge. It did.

After the opening address, the president declares the convention officially in session, and directs the secretary to read "the call" or place it in the record. But the ceremonies do not cease when he assumes his duties as permanent chairman. There is the rite, common in many conventions, of a local committee presenting him with a gavel. Often he asks all present to rise in a silent tribute to departed members. He reads to the delegates greetings from the President of the United States (now customarily sent to the larger unions) and from other important dignitaries. The secretary reads numerous greetings that pour into the convention from unions at home and abroad, and from sympathetic organizations and individuals; and the opening session usually ends with an address by a special guest whom the president has invited for the purpose. Then as the convention gets down to business, the president intersperses the proceedings with speeches by labor leaders, fraternal delegates, friends of labor, government officials, politicians, and publicists, and this continues through most of the sessions. The rules of some unions specifically authorize him to interrupt the business of the convention for addresses by guest speakers.

The ceremonial period may be short or long, depending on the size of the union and the number of invited speakers, but the pattern is the same in every convention. Its ritual values are obvious; it indoctrinates, builds morale, dedicates to duty. Like a prologue to a play or a circus parade, it tells something of the events to come, and the parts to be played by the various attendants.

DURING the preliminary period the convention has been an informal meeting of officers, delegates, union members, friends, guests, and visitors. The accredited representatives have not been officially seated; the convention has not been organized as a constitutional body. The first duty of the president, therefore, after reading of the call, is to announce committee appointments and request the credentials committee to submit its report. At the 1946 convention of the CIO Auto Workers, the president called the rules committee first, and a delegate rose on a point of order: "This convention," he said, "cannot adopt rules until the delegates have been seated. All actions so far are strictly illegal, according to the Rules of Order. The credentials committee has not reported. There are no delegates." The president acknowledged his error, and asked the credentials committee to come to the platform.

The credentials report consists of a list of local unions with names of their elected representatives, the number of votes each delegate and each local may cast, and a certification that the credentials are in good order. It is normally a preliminary report prepared at the national headquarters where credentials sent in by local unions are checked to make sure that constitutional qualifications of representatives and locals have been met. The committee or a sub-committee consisting of national officers usually meets prior to the convention for this purpose. This first list of delegates is rarely complete; some credentials have not been received, others require additional information or have been challenged, and there may be contesting delegations. These are dealt with in subsequent reports after further investigation and hearings. The preliminary report is usually concerned only with the credentials that are clearly in good order.

As the committee's secretary reads the report, delegates check names and votes on a printed copy which has been distributed. There is whistling or applause when a local with a large number of votes is announced, or the secretary may interpolate, as one did at a Machinists' convention when a single delegate appeared from a local with 100 votes: "I imagine he's going to be popular with all the delegates." After the reading, questions come from the convention floor about omitted names, disputed credentials, division of a local's votes among its representatives, and about possible errors in the list. The omissions are explained and obvious errors are corrected, but inquiries about disputed credentials are referred to the committee which, after investigation and hearings, will submit further reports. Ordinarily the list of unchallenged delegates is approved, and an ample majority of accredited representatives is thus seated to organize the convention as a constitutional body authorized to decide disputes about credentials and any other matters.

Sometimes, however, delegates insist on discussing the questioned credentials, and organization of the convention is delayed by the debate. In such cases arrangements are usually made to seat the unchallenged delegates, and shortly thereafter to take up the report of the committee on the contested credentials. After such a proceeding, the Boilermakers in 1944 spent the better part of two days arguing about seating delegates from a local with 936 votes in the convention who had been selected by a "governing board" appointed by the national president to administer its affairs because of irregularities in its management. The appointed delegates were finally seated over the protests of another set of delegates elected by the members pursuant to a court order. At the 1945 session of the CIO Shipyard Workers, no important business was done during the first four days until a dispute over seating delegates from one of the largest locals was settled. Then, in a rush, the convention elected officers and referred most of its business to the incoming national executive board.

Credentials disputes take on an importance in union conventions not common in most parliamentary bodies. They are often the means by which major problems of union policy, law enforcement, and relations between national and local union governments are decided. The convention pays little attention to contests between individuals within a local union. As to these it is impatient of discussion, and usually adopts committee recommendations. But when contests grow out of disputes involving more than one local, or a district organization, or the authority of national officers over subordinate unions, then seating of challenged delegates becomes a main item of business.

Occasionally control of a convention depends on the decision it makes in a credentials dispute. When a rebel New York local succeeded in getting its delegates seated at the 1932 session of the Pattern Makers, its leaders took over the management of the convention with the aid of allied delegations previously seated. Young unions, before they have had enough experience to work into their constitutions detailed policies of structure and government, often settle such problems by accepting or rejecting credentials. The Bricklayers in 1868 refused to seat delegates from a second local union in New York City, and thereby determined that the national organization would charter only one local in a city. The Typographical Union in 1880 established a policy of authorizing new local unions to admit printers who had "scabbed" before the trade was well organized by settling a credentials controversy between two sets of delegates from a St. Louis local.

At the Mine Workers' convention in 1912 the credentials of a number of delegates from a local in the Pittsburgh district were protested by the district officers. Some time previously the challenged delegates had been leaders of an opposition group which went so far as to hold a rump district convention. The leaders were expelled, and the national executive board settled the controversy by upholding the authority of the district officials; but it also directed that there be no personal recriminations. The grounds for challenging the former rebels were that their expulsions had not been appealed and reversed. Their defense was that the provision against recrimination had set the expulsions aside and therefore they were qualified to represent the local. The committee reported "without recommendation," giving as its reasons the "importance of the decision [to be] rendered, and in order that no injustice be done anyone." A whole day was spent in debating the case, and the convention upheld the chairman in ruling that the challenged delegates had the right to argue their case on the floor. But in the heat of debate, they were drawn into reiterating their former rebellious convictions, and they were denied seats. A motion to exclude them from the convention as visitors, however, was defeated.

In 1945 the Machinists' convention settled a long standing dispute between the national officers and a large local union on the West Coast by refusing to seat its delegates. For almost ten years the local had opposed the national administration, and at times refused to carry out its orders. Previous conventions had been reluctant to impose discipline on the local, hesitating at the possibility of losing its 12,000 members. It had refused to pay an assessment levied on all local unions by referendum vote of the members, and it was engaged in a protracted strike jointly with a CIO union, without authorization by the national officers.

The credentials committee reported against seating the local's delegates because of the past-due assessment, though two previous conventions had accepted its credentials despite the delinquency.

But the constitution was clear: No local was entitled to representation that "was not in good standing, free of delinquency of any nature." The local had supporters, mainly from the West Coast, and they contended that the national officers were using a technicality to destroy the local, that the convention should insist on the more fundamental interest of the union to hold on to the 12,000 members and to maintain unity. Since the strike was still going on, they argued, this would be a terrible time to slap the strikers in the face.

The national officers urged that the union's law must be enforced, that other locals had paid the assessment though financially less able than the recalcitrant one, and that it was unfair to bring the strike into the discussion because it was unauthorized. The president relinquished the Chair, spoke from the floor (in many union conventions the chairman disregards this procedure), and stressed the authority of the union: "The constitution is an agreement among ourselves. We set it down ourselves. We live up to our agreements. This [convention] is the Grand Lodge, not the national office in Washington."

On a division, the credentials committee was upheld by approximately a 2 to 1 vote. Then a delegate from San Francisco who had led the defense rushed to the platform and handed the president a $1,000 bill, "out of his own funds," to place the local in good standing. For a moment, the convention seemed relieved; the issue might be settled and unity restored. But two men shouted from the balcony that they represented the local and did not want their debts paid for them, and the ousted delegates defiantly walked out of the hall. The president returned the $1,000 bill to their disappointed friend, and delegates were solidified in upholding the laws of the union, and the authority of the national officers was strengthened.

A few minutes later, however, the convention, in deciding another dispute, showed its own superior authority. The committee had rejected the credentials of an old union member because he was employed by a state government and not doing machinist's work. Although the president pointed out that the constitution required members to be working at the trade to qualify as representatives, the convention reversed the committee and seated the delegate. After this was done someone asked if this had set aside the constitution. The president answered: "No, the convention violated it."

Like any parliamentary body, the convention is the final judge of the qualifications of its members. Occasionally it directly ousts a delegate who has already been officially seated. This may be done for misconduct on the convention floor, or for other reasons. Thus on a motion, the Woodworkers at their 1944 session expelled two delegates for violation of the constitutional provision barring Communists. The normal practice is, however, to refer such controversies to the credentials committee and await its report and recommendation before action is taken.

AS IN THE CASE of seating delegates, most of the other business of the convention is also done by acting on committee reports. The committees vary in number and size, but some are standard in practically all union conventions. The credentials committee is one of these, the others deal with rules and order of business, officers' reports, constitution and laws, resolutions, appeals, and audits or finances. Various unions have other regular or standing committees (union label, research, education, legislation, insurance, health and welfare, etc.), and the convention creates special committees as needed. The miners, steelworkers, and some other industrial unions also have large, standing wage scale committees, which recommend wage and bargaining policies to the convention. When the general assembly is not in session, they function much like conventions and determine the policies which are usually approved by the next session of the regular convention.

The committees are now generally appointed by the president or the executive board, subject to approval by the convention. Election of committees by the convention, a common practice when the delegate body was small, is now rare. The Woodworkers provide that the delegates from each district, meeting in caucus, shall elect one member of each standing committee. The Railroad Telegraphers' convention elects a committee on committees composed of three delegates which selects the members of the regular committees. There is much sentiment for electing committees, and new organizations tend to use the method until they find that it wastes too much of the convention's time. But the feeling for convention-elected committees bobs up even in old unions whenever substantial numbers of new representatives appear in the delegate body.

The Machinists spent four days at their 1920 convention arguing whether committees should be elected or appointed, and finally decided that appointment was the only practical choice. But again in 1936 the question came up on a rules committee recommendation that the convention elect the committees. President Wharton reviewed the experience:

I think because there are a number of delegates who perhaps never had the privilege of attending a convention of our organization before, it might be advisable to explain what we went through under the old law. I think it was in effect for eight years. The constitution at that time provided that committees be elected from the floor of the convention. . . .

The confusion resulting from the attempt to nominate nine members for each of these committees was so great that it consumed about three days' time of the convention just to elect the committees. You can very readily compute the cost . . . and you will find that it runs into a good many dollars per minute. At the Atlanta convention we called attention to this law, and asked the convention to permit the Executive Council to appoint the committees and submit them for . . . approval or rejection. The record will show that there were no exceptions taken by the delegates. . . . That resulted in the present law.

He suggested that the recommendation be stricken from the committee's report, and again there were no objections.

Apportionment of representation on a committee is a constant cause of dissatisfaction. Back of this problem is the size and increasing business of the convention which have transferred to committee rooms the basic decisions that determine most convention action. Hence the urgency with which locals and factions try to get representation on the committees. To quiet clamor for additional representation, the president of the CIO Electrical Workers told the 1944 convention:

I stated when we started to read off the names of these committees that due to the growth and the size of this organization, it was extremely difficult to spread the committees . . . so that every district would have representation. The great majority of local unions present at this convention have no representation on any committee. At the same time we find delegates here rising that already have two or three delegates serving on committees, requesting additional members from their local unions to serve on committees.

In this instance, the union's constitution provided that in addition to the appointments of the executive board the convention should have power to elect other members to any committee that they see fit, but that no more than one member from any local should serve on any one committee. The Typographical Union, in its laws, "calls to the attention of the executive board the importance of giving to the smaller unions a fair and equitable apportionment." The Railway Clerks are more strict: "No delegate shall be eligible to serve on more than one committee during the entire session of the convention." Most unions leave the matter to the discretion of the executive who also usually designates the committee chairmen. To avoid convention criticism, the officials generally try to give adequate representation to small locals, to branches of the trade or industry, and to geographical areas; but they always find it a difficult task, and delegates are often told they will have to be content with the right to appear and present their views at committee hearings instead of serving as members.

When opposition groups are well organized and act in the open, they are commonly given representation, though they may be kept off key committees. But in unions with a closely knit officialdom (e.g., Carpenters, Miners, Steelworkers, Teamsters, and the garment organizations) the same persons head the main committees in successive conventions to make sure that nothing untoward happens. These are generally officers or paid staff representatives, and care is taken to name committee members who are considered "safe." On all important matters, the committees report what has been previously approved by the officials, and the convention rarely changes or rejects the recommendations. Dissatisfaction breaks out on the assembly floor from time to time, but it is usually stifled by overwhelming majorities. For the most part, delegates are content to "back up" their leaders as they are repeatedly urged to do.

FOLLOWING the seating of delegates, the next business of the convention is to adopt rules governing its procedures. The rules committee goes through the formality of submitting a report consisting of a set of rules which varies little from one session of each union's convention to another, and it is generally adopted in routine fashion without discussion. Most of the rules are restatements of the principal parliamentary laws, and they normally provide that Cushing's Manual or Roberts' Rules of Order shall be the guide on all matters not specifically covered. A few rules have grown out of convention experience, but substantial changes in the rules are infrequent. Some unions set forth the rules in their constitutions. A comparison of the Typographical Union's convention rules in 1885 and in 1945 shows little difference, except verbal revisions to clarify details and modifications made necessary by growth in size of the delegate body. Although the rules remain much the same from convention to convention, there appears to be no sentiment for dispensing with the committee report and using instead, a motion to adopt the rules of the previous session.

The rules committee has no other function than to report the rules; it is not a steering committee and does not control the agenda or convention calendar. It often does include in the rules the convention's "Order of Business" and a special order fixing the time when the delegates must begin nominating and electing national officers. But these provisions are prescribed in many union constitutions, and the rules committee is discharged immediately after the rules are adopted. The union president in large measure controls the order in which specific items of business are presented for consideration by the delegates at the daily sessions. As already mentioned, he may interrupt the proceedings at any time to introduce a guest speaker, and he may call for committee reports in part or in whole as he deems necessary. He adjusts the order of business to meet the exigencies of the convention, and he is in a position to bring up subjects for convention action at such times as he may consider it advantageous to do so, though he may be overruled by a two-thirds majority of the delegates.

A change in the rules that gives the union executive greater control over convention procedures has been spreading among the larger organizations in recent years, although it has met vigorous opposition wherever it has been introduced. It will be recalled from the previous chapter that delegates at the Steelworkers' founding convention repeatedly objected to a rule which prohibited amendment of a committee report or recommendation until it had been voted "up or down" by the convention. This rule reverses the procedure followed by most conventions both of CIO and of AFL unions, whose rules usually provide that reports and recommendations of committees shall be subject to amendment and substitutes from the floor of the convention, as in the case of other motions or resolutions. With one or two exceptions the unions that have adopted the change have done so since World War II.

The new rule seems to have originated in the conventions of the United Mine Workers, although the Glass Bottle Blowers adopted it at their 1920 and 1922 conventions, their president claiming it was a precedent set by Samuel Gompers. But a newly elected president told the 1925 convention he "never liked that idea," and the union returned to the old rule. In the Miners' convention the first step toward changing the practice with respect to amending committee reports was taken by President White in 1912 when he held out of order a substitute for a committee recommendation on the ground that the recommendation was itself a substitute for a number of resolutions on the same subject that had been referred to the committee. This ruling did not necessarily bar amendments to committee reports, but at the 1918 convention another presiding officer laid the basis for completely changing the old rule by refusing to entertain a motion to defer consideration of a committee report. A delegate asked: "Can't I move to defer action?" The Chair answered: "No. The committee's report must be voted up or down; you can't defer action."

Until 1927, however, there was nothing in the Miners' rules that could be pointed to as barring motions to modify or change committee recommendations when they were being considered on the convention floor. That year the rules adopted by the convention without dissent contained the sentence: "Committee reports on specific subjects shall receive prior consideration." Later in the proceedings when this was held to bar an amendment to a committee report, the chairman replied to a protest: "That is a standard rule of procedure and it has been the rule of the convention for a number of years." Since that time the provision has been in the rules of all Miners' conventions.

The precedent set by the Mine Workers was passed on to the Congress of Industrial Organizations. When the first constitutional convention of the CIO met in 1938, it adopted verbatim all the Miners' convention rules. As in the case of the Miners eleven years earlier, this was done at the beginning of the session without objection; but when the constitution committee submitted its draft of a proposed constitution, a motion to send it back to the committee for further consideration was held out of order. This brought vigorous protests from several presidents of affiliated unions who wanted to defer action until they had an opportunity to be heard by the committee and printed copies of the document could be made available to the delegates. The chairman's ruling prevailed, and at the next morning's session John L. Lewis, then President of the CIO, added his voice to silence the protests.

Under the rules adopted by this convention, the convention is obligated to pass on these recommendations of the committee. The report may not be amended or recommitted or tabled until this convention expresses itself on the merits of the recommendation of the committee. . . . After the convention rejects a proposed section it becomes the property of the convention subject to amendment, recommitment, change modification, or to be tabled, as the convention wills.

The whole purpose . . . is to create a committee, the members of which are more or less experts on a subject, to crystallize the viewpoints and thoughts and opinions, and set them down in concrete form. The convention basically and inherently has the right to that expert opinion from the committee, and the convention cannot let the amendment of a man who merely has an idea destroy the work of a committee, or change the whole subject of debate from the committee's report to his own personal idea.

There can be no amendments to this committee's report until the convention has expressed itself on a section, and the rules will not be changed, and it will not help any delegate to rail against the rules, and we do not propose that the time of the convention shall be taken by delegates in filing protests against the rules.

Although the annual conventions of the CIO thereafter were governed by the new rule, many of the unions affiliated with the CIO permitted amendments and substitutes from the floor in their own conventions, and some, like the Rubber Workers and the Oil Workers, continued to carry the old, standard provision quoted above. Those that followed the example of the CIO in copying the Miners' rule included the two largest affiliates, the Automobile Workers and the Steelworkers, and also the Amalgamated Clothing Workers, Textile Workers, Transport Workers, and the Woodworkers. The Newspaper Guild followed the same procedure as a result of a ruling by the Chair in 1944 which was upheld by the convention. In addition the United Electrical Workers and the Longshoremen and Warehousemen adopted the same rule.

Harry Bridges, the president of the latter union, was one of the delegates at the first CIO convention who urged recommitting the constitution committee's report, and he denounced the rule that prevented this as undemocratic. But at the 1945 convention of his own union when the same rule was adopted, he justified it much as Lewis had done. Said he: "These committees may labor long hours in the night or in the day. They are large committees, all of them composed of twenty or more people, and they put in a lot of time. However, often somebody who has spent the night before building up a halo for the next day suddenly gets a bright idea and gets up and says, 'I amend the committee's report.' That does not give much consideration to the work, the judgment and the effort that a committee has put in, maybe for many hours."

The conventions of the American Federation of Labor continued to use the old standard rule, but some of its affiliates in their own assemblies also required a vote on committee recommendation before amendments or substitutes could be considered. A rule of the Paper Makers provided that "Reports of committees are not subject to amendment" though a motion to recommit is in order, and the Bricklayers' rule reads: "All reports of committees . . . when read to the union shall be considered accepted without vote unless objections are made thereto. At the 1944 convention of the Typographical Union, President Randolph made a ruling barring amendments, but said he would entertain motions to recommit. The Committee on Laws had recommended unfavorably a proposal regulating apprenticeship, and two delegates offered amendments, one that the proposal be sent to a referendum vote of the membership. Randolph explained:

I realize they [amendments] have been tolerated in the past and caused great confusion and the rules of the convention provide that all propositions shall be in writing. . . . I will rule that they are not in order. If there is a motion made to recommit with instructions to change, that is in order. That gives opportunity to the committee to work on it and report it again and have debate on the change without confusion.

After the committee's recommendation was adopted the motion for a referendum was renewed, but Randolph ruled it out of order at that time, too, because the effect of approving the committee report was to defeat the proposed apprentice regulation.

There is much to be said for the contention that recommendations of a committee which has studied a proposal should not hastily be changed by a delegate with a persuasive tongue who has given little thought to the subject. This may result in binding union officers to ill-considered policies which they have had no part in framing and to which they are opposed, while the convention does not elect to office the delegate who succeeds in committing the union to a thoughtless policy with an appealing speech. But the committee members who are informed on the subject have no less opportunity in discussion on the convention floor to persuade the delegate body to a wiser course than those who offer thoughtless amendments. Implied in the argument for the new rule, therefore, is a certain lack of confidence in the ability of the delegates to choose between a studied recommendation and a reckless amendment. Certainly the manner in which the miners' rule has spread to other unions bears out this implication; and wherever the rule has been adopted it has plainly worked to strengthen and control of the convention by the union executive.

AFTER the rules are adopted there is usually a lull in activity on the convention floor. As the president of the Machinists' Union explained at its 1945 convention:

There is a period in every convention when it is practically impossible for the convention to proceed with its business . . . , many delegates are absent from the floor in attendance upon committees, and it has been most desirable to take two or three half-days off during the first week to give the committees an opportunity to consider the matters before them. . . . That is not an unusual situation, . . . and the time for receiving resolutions only expired yesterday. There are a great number of committees. Approximately 135 delegates are serving on committees, and they are in session most of the time, with delegates appearing before them in connection with matters in which they are interested.

The recesses do not mean that the convention's business is being neglected. On the contrary, the hearings and deliberations of the committees are a means of expediting its work. Differences are adjusted in committee rooms, many issues are resolved, and lines are drawn for floor debate on the disagreements. Attempts are also made to keep the convention in session while the committees are at work. The president introduces guest speakers to take up the slack time on the floor, noncontroversial matters are disposed of, and if controversy does arise, a call is sent out to all committees that an important vote is to be taken. This, however, interferes with the work of the committees, and their members and delegates appearing before them often do not want to miss noted or entertaining speakers. At the 1943 Paper Makers' convention, the committeemen got special permission to hear a Welsh orator, and again to listen to an address by the president of their sister union of Pulp Workers, so that committee reports were long delayed. The Ladies Garment Workers had so long a list of speakers at their 1944 convention, and they put on so good a show, that all delegates wanted to be present. As a result committee work was crammed toward the end of the convention when recesses had to be taken.

Many unions require the more important committees to meet in advance of the convention to consider resolutions and constitutional amendments which are sent to the national's headquarters before the delegate body assembles. But this helps little to avoid the recesses, for the rules usually permit introduction of resolutions on the first and second days of the session, and if delegates are to have an opportunity to be heard on the merits of the proposals, the hearings must be held during the convention period. Some unions, however, make it obligatory to file all resolutions with the national secretary at least ten days before the convention meets and in these the practice has developed of preparing committee reports without hearings before the delegates assemble. Thus the recesses that mark most conventions during the hearing period are sometimes avoided.

Business comes to the convention in three main forms: resolutions, reports, and appeals. The resolutions are by far the most numerous; practically all matters on which the local unions and their representatives desire convention action, including amendments to the constitution, are introduced in the form of resolutions. The reports are mainly those the officers submit, but there may be other reports by individuals or special committees assigned to investigate particular subjects. Recommendations of the regular committee are also referred to as reports, but these deal with the resolutions previously introduced. Appeals come up through the judicial processes of the union. They are certified to the convention by the national secretary when members or local unions are dissatisfied with decisions of the president or the executive board and have conformed to procedural requirements set forth in the constitution. A committee on grievances or appeals hears them and the convention acts on its recommendations.

In small conventions, resolutions are still introduced and read on the assembly floor, and the president announces the committee to which each one is referred. The larger conventions no longer follow this procedure; their numerous resolutions are referred to committees without being read to the delegate body even by title. After committee appointments were announced at the 1944 convention of the Amalgamated Clothing Workers, the president called the committee chairmen to the platform where each one was given a folder containing the matters referred to his committee. Usually this is done behind the scenes by the national secretary or his staff. The resolutions are distributed according to subject matter; the committee on resolutions gets only those that are not referable to other standing committees. In some large conventions, committees report out the original resolutions with recommendations for concurrence or nonconcurrence, as is usually done in small conventions. In others where the practice is to prepare substitute resolutions before the convention meets, a rule commonly provides that resolutions will be read by the committees on request of the delegates introducing them.

In earlier years it was customary for the officers to submit their reports to the convention in person, each one reading his own, and the delegates proceeded to discuss them, and to act on their recommendations. Much of the convention's business was introduced and disposed of in this way. Some small unions still follow this procedure, but the general practice now is to refer the officers' reports to a committee in the same manner as resolutions. They are usually printed documents, and the larger unions distribute them to the locals some time before the convention, or to the delegates when they assemble. Although the secretary may read a digest of the reports to the delegates, the convention does not act on them directly, but waits for the recommendations of the committee to which they have been referred. Normally, this is the committee on officers' reports, but it may reassign portions dealing with particular subjects to other committees, and some constitutions provide that officers' specific recommendations must be drafted in the form of resolutions and processed like those submitted by local unions and ordinary delegates. The printed reports have become too long and discursive to raise issues sharply, and they have lost their importance as a medium of presenting business to the convention. "From a close study of the Officers' Report," said the Machinists' committee on officers' reports in 1940, "we find only one direct recommendation to this convention."

The dullest part of the convention is the reading of the report of the committee on officers' reports. It rehashes the main points made in the printed reports with running comments approving the officers' work and the policies they have pursued. All acts of the executives since the preceding convention are usually endorsed, and their efforts and qualities of leadership are praised, especially those of the president. Often the report is read in sections, and the convention adopts as a matter of course a committee motion to approve. As each section is read, or at the end if the whole report is read without interruption, the president and other officers, or a delegate occasionally, may rise to emphasize the importance of some subject, but otherwise there is usually no discussion. Except in the rare instances when a strong opposition openly strives for control of the union, the report is adopted by acclamation.

Typical of the tone of the report on officers' reports are the following excerpts:

OPERATING ENGINEERS (AFL), 1944

Your committee has been privileged to review . . . a report which is as fine as any that has ever been given by a general president of a labor organization to the members. This report has not been merely an account of General President Maloney's excellent stewardship; it has also been a highly personalized account of what the future will hold for us if we continue to cooperate for the attainment of our common goal. . . . No greater proof of the existence of the democratic process within our organization can be given than the fact of our presence at this convention which has been called to order in the American way, in full compliance with the provisions of our International constitution. . . .

During these times when much slander is heard . . . regarding the management of union funds, it is a distinct pleasure to report to our fellow members that our General Secretary-Treasurer has conscientiously administered our financial affairs with honesty and integrity. . . .

Your committee has considered the report of the Board of Trustees. These men have shown a high regard for the trust which we have placed in them . . . as auditors for the International Union. . . . Their report fully confirms the correctness of the General Secretary-Treasurer's financial report.

AMALGAMATED CLOTHING WORKERS (CIO), 1948

This [officers' 180-page] report relates to you in detail the achievements of our great organization since the last convention. It is not only the record of twenty General Officers and members of the

[Executive] Board, it is the story of dozens of joint boards, hundreds of local unions, thousands of officers and staff members, hundreds of thousands of members. It is the story of a democratic and powerful force in the community. It is, in short, the impressive record of a great union during two crucial years.

Your committee has reviewed the full text of the report. We find it to be an accurate and complete account of the period. . . . The committee has the privilege of recommending adoption of the report and approval of all the acts of the General Executive Board and the General Officers taken since the last convention.

The International Woodworkers' Union furnishes one of the rare examples of a contesting faction criticizing officers' reports. At its 1944 and 1945 conventions the committee divided, a minority disagreeing with various sections of the reports: "The report of officers to this eighth constitutional convention . . . is notable, not for what is included, but for what is omitted." The minority represented a Communist group which had previously been in control of the union and had been ousted from office. It was fighting a losing battle against a constitutional amendment adopted in 1941 which provided for expulsion from the union of "any member accepting membership in the Communist Party."

APPROVAL of officers' reports may come early in the convention or it may be sandwiched in between other committee reports later in the proceedings. Except for the committees on credentials and on rules, there is no fixed order in which committees submit reports to the convention. The order of business may list the committees, but they rarely report in the order listed, and often there is only the heading "Reports of Committees." Also, the convention does not normally complete action on one committee's report before it takes up another. The common practice is to consider partial reports as any committees are ready to submit them, although the Bricklayers do not permit any committees to report till all are ready. At the 1941 assembly of the Locomotive Firemen, for example, the constitution committee began reporting in the afternoon of the first day, June 7, and it continued to submit partial reports, intermittently with partial reports of other committees until August 13, when it presented its final report. Most conventions are in session only for a week or two, but their practice is much the same.

This procedure leaves much to the discretion of the union executive as to the order in which business is brought to the convention floor. Though the sequence is largely determined by the readiness of committees to submit reports, it is also planned by the president and convention managers. The Machinists' 1940 convention illustrates how both factors operate. At the beginning of the second day's session, the president asked: "Is the Resolutions Committee ready with a partial report?" Its chairman answered: "Yes. . . . We have one resolution here. . . . This was referred to [us] by the Executive Board after the resolutions were printed. I do not think you will find it in the printed reports." He then read a resolution proposing to "endorse the candidacy of [Franklin Roosevelt] and promote his reelection to the Presidency of the United States." The committee asked unanimous support for the resolution, and it was adopted with no contrary votes.

The union president asked for no other committee report that day, but presented five guest speakers to take up the time. The resolutions committee did not begin to report on the printed resolutions until the next day, and this was interrupted by two more guest speeches. On the following morning, the president told the delegates he would call the committees in the order in which they appeared in the rules. Only the committee on ritual responded, and what it offered could not be acted on for technical reasons. The president continued: "That is a list of all committees. While I do not want to appear impatient, this is Thursday of the first week, and we have a tremendous amount of work to do. I was hoping that some of the committees would have a partial report, and I hope by this afternoon's session that some of the committees will have partial reports, so we can get to work."

At times the convention adopts a special order which sets the day and hour when a committee report on a particular subject shall be taken up for consideration, but generally the president and convention managers can plan the timing of important items, and they may do this for dramatic effects. It is not uncommon for a resolution to be brought up for convention action after a guest

speaker has discussed the subject. At the United Electrical Workers' convention in 1944, the president introduced a soldier fresh
from the battlefield to address the delegates, and immediately
thereafter a committee reported a resolution to affirm the wartime
no-strike pledge. It was quickly adopted, though a good deal of
sentiment against renewing the pledge had been previously expressed by delegates. This convention also heard a speech by
Philip Murray. When he finished a committee reported a resolution praising his leadership, which was adopted with loud acclaim.
The Ladies Garment Workers, meeting the same year, had a carefully arranged program with each day's session given over to a
special event.

Such planning for effects does not necessarily mean that the
convention is bossed by the union executives, or that it functions
largely to register approval of their acts and wishes. Some of the
delegate bodies give many indications that they operate in this
manner, but others are governed by union laws which guard their
independence against executive domination. In some conventions
the committee on constitution or laws is given a special status, and
the greater part of the time of their sessions is devoted to consideration of its reports. By constitutional provision or convention
law special rules govern selection of its members and action on its
recommendations which do not apply to the other committees.
Its members may be elected while others are appointed, and its
recommendations may require several readings before the delegates can finally act on them. Some organizations also require
ratification of convention action by vote of the union membership.

The Typographical Union's assembly in 1944 spent about three-
fourths of its time in considering the report of its committee on
laws. The Locomotive Firemen considered the report of its constitution committee on each day of the first five weeks of its six-
week meeting in 1941. The same year the Railway Conductors
similarly devoted the greater part of their session to considering
revisions of the union's constitution and statutes recommended by
its "jurisprudence committee."

On the first day of this Conductors' convention, when a recommended change in the constitution had been read, a delegate

asked: "We get a chance at this at a second reading, do we not?" The president answered, "Oh, yes. This is the second reading. You get a chance on third reading. . . . Therefore if something gets by you, you don't need to be concerned or excited about it. You will have an opportunity at the third reading." The Railway Clerks' convention in 1947 heard a fuller explanation of this procedure from the president:

By way of explanation to the delegates that are unfamiliar with our procedure we distribute a copy of the law committee's report and that distribution becomes the first reading of the report. I am making the distribution of the report at this time because I want you to have the benefit of the report overnight, and we will undertake to hear from the committee and deal with the report tomorrow. When we do that, that will constitute the second reading. Action on the second reading is by majority vote. After we finish the second reading at a later date in the convention, we will take up the report for a third reading. It is necessary to have a two-thirds majority to change the constitution and statutes . . . and the protective laws.

The Machinists' Union goes farther than any other in providing regulations to assure that its members and local unions, as well as convention delegates, will have ample opportunity to participate fully in the processes of law making and constitutional revision. Its law committee is elected by referendum vote of the membership concurrently with the election of national officers, while the other committees are appointed by the executive. Ninety days before the convention, each local lodge is required to elect a committee on revision of the constitution which studies amendments proposed by members and makes recommendations to the lodge meeting as to their merits. Those approved by the membership are forwarded to the national secretary who compiles and prints them in a circular which must be mailed to all the lodges thirty days prior to the convention. No amendments may be considered by the delegate body which have not been submitted in time to be included in this circular, and all amendments adopted by the convention are subject to ratification by a referendum of the union's membership. The Typographical Union, most rail transportation brotherhoods, and some other of the older unions have similar though not as detailed regulations, but ratification by the membership is not commonly required. The printers, like the machinists, do make such ratification obligatory.

The conventions of these organizations (typical of a minority of American unions) concern themselves mainly with problems of internal government and with regulations governing employment of their members. They spend relatively little time on political or social issues. They elaborate and develop their constitutions by statutes and by-laws as well as amendments, and they also legislate on matters that are ordinarily the subjects of collective bargaining. They enact "protective laws" classifying work, regulating apprenticeship, establishing seniority, and fixing working hours, minimum wage scales, and standard grievance procedures to be included in contracts with employers. Sometimes these are embodied in the constitution, more often they are compiled as general laws or rules. The Typographical convention, for example, has in recent years legislated (not merely passed resolutions) on such subjects as vacations, severance pay, shorter work days, duration of contracts, arbitration, and priority (seniority). This union's president, Woodruff Randolph, writing in the August, 1952, issue of the *Typographical Journal* when the convention was about to assemble, explained the rationale of these laws as follows:

It has been our history that when improvements become generally established, the General Laws nailed them down and caused stragglers to be brought in line.

It is the predominance of delegates from smaller [local] unions which assures a safe judgment on such matters. The delegates from the larger unions sometimes propose changes in the General Laws to raise our standards before establishment through collective bargaining, but conventions have rejected such proposals.

A certain area of resiliency is necessary between the minimum standards and our best accomplishments. Otherwise we would be legislating our desires rather than recognizing the difference between the bargaining power of a small and a large [local] union.

All [local] unions are brought to the realization that the large and small unions are dependent on each other when trouble appears. This interdependence assures unity and determination to survive.

Such laws governing working conditions and relations with employers enable the convention to maintain control over collective bargaining activities of the union, as the statutes, by-laws, and convention laws enable it to control its own operations and the internal management of the whole organization. The various laws are the means by which the delegate body assures a government of laws, prevents domination of its sessions both by the executive and by the larger locals, and maintains its supremacy as custodian of the organization's sovereign powers.

An incident at the Typographical convention in 1944 illustrates the care that is taken to guard against delegation of powers to executives even in minor matters. Delegates from a number of Mailers' local unions submitted a proposal to "instruct the secretary-treasurer to make such changes as are necessary in the Book of Laws" so that where the words "printers or composing rooms" were used they would include also "mailers and mailing rooms." Although the committee on laws was "in entire sympathy with the desires of the delegates from the mailers' unions," it nevertheless reported unfavorably on the proposal, explaining: "The authority here granted to the secretary-treasurer would embrace matters properly the subject for convention and referendum action. The purpose can be better achieved by gradual revising by conventions." The fact that there was general agreement on the desirability of the proposal makes its rejection by the committee and the convention the more emphatic in insisting that union law governing procedures must be followed.

MOST CONVENTIONS do not attempt to regulate work and pay by union laws, even to the limited extent of setting minimum standards. They leave all such matters to be governed jointly with employers by collective bargaining agreements. Instead of laws, they adopt resolutions embodying programs for bargaining and "demands" to be served on managements. The demands are rarely granted in full; usually they are compromised, in part withdrawn, and management counter-proposals often have to be accepted in order to reach agreement. At times, too, some issues are submitted to arbitration whereas union laws are not subject to compromise or arbitration.

Nor does the committee on constitution have a special status in most conventions by provisions in the union constitutions requiring election of its members and special procedures in voting on constitutional amendments. The common practice is not to differentiate this committee from other convention committees. The union president usually appoints the members of all committees, and procedures for voting on their reports and recommendations apply alike to all committees. Amendments to the constitution and resolutions are alike adopted by majority vote, and no more than one reading of amendments is required.

This type of convention procedure is particularly characteristic of industrial unionism. In former years when most unions were craft organizations, the law-making type of convention was the more numerous. But as craft unions have broadened their memberships to include miscellaneous production workers and unskilled laborers and new industrial unions were formed, the tendency has been for more and more of the delegate bodies to take on the characteristics of the industrial type. This trend has also been furthered by merging of unions and absorption of small organizations by larger ones, as well as by the increasing concern of all unions with political and social issues. Thus conventions which attempt to regulate wages, employment, and relations with managements by union laws have become relatively few, and those that function mainly by passing resolutions for the guidance of national officers and local unions have come to prevail.

All conventions do some law making, just as all perform judicial functions. But the majority limit their legislation to amending or revising the union constitution in order to improve the structure and administration of the organization. The typical union convention today does not enact laws to regulate work, wages, health, or welfare of the membership, such regulations being subject to negotiation and agreement with employers. The legislation it is mainly concerned with are the laws under consideration or adopted by the U.S. Congress or state legislatures, which they resolve to support or condemn.

The 1954 convention of the United Steelworkers adopted a legislative program urging repeal of the Taft-Hartley Act, a higher legal minimum wage, improved social security, a national health insurance system, and expanded government housing program, federal aid to education, a "progressive" tax policy, regional development of river resources, a strengthened program of civil rights and civil liberties, and more adequate Congressional procedures to protect the rights of witnesses. A foreign policy resolution urged the government to provide "effective leadership in unifying our people in the struggle against communist totalitarians"; and the delegates voted to "indorse and support" the efforts of their president, David McDonald, to promote expanded international trade. They also pledged the union to work "unremittingly" to achieve guaranteed annual wage plans in industry.

The resemblance between these resolutions and the planks of a political party platform is obvious. This is normally expected of a large industrial union convention like that of the Steelworkers with almost 3,000 delegates representing a claimed membership of more than a million. But also meeting in 1954 was the convention of the Brotherhood of Railroad Signalmen with only 208 delegates, and it functioned in much the same way. This is a union of craftsmen, much concerned with working rules, but the convention neither changed existing working rules nor adopted new ones. Instead it passed resolutions urging legislation by the U.S. Congress to facilitate bargaining with employers about rules, wages, and other matters.

One resolution at the Signalmen's convention, referring to a "rules improvement program" under negotiation with the railroads, stated: "The Carriers immediately began their stalling and delaying actions by every quirk possible, even to the extent of entering the civil courts, . . . and, further, served counter-proposals . . . which are insults to our intelligence." It went on to condemn the "Carriers' actions in delaying these negotiations and in the handling of other matters vital to our wages and working conditions." An accompanying resolution urged amendments to the Railway Labor Act which would require managements to enter into conference about any request for improvements "not later than 60 days from date of notice served," and requiring also that any settlements reached "shall be made retroactive to 60 days from the date of original notice."

Other resolutions calling for Congressional legislation dealt with competing air and highway truck transportation. One condemned the U.S. Post Office for flying "3-cent mail between some favored cities," another for permitting the trucking of dangerous explosives over public highways. The national officers were directed to seek legislation to prohibit such practices. On the other hand the convention expressed satisfaction with amendments to the railroad retirement and unemployment insurance acts which Congress had adopted to increase benefits and make other improvements.

While this program was less ambitious than that of the Steelworkers, it showed the same major concern with national legislation, though more limited to the immediate interests of the members. At the same time it followed the pattern of industrial union conventions by outlining its collective bargaining program in resolutions rather than attempting to adopt union rules or laws by convention action. In addition to the resolution about the Rules Program referred to above, there was another calling for a "substantial increase" in rates of pay, and one directing the national union "to negotiate rules providing for living expenses and week-end travel time to and from home for signalmen assigned to work in camp cars."

Normally, a union embodies neither its legislative nor the economic or collective bargaining program in a single resolution; each is usually made up of a number of separately adopted resolutions. But all of these do not necessarily come to the convention floor from the committee on resolutions. Some conventions have other committees which are specialized to report on resolutions dealing with certain parts of the programs. There may be a committee on legislation or on political action, a wage policy or scale committee, a committee on education, on social security, or on other subjects. Such additional committees are common in the larger conventions.

The reports of these committees consist of a series of recommendations for approval or disapproval of individual resolutions. The committee chairman reads them one at a time, and states that the committee recommends concurrence or nonconcurrence. He then moves that the recommendation be adopted, but in some conventions a rule provides that all committee recommendations shall be considered motions to adopt. The presiding officer calls for discussion, and thereafter the delegates vote on the motion to concur or nonconcur. The same procedure is followed by the committee on constitution and the appeals or grievance committee. As previously noted, the convention considers portions of several committees' reports at a single sitting, and normally each committee submits a number of partial reports at several sessions before it completes action on all its recommendations. Its whole report as adopted is then approved, and the committee is discharged.

The period of debate on the convention floor develops as the motions to adopt resolutions, constitutional amendments, and appeals are thrown open for discussion. At first the discussion is leisurely; the end of the convention is some days off, and delegates feel there is plenty of time for expansive talk. Time-limit rules on speakers are not strictly enforced, and efforts to "rush the convention" are resisted. But the total time of the convention is limited, and when the talking threatens to make night sessions necessary, then time limits are strictly enforced, and motions to close debate become frequent and are quickly adopted. Delegates are aware that the next item of business after committee reports is election of officers, and that the convention must end shortly thereafter.

Much of the discussion is likely to be noncontroversial. On recommendations that proponents and opponents have agreed to in committee meetings, there are likely to be speeches which merely reiterate reasons for approval; and the convention usually adopts committee recommendations whether concurrence or noncurrence is recommended. Sometimes the debating period ends abruptly because a specified time has been fixed for nominating and electing officers, which marks the beginning of the final phase of the convention. But with or without such a fixed time, there is usually a rush to complete action on committee reports. Frequently, parts of some committee reports are left for consideration after the elections, and often the convention refers remaining measures to the incoming national executive board for such action as it may deem necessary.

Resolutions adopted by the delegates do not have the effect of laws. They declare the organization's policies, proclaim its immediate or short-term aims, and instruct the national officers and local unions to direct their efforts toward achievement of the stated goals. The legislation enacted by the convention is generally limited to amending or revising the constitution and it is the responsibility of the committee on constitution or laws to report on all proposed changes, with recommendations for adoption or rejection. Consideration by the delegates of this committee's recommendations is much the same as when the original constitution is adopted at founding conventions, described in some detail in the preceding chapter. Noteworthy here are some unusual procedures of the United Mine Workers' convention in amending the union's constitution at its 1944 session.

The committee on constitution proposed to change the provision for biennial meetings of the delegate body to quadrennial sessions to be called the "Constitutional Convention" and to provide for a "Scale and Policy Convention" to meet every two years between the constitutional sessions. When the committee recommended approval of this change together with a proposal to elect national officers for four-year instead of two-year terms, a delegate rose to oppose lengthening the period between conventions. Said he:

Mr. Chairman, I am heartily in accord with the election of International officers . . . every four years, or eight years or as many years as necessary. I am for these officers as long as I will remain a United Mine Worker.

But, Mr. Chairman, I think four years is too long for us to wait for a convention.

The chairman of the constitution committee answered:

I think there is some misunderstanding. We do not propose to wait four years for a convention. The committee specifically reports as follows: "The next International Scale and Policy Convention shall be held . . . in October, 1946, and the next International Constitutional Convention shall be held . . . in October, 1948."

The reason for that is because the officers are elected and will have been elected for four years . . . but in so far as the policy of our organization is concerned, as affecting our wage scale, we propose to meet every two years, the same as we always have.

Another delegate then indicated an additional reason for opposing the amendment:

I am for that change in the officers every four years, yes, although I heard it said on the street last night that John L. Lewis would get that because he is a dictator. I don't call John L. Lewis a dictator, and I did not agree with that man at this time, but I do think we should have our conventions the same as we do now, every two years.

Immediately thereafter the previous question was called for, but Lewis presiding, interrupted to assure the delegates that the amendment would do nothing more than make the constitution amendable every four years instead of every two years.

President Lewis: "Before the Chair puts the question, let the Chair ask the committee what is involved in this recommendation, except that the constitution will be amendable every four years, and otherwise the convention will be held as usual. Is that it?"

Committee Chairman Brennan: "That is exactly it. The constitution will be amendable every four years, but the convention will meet every two years to map out a policy for the next two years."

The vote on the amendment was by show of hands, and Lewis announced: "The Chair is of the opinion that the amendment has been adopted by the overwhelming vote of the convention, and the Chair so declares."

But while the delegates were assured that the amendment would merely make the constitution amendable every four years and otherwise the convention would meet as usual every two years, it became evident later in the proceedings that the assurances were somewhat misleading. After the convention had completed action on the entire report of the constitution committee, it considered next the scale committee's report, and this recommended in part as follows:

We the members of your Scale Committee, having carefully examined all resolutions forwarded to this convention bearing upon wage scale matters [nearly 300], and we hereby recommend the following as a substitute for all such resolutions:

"A National Policy Committee shall be established composed of the International officers, the International Executive Board, the executive officers of each bituminous district, and an additional number of district wage scale committee members, selected by the respective districts. . . .

"The General Wage Scale Committee, created by the National Policy Committee, shall propose and endeavor to secure the abolition of all discriminatory tonnage or day wage differentials. [Additional paragraphs listed other wage agreement proposals.]

"All wage scale resolutions submitted to this convention, . . . should be referred to the Policy Committee as a guide to assist them in the presentation of wage proposals to the coal operators in the Joint Conference. . . .

"For the basis of representation at the next Policy Committee, we recommend that each bituminous district be represented, first by the officers of the district, and then with election of committeemen directly by the members of the district or through a convention held by the district, or whatever plans a district may map out for the selection of such representatives."

The committee secretary gave a lengthy explanation of the entire substitute resolution, and immediately thereafter a delegate moved "that debate cease and that the report of the scale committee be adopted." Several delegates rose to ask that wage scale resolutions they had introduced be read and discussed, but the Chair ruled them out of order because of the pending motion to close debate. This was carried, and according to the printed proceedings: "The motion to adopt the report of the Scale Committee, as analyzed by the secretary of the committee, was carried by unanimous rising vote."

It is to be noted that the national policy committee and the general wage scale committee established by the adoption of this report were not mentioned to the delegates when they approved the constitutional amendment. Nor is there any mention of these committees anywhere in the revised constitution adopted at the same session in 1944. The last paragraph quoted above from the report hardly squares with the assurances given the delegates that the only change made by the amendment was that the constitution will be amendable every four years, and otherwise the convention will be held as usual every two years. This paragraph provides for representation "at the next Policy Committee," not at the next "Scale and Policy Convention," as the amendment reads. Similarly, another paragraph refers all wage scale resolutions to the policy committee, not to the next convention. The union's constitution prescribes that: "Representatives to the International Convention shall be elected directly from local unions"; but the adopted report did not provide for such election. Instead, district officers and committeemen, who could be selected by "whatever plans a district may map" were authorized to serve as delegates to the policy committee "composed of the International officers, the Executive Board, and the executive officers of each bituminous district."

It appears, therefore, that the scale committee report or substitute resolution did not provide for a convention of delegates as prescribed by the constitution, but rather for a meeting of the officers who made up the membership of the national policy committee together with the general wage scale committee whose members were to be selected from the district scale committees. That the intent of the constitutional amendment and the report was merely to hold a meeting of the policy and scale committees rather than a convention seems to be confirmed by a constitutional amendment adopted in 1946 which eliminated the provision for a scale and policy convention. The constitution now provides for one convention to meet every four years.

Nevertheless a scale and policy convention of delegates elected from the locals was held in 1946, and the only difference between this and the regular convention was indicated in the call for its assembly which stated: "No constitutional amendments will be considered at this convention." Except for the absence of a report from the constitution committee, it functioned like the normal convention with reports from all regular committees, including the scale committee. Perhaps this was done because of the promise to hold such a convention, but after the constitution was amended in 1946 to eliminate provision for a policy convention, no such convention has been held. Thus the United Mine Workers convention now meets regularly every four years instead of every two years, which seems to have been the purpose of the 1944 amendment.

A wage policy or scale committee is usually found only in those conventions which bargain on a national or industry-wide basis. It reports to the delegate body like other convention committees and the delegates determine bargaining policies and programs on the basis of its recommendations. Most unions that bargain nationally hold their conventions annually or biennially, so that convention-approved programs are ready for negotiations with employers. The Miners' wage agreements generally run for two years, and by changing the convention sessions to every four years, there would be no opportunity for the delegate body to determine the nature of the demands to be proposed for negotiation when the agreement expired in the middle of the period between conventions. The delegates who objected to quadrennial conventions apparently feared that the executive officers would decide what wages and employment conditions the union would request on these occasions instead of the convention determining these matters. The fact that the delegates' wage scale resolutions submitted to the convention were all referred to the newly created policy committee seemed to justify their apprehensions; and since the provision for the so-called scale and policy convention was dropped from the constitution, the officers constituting the national policy committee determine the bargaining programs and policies when new agreements are to be negotiated midway between the sessions of the convention.

BY THE PROCESS of adopting or rejecting a recommendation in a committee report, the convention also performs its judicial functions. The delegates as a body are not only lawmakers, they also serve as judges, sitting as the highest court of appeal in cases involving interpretation or application of the union's constitution and laws. The convention's committee on appeals or grievances hears appeals from decisions of the national executive board which acts as an intermediate court of appeal from local unions where disputes about members' rights and grievances against local officers are first heard and decided. The committee's report consists of findings of fact in each case together with its conclusions and a recommendation for sustaining or denying the appeal. The vote of the convention is the final step in the judicial process within the union.

In Chapter XI this subject is discussed in some detail with illustrative cases, including those that are appealed to the convention. Here it is sufficient to note that the number of cases brought to the convention generally declines as the union grows older. This is due partly to the precedents set by convention decisions and partly also because the right of appeal to the convention has been restricted to make decisions of the national executive board final in certain types of cases. Penalties of expulsion from membership and charges of malfeasance in office are generally appealable to the convention. But whether it is the convention or an executive board that exercises final judicial authority, neither provides an independent judiciary in the American tradition. The atmosphere of a convention and decisions by vote of hundreds or thousands of delegates are hardly calculated to assure trials in accordance with due process of law in the sense that this is understood in the United States.

The final important business of the convention is to elect the union's national officers, although as already indicated this may be made a special order of business before action on committee reports have been completed. Not all conventions perform this function, however. A minority of the organizations (about 30 percent) provide in their constitutions for electing officers by referendum vote of the members. In most unions the elective officers are the president, a specified number of vice-presidents, and the secretary-treasurer who together form the national executive board or council. In the larger industrial unions, a representative of each district is also elected to the executive board, and those organizations have only one or two vice-presidents. The district representatives are commonly elected only by those delegates who represent the respective districts. Terms of office are from convention to convention, and even where officers are elected by referendum vote, their terms correspond to the number of years between conventions. Some of the unions that elect officers by referendum provide for nomination of candidates by the convention;

others require nominations to be made by a specified number of local unions.

As the policy resolutions adopted by the conventions resemble platforms of political parties, so their methods of nominating national officers are characteristically like those of the quadrennial political conventions which nominate party candidates for President and Vice-President of the United States. But union constitutions do not limit the number of terms that an officer may serve, and it is customary to reelect the same officers repeatedly in convention. This is particularly true of the president and the secretary-treasurer, who normally continue to be reelected as long as they are willing to serve in practically all well-established unions that have reached a degree of stability. The same is largely true of the vice-presidents, though there are likely to be more contests for minor offices, whereas the president and secretary-treasurer are commonly reelected by acclamation.

Typical of the nominating speeches is one delivered at the 1940 Teamsters' convention by David Beck, then a vice-president of the union. He was renominating Daniel Tobin, who had already been president for more than thirty years and who continued to be elected until he retired a decade later. Said Beck:

I want to take this opportunity to nominate for office as the president of this great International Union a man who I know will have no opposition. I am not going to attempt to eulogize him because eulogies are not necessary . . . practically every man in this convention knows him personally, because he is the kind of an International president who mingles with his men . . . we know he has never lost contact with the membership of this International Union.

I could go back into history and could recite his progress from the time that he was a humble truck driver . . . until the great achievement he accomplished . . . , perhaps the greatest achievement of any labor man in the United States, when he not only introduced the President of these United States to this Teamsters' Convention and to 40,000,000 people listening [on radio], but he and no one else was responsible for bringing that President to this convention hall. That achievement brings honor to him. It has redounded to the credit of this organization . . .

But far more important is the splendid leadership he has given to this International Union . . . the great progress he has made in the trade union movement, . . . he has been able to say "yes" and to say "no." He is known as a great disciplinarian, a man who lives rigidly through his conscious understanding of law. . . . I could go on and on. Every honor that labor could afford this man, . . . every gift of our government, every gift of fraternal associations has been heaped upon him, but I know there is no honor that can be given greater than you can give him tonight by again electing him to the office of general president.

The Bridge and Structural Iron Workers meeting in 1944 heard its president renominated in the same vein, but with added emphasis on the importance of sticking to old leaders:

This organization has shown it has leadership. We can look back to the days gone by and remember where the Iron Workers used to hold their convention, and you see now where we hold them today, in a first-class hotel in our big cities. That means leadership.

Leadership has brought this organization where it is today. A lot of times you hear fellows say, "Let's have new leadership, the old fellow is out of date." You know what you have got and you had better hold on. . . .

So let's hold our own now and keep our old leaders in office.

A younger president (Walter Reuther) who had held the office for relatively few terms was renominated at the 1951 convention of the United Auto Workers with a somewhat different appeal, more attractive to the membership of a CIO industrial union:

Brother Chairman and Fellow Delegates: I rise to place in nomination for president of this great union the name of a member . . . whose name is synonymous with freedom and the rights of workers everywhere. His brilliant leadership, coupled with determination and dauntless courage, have gained for him the devotion and respect of the members of the UAW and the admiration of free workers throughout the world. His vision and foresight during the years of World War II have brought him in prominence in the present world crisis. . . .

Feared and hated by the forces of reaction and totalitarianism he is beloved by freedom-loving people everywhere for his dauntless and relentless fight to build and strengthen democracy. Under his leadership, the UAW has made more progress than any union in the world, and continues to lead in the fight to better the conditions of American workers.

The nominations are usually seconded by delegates with brief remarks echoing similar sentiments, and other chief officers are nominated in the same manner. The nominees referred to in the quotations were the incumbent presidents who were to be retained in office, as the delegates were well aware.

The convention of the Amalgamated Clothing Workers has a unique method of naming candidates for its top officers, though others are approaching it. This is, in effect, nominations by demonstrations. When nominations for the office of general president were called for at its 1948 session,[1] the proceedings show the following:

VOICES FROM THE FLOOR: Potofsky! Potofsky!
(*There ensued a demonstration and parade.*)
EXECUTIVE VICE-PRESIDENT BLUMBERG (in Chair): Jacob S. Potofsky . . . has been nominated. (*Applause and cheers.*) Are there any other nominations?
VOICES FROM THE FLOOR: No! No! No!
BLUMBERG: There being no other nominations, Jacob S. Potofsky's name will go on the ballot as candidate for general president. (*Cheers and Applause.*) We are now open for nominations for the office of general secretary-treasurer.
VOICES FROM THE FLOOR: Rosenblum! Rosenblum!
BLUMBERG: There being no other nominations, Brother Frank Rosenblum has been nominated for general secretary-treasurer.· . . .
(*There ensued a demonstration and parade.*)
VOICE FROM THE FLOOR: How about the executive vice-president?
BLUMBERG: The executive vice-president is a candidate for reelection.
DELEGATE SALERNO: I nominate Hyman Blumberg for executive vice-president.
(*There ensued a demonstration and parade.*)

The Advance, semi-monthly journal of the Clothing Workers, gives a more graphic description of the demonstrations at the 1954 convention in its issue of June 1 that year:

Despite requests that demonstrations be held to a minimum, 1,500 thundrously applauding, whistling, hornblowing, stamping, and confetti-throwing delegates . . . unanimously nominated [the president, secretary-treasurer, and the executive vice-president] for another two-

---

[1] Jacob Potofsky, who had long been secretary-treasurer was appointed president by the union's national executive board in 1946 when Sidney Hillman died. Authority of the board to fill vacancies in the office until the next session of the convention is found in most union constitutions. Hillman served as president from 1914 when the clothing workers' organization was established until his death. Potofsky was first elected president in 1948 and he has been reelected every two years since that time.

year term. The business of the nominations, which climaxed the convention's final session, . . . was repeatedly punctuated and interrupted by the ovations as names were placed in nomination. . . .

Owing to the fact that the . . . nominations [threatened] to run over time limitations, the delegates were requested to dispense with the snake dances and parades, which usually spontaneously arise, but the delegates whooped it up anyhow.

When the nomination for general president was called for by the Chair, shouts of "Potofsky" resounded from every corner of the hall. And for minutes thereafter, a din of shouts, whistles, and stamping filled the hall. The tons of paper and confetti thrown up turned the hall into a myriad of colors.

Order was finally restored, but the demonstration resumed again when shouts of "Rosenblum" greeted the request for the office of general secretary-treasurer. And several moments later, the hall broke out in pandemonium once again in reception of the nomination of Blumberg [executive vice-president].

This is one of the conventions that nominates candidates but does not elect them. Although there was only a single nominee for each of the three principal offices, their names were nevertheless placed on the ballot so that members could vote against them if they so desired. Some of the unions which elect officers by direct vote of the membership provide in their constitutions that the convention may declare a candidate elected if he is the only nominee, or authorized adoption of a motion that the secretary cast a unanimous ballot for such a candidate. The Clothing Workers' 1954 convention also renominated the incumbents of all seventeen vice-president positions which together with the three top offices constitute the national executive board. But there were additional nominations for most of these positions, so that the members had some contests to decide in the election.

At the 1948 convention of the Textile Workers of America, which like most conventions elects its officers, the incumbent president, secretary-treasurer, and executive vice-president, were also the sole nominees. A remark of the president after he was nominated and the laughing response of the delegates show the common understanding that the chief-executive's nomination means that he is to be reelected. The usual cheers and applause following his nomination were accompanied by calls for a speech and the customary motion to close the nominations was adopted. Emile Rieve, who had been president since the union was founded, then said: "You know, it is a little too early for a speech. I have only been nominated, not elected. [Laughter.] According to the rules, the election takes place tomorrow morning; therefore I am not going to make a speech."

Whether national officers are elected by the convention or directly by referendum of the members, the result is generally the same: the president and one or two other officials are continually reelected, and usually there are no contestants for their offices. But an outstanding exception is the Typographical Union in which there are two organized parties which nominate candidates for the top executive positions. It is significant, however, that despite the two-party system and annual direct elections by the members, this union also reelects the same officers over long periods of years, though not as consistently as do the others.[2]

Half a century ago there was much argument that election by the members was more democratic than convention elections. At that time many state governments were amending their constitutions to provide for "direct government by the people" through the referendum and recall of officers. But after 1912 very few of the older unions changed from convention to referendum elections. There was a mild revival of the issue in the late 1930s and early 1940s when the new industrial unions were established, but a majority of the CIO unions also chose the convention method of electing officers. Today little is heard of the old argument. Once a union adopts either referendum or convention elections, this takes on the character of a tradition, and it rarely changes from one to the other. Experience having shown that the same officers are continually reelected under both methods, the question whether one is better or more democratic than the other has lost its former importance.

[2] For an historical account of the two-party system in the ITU, see S. M. Lipset, M. A. Trow, and J. S. Coleman, *Union Democracy* (Glencoe: The Free Press, 1956), chap. 3. For evidence relating the continuance of the system to the survival of printers' social clubs and autonomous local chapels, cf. chaps. 5, 12. See, also, C. Kerr, *Unions and Unions of Their Own Choosing* (New York: The Fund for the Republic, 1957).

The rare occasions when conventions do consider changing the method of electing officers come when a faction achieves enough strength to reach for control of the union. The original constitution of the Newspaper Guild adopted in 1933 provided for elections by the convention. At the eleventh annual session in 1941, this was changed to referendum elections. During the intervening years, a faction reputed to be Communist-controlled succeeded each year in electing its candidates for national executive officers. The opposition believed that the incumbents held power through the support of only a small minority of the members who were active in local union meetings and controlled the election of convention delegates. It therefore proposed referendum elections to get bulk of the membership to vote for officers. The referendum did result in a victory for the opposition, and it also won a majority of the delegates to the convention, which it has since maintained. An intrenched Communist administration of the United Electrical Workers' Union was easily able to defeat a similar proposal to substitute referendum for convention elections at its convention in 1944. This organization and ten others were expelled from the CIO in 1949 for following the Communist line. No Communist issue was involved in the 1930 convention of the Pattern Makers League where a faction opposed to a group that had long controlled the union lost by a close vote an attempt to change from convention to referendum elections. But the next convention in 1934 voted for a referendum election, and though the opposing faction succeeded in winning control of the union, subsequent elections have been by the convention, and the union's current constitution so provides. The Brewery Workers in 1946, then also torn by factions, rejected a constitutional amendment for electing officers by the convention, thus insisting on their right to elect the same officers every three years.

When the issue of referendum versus convention election arises, debate usually centers on whether direct election of executives by the members is more democratic than the indirect method of election by the convention. Actually, however, there is no evidence that union governments are more democratic as their officers are elected by one method or the other. The same undemocratic tendencies appear in the smaller number of organizations which elect by referendum as in the much greater number in which the convention chooses the executives. The miners' delegate quoted above who "heard it said on the street" that John Lewis would get the constitutional amendment he wanted "because he was a dictator" was in a union which elects by referendum; and there is no less a proportion of union presidents with similar reputations in the organizations where convention delegates do the electing. What the evidence does show is that the factors which influence the selection of union leaders are little affected by the difference between the referendum and the convention.

These factors are: 1) a large proportion of members are passive and do not attend union meetings or vote in referendum elections; 2) factional organization develops within the active minority; and 3) the need for maintaining united action against employers stimulates growth of a dominating machine by which leaders are kept in office and their policies continued. That these are the controlling influences in the selection of union officers is evident from the nature of the debates on the relative merits of referendum and convention elections.

Thus the convention of the Pattern Makers League in 1930 heard a delegate remind his fellow representatives that "there are many members who carry cards but do not take interest in the organization and do not attend meetings, and as a result a majority of members do not vote, but a minority of the members control in an election." He represented the views of the faction that favored the referendum as a means of wresting control of the union from the incumbent leaders whom the convention had repeatedly re-elected for many years. Another delegate answered in behalf of the incumbents who favored convention elections: "Those who vote and are interested in the union are really the bone and sinew of the organization, and the League will gain a great deal from their votes and can forget the others."

At the 1944 convention of the United Electrical Workers, both sides argued that democracy required the election method they favored. Whereupon a delegate declared: "I say if you want to talk about democracy, let the same democracy elect the president of a union as elects the President of the United States." To this a supporter of the incumbent administration replied: "A convention in which the key people—the leadership of the locals who have been selected by their membership to come to this convention—are a far better representation of democracy than any vote or referendum which can be manipulated by any group who will try to manipulate such an election."

This answer reflected the Communist influence in the union, but it was substantially the same as that made fourteen years earlier at the convention of the Pattern Makers League which has been untinged by Communism. Both preferred convention elections because the delegates are mainly active unionists better informed on union affairs and better qualified for national executive positions than the rank and file members. The Communist angle appears in the charge that only referendum elections can be manipulated. Actually, as the pattern maker stated, minorities control both convention and referendum elections, for the passive majority does not attend local meetings where the "key people" are selected as delegates any more than it participates in referendum voting.[3]

Thus the results of the elections are the same whether convention delegates elect the national officers or the members directly do the electing. In either case "a minority of the members control in an election." In this minority, factions develop which frequently contest elections in the early years of a union organization, and then develop a dominating minority that reelects the same officers

[3] The charge that direct elections by the member could be manipulated was merely an example of Communist double-talk. Where Communists control unions that elect officers by referendum, they argue just as vehemently for this method. The United Electrical Workers and ten other unions were expelled from the CIO in 1949 because they followed the Communist line. Of the eleven unions, at least five elected officers by referendum. Prior to 1949, the National Maritime Union had purged itself of Communists, but while it was dominated by them its constitution proclaimed: "The membership . . . is guaranteed the right to elect all officials of whatever description by secret ballot." This still appears in Article III of the constitution as revised in 1949, but Article XVI adds "that members of Nazi, Fascist, or Communist organizations shall not be admitted to membership in the union."

for practically as many terms as they are willing to serve. It is these factors, rather than the particular method of electing officers, that determine the extent to which democratic standards in union governments are maintained and advanced or undemocratic tendencies are developed or promoted. To understand the operations of these factors it is necessary to examine the nature and functions of the union executive.

X

THE UNION EXECUTIVE

THE EXECUTIVE POWER in union governments is divided between the president and a national executive board or council. The board is usually composed of all its national officers, but some constitutions exclude officers from its membership (except the president) and provide for election of board members who hold no other office. As a body, the board has superior authority over the president; his acts are generally subject to its approval, and it may suspend him from office on proved charges. But normally it meets only for short periods twice, three, or four times a year, and when it is not in session the president has authority to assign duties to the individual members of the board and to supervise their work. He is the chief executive officer, responsible for conducting the affairs of the union; and as some constitutions provide: "He shall see to it that all other officers perform their duties."

Practically all union constitutions give both the president and the executive board judicial as well as executive powers. Most of them assign the powers in language similar to the following from the Machinists' constitution: [1]

Between conventions all executive and judicial powers . . . shall be exercised by the Executive Council. . . .

The International President . . . shall enforce the laws of the International Association of Machinists; decide all questions of order and usage and all constitutional questions, subject, however to an appeal . . . [to the executive council and to the convention].

Some constitutions also delegate legislative powers to the execu-

[1] Constitution (1946), Art. III, p. 11; Art. IV, p. 13.

tive board and the president. The Operating Engineers' constitution provides: [2]

> All powers of the general convention . . . , when not in session, pass to and vest in the General Executive Board. . . .
>
> All powers heretofore vested in the General Executive Board when in session shall, when the same is not in session, pass to and vest in the General President. All of the acts and decisions of the General President shall be reviewable by the General Executive Board and shall continue in full force and effect until reversed by action of the . . . Board.

The Musicians' president is given authority, "where in his opinion an emergency exists," to issue executive orders to annul the union's constitution and laws or any portion thereof (except finance regulations) and "substitute therefor other and different provisions of his own making." His power in this respect is made absolute.[3] On the other hand, the Boilermakers' constitution emphasizes that "executive and judicial powers only" shall be vested in the executive council when the convention is not in session; and the Railway Conductors provide that the legislative power may, in part, be delegated to the members for voting on constitutional amendments, "and in no other manner."

The president's powers are shared to a limited extent with other elected executive officers specified in the constitution. Normally these are: a secretary-treasurer, a first or executive vice-president and a director of organization, though titles vary. The Brotherhood of Locomotive Engineers has a "Grand Chief Engineer" and a "First Assistant Grand Chief Engineer" instead of a president and first vice-president. Some unions elect an "Assistant President," and some combine the office of secretary-treasurer with that of the president, in which case there is likely to be an office of corresponding or recording secretary. Others have both a treasurer and a secretary. A few make the editor of their monthly journal an elective office, and in some the director of organization is appointed by the president, though others elect this officer.

The number of vice-presidents varies in different unions from one to more than twenty, and they usually serve as members of

[2] Constitution (1944), Art. V, p. 17; Art. VI, p. 21.
[3] Constitution and By-laws (1949), Art. I, p. 19.

the national executive board. But those that have only one or two vice-presidents generally fill out the membership of the board with representatives elected from districts or territorial regions. There is little difference between a vice-president and a district representative, except that the former are often elected at large. Otherwise a vice-president is usually assigned to a district where he has the same duties as a district director who usually represents the area on the executive board. Some constitutions require vice-presidents to be elected from the districts.

The president of the Pattern Makers League is its only elected national officer. In addition it has a five-man executive board who hold no other national office. Other small organizations have a complete set of officers, but only one of them salaried on a full-time basis, the rest being part-time officials. The president of the Newspaper Guild is such a part-time officer; its executive vice-president being the only full-time officer. Thus the executive vice-president exercises many of the powers and performs most of the duties of the president. The Mechanics' Educational Society has a similar arrangement with its secretary-treasurer as the chief executive officer.

Many of the older unions began in this way with a single full-time officer, usually the president. The powers thus concentrated caused dissatisfaction, and led to the development of the executive board as a controlling authority rather than an "advisory board" which it still is in the Brotherhood of Locomotive Engineers,[4] although with power to suspend officers. In 1863, William H. Sylvis, President of the Iron Molders' Union was its only officer. When he assumed office, the constitution did not provide for an executive board. "All power—executive, judicial, and even legislative was vested in the president." [5] He almost singlehandedly rebuilt the union after it had disintegrated during the first years of the Civil War. His personal control of the organization became the subject of controversy, and when an executive board was created, he dismissed most of its members. He was found guilty of misappropriating funds, but was later exonerated. It took a special

[4] Constitution (1942), Sec. 14a, p. 15.
[5] T. W. Glocker, *The Government of American Trade Unions*, (Baltimore, Johns Hopkins University Press, 1913), pp. 177, 187.

convention to remove him from office. Despite the controversies he caused, he made great contributions to the government of American labor union, setting the pattern of many of its administrative methods and policies.[6]

The national executive board, as it exists among present-day unions, takes two forms. A majority of the unions include the president and other national officers in its membership together with all the vice-presidents, or with representatives elected from districts or territorial regions. A substantial minority of the organizations, however, exclude the officers from the board, and provide for election of a separate group of board members, though some of these permit the president to serve as chairman with the right to vote only when the members are equally divided on any question.

The old Iron Molders' organization, now known as Molders and Foundry Workers Union, is in this minority group. Apparently as a result of its early experience, its constitution now provides that "No member of the Executive Board, except the President, shall be eligible to hold any other elective office . . . but [the president] shall have no vote on any question before the Board except in case of a tie vote." [7] The Plumbers and Steamfitters' constitution accomplishes the same purpose by restricting membership on the executive board to "six vice-presidents (three plumbers and three fitters), allotted to districts," each consisting of a group of states. This union has no other vice-presidents, and also permits its president to serve as chairman of the board, but voting only in case of a tie.

The Pattern Makers League excludes the president from its executive board, which consists of five elected members who serve also as a board of trustees. Its constitution provides that the board "shall have general supervision of the League." The Brotherhood of Electrical Workers has an executive council composed of nine members, one elected from each of nine districts, and the council chooses its own chairman. (The president, secretary, treasurer, and twelve vice-presidents are all excluded from membership of the

[6] Jonathan Grossman, *William H. Sylvis, Pioneer of American Labor* (New York, Columbia University Press, 1945), Chap. IV.

[7] Constitution (1945), Sec. 43, p. 24; Sec. 32, p. 18.

board.) Equivalent to an executive board is the "board of directors" of some of the rail transportation organizations. The Brotherhood of Locomotive Firemen and the Switchmen's Union each elects at its convention from among the delegates a five-man board of directors which chooses its own chairman and secretary. The Railroad Trainmen and Maintenance of Way Employees use the name "executive board" for similarly elected five-man bodies from which all national officers are excluded.

Most unions, however, include the officers in their executive boards, together with all the vice-presidents or district representatives. Typical constitutional provisions are:

The President, General Secretary-Treasurer, and the twenty-three vice-presidents, shall together constitute the G.E.B. [General Executive Board].[8]

One Executive Board member from each of the districts over which the United Mine Workers has jurisdiction . . . shall constitute the International Executive Board. . . . The President, Vice-President, General Secretary-Treasurer, and the twenty-three vice-presidents, shall be members of the Board by virtue of their positions.[9]

The general officers shall be a President, a Secretary-Treasurer, and thirteen vice-presidents. . . . These are hereby constituted the General Executive Board of the International Union.[10]

There shall be an Executive Board composed of the President, Secretary, ten vice-presidents, and the Treasurer.[11]

Some of these unions, though including the officers in the board, limit the additional members to the elected trustees who have charge of union funds and property, or to a few elected members who are neither vice-presidents nor district representatives. Examples are the Railway Conductors whose "board of directors" consists of three trustees in addition to its president, senior vice-president, and secretary-treasurer, but does not include eight other vice-presidents; and the Musicians provide for election at large of a five-man executive committee which together with the president, a vice-president, and the secretary-treasurer constitute the executive board.

[8] Ladies' Garment Workers Constitution (1940), Art. IV, p. 18.
[9] Coal Miners' Constitution (1944), Art. VII, p. 12.
[10] Hotel & Restaurant Employes Constitution (1943), Sec. 85, p. 28.
[11] Pulp, Sulphite & Paper Mill Workers Constitution (1947), Art. V, p. 8.

THE TYPOGRAPHICAL UNION has gone farther in reducing the size of its executive council by making its national officers (president, secretary-treasurer, and three vice-presidents) the only members of the council. It has thus practically eliminated the division of executive power between the officers and the council. Explaining the purpose of this concentration of powers in the officers, the then president of the union told its 1927 convention: "To permit the members to properly place responsibility for the ails of the executive officers, there should be no divided responsibility." This concentration of powers was adopted by constitutional amendment in 1900 with a good deal of opposition. But at the convention in 1913 a delegate who had doubted its wisdom testified to its beneficial results and to the direct control of the executives by the membership.

Many of us were afraid at that time we were making the Executive Council too small. But we took the risk and the fruits of that action are apparent today in the history of the Typographical Union. It has made the greatest progress since the [1900] convention . . . , and it has been due absolutely I think to the centralizing of authority and responsibility in the bands of a few men. . . . When [they are] not absolutely responsive, we get a crack at them every two years, and they know it.

The convention of this union meets annually, the officers must stand for reelection by referendum every two years, and the organization is unique in permitting two political parties to function openly (Progressives and Independents) which nominate candidates to contest the elections. The constitutional provisions and the organized parties have stimulated a majority of the members to participate in the elections—60 to 70 percent in recent years, whereas only about 10 to 15 percent turn out to vote in other unions which election national officers by referendum. Apparently the members are confident of their ability to control the powers concentrated in the officers, for there has been no serious effort to restore the division of executive powers.

Despite the division of powers in practically all other unions, most of them show the same concentration of powers in the officers as in the Typographical Union, but the direct membership

control to enforce responsibility is usually lacking. The constitutional authority of the executive boards to supervise and control the officers' powers is largely vitiated by the provisions for
making the officers members of the boards with full voting powers.
They are therefore in a strong position to influence the decisions
of the boards. This is particularly true where the officers are a
large proportion of the board members. But even in boards where
district representatives or vice-presidents are a substantial majority
of the members, they are subject to the orders of the president, and
hardly in a position to oppose his wishes on questions that he
considers important. As a result, the tendency in most unions is
for the officers, and particularly the president as chief executive,
to control the board rather than to be controlled by it. Only in
the relatively small number of unions which bar the officers from
membership on the board is it in a position to exercise effective
control over the officers.

Although the actions and decisions of both the president and the
executive board are generally appealable to the convention, this
has proved no more effective a check on the powers of the executive officers than has the constitutional authority of the executive
board to supervise and control their activities. Indeed in most
unions where the officers control the board they also control the
convention. The factors which determine the election officers
(referred to in preceding chapter) also determine the choice of
executive board members and convention delegates; and the
responsibility of the president and other principal officers is to the
"machine" of active members rather than to the majority of the
unions' memberships. Unlike the Typographical Union with its
two functioning parties, unions generally have in effect one-party
governments. Parties are usually decried as dangerous factions
threatening the unity that is essential to the existence of labor
organizations. Factions exist, nevertheless, and stable union governments are maintained by a dominating faction or machine
which does everything it can to suppress other factions in the interest of unity.

References to "the machine" are not infrequent in convention
proceedings. Discussing the method of filling temporary vacancies

in officers' positions due to death, retirement or resignation, an old and experienced delegate told the Machinists' 1936 convention:

> I know the machine that has been built up in our organization on this referendum vote. I know that deaths have occurred, retirements, resignations, and the fellows that have been appointed to fill the vacancies; and I know it is the machine that reelects, no matter where they come from. I don't like it, brothers, any more than you do, and I would like to find some way of changing it. I don't think the amendment that we should elect each man from a particular district is going to do it.
>
> I don't think, on the other hand, that the present method of selecting them through the machine is a good thing. After some of these seven men have died or resigned, instead of the machine appointing a man to take their places, there should immediately be a referendum vote, and a lot of you young fellows that want to come up in this organization will have an opportunity of supplanting some of these old worn-out members.

The issue in this case was whether executive board members should be elected from districts or at large. But the delegate was concerned with the more important problem that in either case when a temporary vacancy occurs, the office is temporarily filled by someone picked by the officialdom of the union, and the machine sees to it that the man thus picked is generally elected to fill the office permanently. He thus made plain the continual reelection of the president and other executive officers as long as they are willing to serve, as well as how their successors are chosen.

When a vacancy occurs in the office of president or in that of a vice-president, it must be temporarily filled until the next convention meets to choose a new one or a referendum election can be held. Union constitutions provide two methods of filling such vacancies. Most commonly the executive board is authorized to appoint a temporary successor or the president may appoint subject to approval by the board. Others provide that the first vice-president shall succeed to the vacancy for the remainder of the term. Similarly the second vice-president moves up to the position of the first when that becomes vacant, the third to the second, and so on.

The Machinists' constitution restricts such temporary appointments to the period necessary to hold a special election, except when the vacancy occurs within a year prior to the regular elections. The Typographical Union and the Newspaper Guild have similar provisions unless the vacancy occurs within six months and three months, respectively, before the regular elections. But most constitutions do not provide for such special elections. They authorize the executive board to make the temporary appointment, and the machine sees to it that the appointee is elected to fill the position for the next term and reelected for succeeding terms like the other officers. Thus the circle of incumbent officers forms a sort of self-perpetuating body designating the successors to the various executive positions.

One result is that a new president is almost always chosen from among the other national officers, and other executives are similarly selected from the members of the executive board. This has certain advantages, for it makes certain that the new president or other principal officer will have executive experience before taking office. But it limits the opportunities of the younger promising leaders who have had experience as officials of local unions and other subordinate organizations to achieve national office. Hence the complaint of the machinist delegate quoted above that the top offices were occupied by old men and his plea that the younger local leaders be given more opportunities "of supplanting some of these old worn-out members."

More serious are the abuses that result from such concentration of power in the hands of the national officers, despite the constitutional provisions for executive boards, appeals to the convention, and referendum elections to check and control their authority. Some of these abuses as they affected the rights of individual members were discussed in Chapter IV. Others are illustrated by the capture of the machines and the national offices by Communists and racketeers, as in the cases of the eleven unions expelled by the CIO and the expulsion of the Longshoremen's Union from the AFL in 1954. But an extreme example of nepotism in the Carpenters' Union is illuminating as to other possibilities of abuse.

A first vice-president of this union, who was elected in 1936 to serve until 1940, died in the middle of his term. President William Hutcheson appointed his son (an employee of the national union) to fill the vacancy for the unexpired term, and told the executive board about it afterward:

> While according to the constitution the second vice-president automatically becomes first vice-president; however, Vice-President Meadows requested that he be permitted to remain second vice-president,[12] therefore the vacancy to be filled is that of first vice-president, and in conformity with the constitution of our Brotherhood, and authority vested in me as General President, I have appointed Maurice A. Hutcheson to that vacancy.
>
> This action and appointment was approved by the General Executive Board.

Had the constitution been followed, the vacancy to be filled would have been that of the second vice-president, but putting the son in that position would not have placed him as directly in line to succeed to the presidency of the union. Approval of the temporary appointment for the unexpired term assured his election at the 1940 convention for the next full term and for succeeding terms. In 1940 William Hutcheson had been president of the Carpenters' for about twenty-five years. He was looking forward to retirement and wanted to leave the presidency in good hands. That he confidently expected his son to be elected to succeed him, he made plain in an interview when the son was serving as first vice-president:

> Hutcheson's present benignity derives from his satisfaction over the fact that Maurice is at hand to keep things running as they always have. He says no one in the union has a wider acquaintance than Maurice and if he can't run the Brotherhood "I don't know who can." And it must be admitted that the docile personnel of the general executive board does not appear to furnish a rival for Maurice.[13]

But when the general secretary of the union nominated Maurice for election as first vice-president at the 1940 convention, he told the delegates that it was his idea to appoint Maurice as first vice-president, and that William Hutcheson strongly objected:

> I went to General President Hutcheson and I said: "Bill, I want to talk to you, I have a recommendation to make. . . . The one I have

---

[12] Meadows later was elected general treasurer of the Brotherhood.
[13] "Boss Carpenter," *Fortune*, April 1946, p. 282.

in mind is Maurice." And in the language of the street, Bill Hutcheson hit the ceiling. He wouldn't listen to me. He said, "If I do that and it is approved by the General Executive Board then they will say it is a Hutcheson family affair." I said, "Well, they say that anyhow. They say we have a Hutcheson-Duffy Machine." Of course there is nothing to that but they say it just the same.

Maurice was declared elected first vice-president by unanimous vote of the convention in the absence of any other candidate to oppose him. (The constitution provides for this procedure when there is only a single nominee, contested elections being subject to referendum.) A delegate did attempt to nominate another candidate in a speech with many apologies, but he declined the nomination after another delegate rose to tell the convention:

I don't want to second this nomination because I happened to be at one of those "alley" meetings last night. I want to state here and now that the meeting was held, not for constructive purposes but for destructive purposes. [He intimated it was a "Black Legion" group.] I asked if they could prove to me . . . whereby something was wrong with our organization, and not one could point the finger of scorn at any of our officers.

After Maurice was elected first vice-president at the 1940 convention, he was reelected for several additional terms until 1952 when he was unanimously chosen president to succeed his father who retired early that year.

There is no reason to believe that the son was less qualified for president than any one of the older vice-presidents who would normally be designated by the officialdom of the union to succeed to the presidency, and then be unanimously elected by the convention. The significant fact is the ease with which an extra-constitutional arrangement could be made to bring the young staff employee into the official family as first vice-president and in line to succeed to the presidency. Important, also, is the method by which the attempt to nominate an opposing candidate was discredited. The opposing faction held "alley meetings," its purposes were "destructive," and it appeared to have some connection with a "Black Legion." No one of the group "could point the finger of scorn at any of our officers." This is not untypical of the manner in which opposition to official policies is identified with destructive factionalism, while a dominating faction led by the officers maintain "unity."

The constitution of the Ladies Garment Workers prohibits members from organizing "groups or clubs in the union or outside of the union," except during a three-month period prior to election of officers when committees may be formed to support candidates. It provides further: "If members . . . find it necessary to organize such groups for the benefit of the Union an application shall first be filed with the General Executive Board, and only upon the granting of such application shall such group be organized." [14] At the union's convention in 1944, an amendment was introduced reading: "RESOLVED, That this convention authorize the permanent existence of groups in order to promote and extend democracy and its free and integral function within local unions throughout the year and not be restricted only to the time of elections." The committee on law recommended rejection of the proposal, "particularly since there is ample opportunity for those seeking to organize such groups and clubs for the benefit of the union to obtain permission upon satisfying the General Executive Board as to the need therefor."

In the debate that followed the issue boiled down to whether free organization of groups or parties was destructive of union purposes or whether they could serve to benefit the union. Supporting the proposed amendment, one delegate said:

I believe that the ban by our International on the formation of groups . . . is simply encouragement of . . . bootleg groups. At the same time, destructive elements are given a chance to act as groups, while constructive forces have no way of . . . bringing their issues before the general membership of our union. I do not believe that the U.S. Congress would ever outlaw the Democratic or Republican parties. We, too, are a government, sitting in Congress. . . .

Why not legalize all groups in our union and let them function as political parties in the United States of America?

Another added:

We all know that the destructive elements in our union have a chance to function under different disguises . . . Therefore, at membership meetings they can act as a unit for destructive purposes, whereas when

[14] Constitution (1940), Art. VIII, p. 42.

it comes to proper organization on our part, we are completely de-
mobilized legally and we are not going to function against the wishes
of the General Executive Board.

An opponent of the amendment argued:

The minute you legalize groups, it would mean that this convention
decides that any group may exist, that they may discuss union problems, that they may decide union policies. Group decisions would thus
become binding, and the elected leadership of the local union would
exercise little function indeed. Small groups and cliques, not the local
union, would decide the fate of our locals and sometimes of our International.

President Dubinsky closed the debate:

I am absolutely opposed to any changes in our constitution on this
subject. I think our members are as free as any membership within any
trade-union in this country or in the world to exercise their judgment,
their free opinion. But we are opposed to clique dominations of our
union. . . .

I hope that our union will continue the way we are. There is no
reason for changing it. We are a model organization, and let's not
consider it from a group point of view, here and there. Let's consider
it from the point of view of the general welfare of our entire membership and our entire organizations.

The *Proceedings* then state that the motion to reject the amendment was adopted "with several dissenting votes."

Convention delegates of most unions can usually be relied upon
to respond to such appeals for unity against factional groups and
for support of official policies to promote the welfare of the organization as a whole. When the 1948 convention of the Amalgamated Clothing Workers unanimously nominated its president
for reelection, his acceptance speech said in part:

I was deeply touched by the demonstration and the expressions that
I know came from deep down in your hearts. I take these expressions
as feelings of love for your union. I take these expressions as an approval of the acts of your officers and your General Executive Board.
Your board is of high caliber and has risen to new heights in the last
two years. . . .

I want to say to you that I have sensed throughout this week an
extraordinary communion between the platform and the delegates on

the floor. It was a communion of deep understanding, and this is one of our great assets—that our union is bound together like one integrated family. . . . Anyone who is honest and fair, who has sat through and observed this parliament in action, will return to his home with conviction that, here, the voice of the people and the voice of the officers were as one. There is no division.

Though the "communion" between the Clothing Workers' officers and convention delegates is indeed marked, it is by no means extraordinary as their president emphasized. More or less of the same kind of communion is to be found in most unions which have been in existence long enough to stabilize their governments. Thus the constitutional division of powers between the president, the executive board, and the convention works in practice not as a system of checks and balances, but rather to concentrate executive and judicial powers in the officers as a body under the leadership of the president, while the convention tends to become a body for registering approval of their acts and policies. The delegates, consisting mainly of the active members and sub-leaders who elect the president and the board, generally serve to support rather than to check the powers of the officers when these act in unison as members of the executive board.

In the early years of a union organization, conflicts between the president and the board are fairly frequent and these are fought out on the convention floor. But the differences tend to disappear as it grows older and the active members solidify into a dominating machine which keeps the administration of the union in the hands of tried leaders. As the officialdom of the union and the convention delegates are integrated "like one family," the tendency is to add to the officers' powers rather than to restrict them. Illustrative of this tendency are provisions in some constitutions which transfer from the convention to the executive board final judicial authority in certain types of cases. The United Mine Workers' constitution, for example, now provides:

In all questions of dispute, appeals and grievances . . . the right of appeal of an individual member shall end with the district executive board, and the right of appeal of any branch of the organization shall end with the International Executive Board. This shall not prevent individuals whose membership is at stake from appealing to the Board which body's decision shall be final and binding until reversed by the International convention.[15]

This is one of the reasons for the decline in the number of appeals taken to the convention noted in the previous chapter.

UNION CONSTITUTIONS give the president both general and specific enumerated powers. The grants of general executive powers are worded in some such language as the following:

He shall have full power to direct the affairs of the union subject to approval by the Executive Board.[16]

He shall supervise the entire interests of the United Association.[17]

He shall have supervision over the interests of this Union as its executive officer and chief organizer.[18]

He shall . . . possess such authority while the Grand Division is in session as pertains to his high office, and exercise all executive functions of the Grand Division when it is not in session.[19]

Judicial powers of the chief executive are similarly described in general terms.

The President shall interpret the meaning of the constitution . . . subject to repeal by the Executive Board.[20]

He shall decide disputes or questions in controversy . . . all his decisions being subject to appeal, first to the Executive Board, and then to the convention.[21]

He shall enforce the laws of the International Association, decide all questions or order and usage and all constitutional questions.[22]

In addition to these general grants of power, the constitutions enumerate specific powers in describing duties of the president which are usually set forth with much detail, as for example that

[15] Miners Constitution (1944), Art. III, p. 7; Steelworkers Constitution (1944), Art. IV, p. 7.
[16] Miners Constitution, Art. IX, p. 21.
[17] Plumbers Constitution (1942), Sec. 4, p. 6.
[18] Molders Constitution (1945), Art. IV, p. 17.
[19] Railway Conductors Constitution (1941), Art. IV, p. 10.
[20] Miners Constitution (1944), Art. IX, p. 15.
[21] Auto Workers Constitution (1946), Art. XIII, p. 36.
[22] Machinists Constitution (1946), Art. IV, p. 13.

he shall preside at conventions and executive board meetings, sign checks, give bond, audit accounts, etc., and that he may call and attend meetings of local unions. Usually he is authorized to appoint national representatives, organizers, staff assistants and other employees, and he may suspend or discharge them. He is empowered "at all times [to] exercise a general supervision over all officers of the International Union," or have "full charge" of them, or he must "see that all other officers perform their duties." He assigns duties and directs the work of the vice-presidents as well as representatives and organizers, and he may deputize any of them to act as his personal representative.

He has authority to suspend a national officer and the officers of local unions; and he may appoint a temporary administrator or governing board for such locals or other subordinate organizations. He is empowered to fill vacancies in office and to suspend individual members of the union. Typical of these grants of authority is the following from the Machinists' constitution:

The International President shall have the direction and supervision of all district and local lodges, with full authority to suspend individual members, or district or local lodges for incompetency, negligence, insubordination, or other failure to properly perform their duties . . . and for violation of the provisions of the constitution of the Grand Lodge or the constitution of local lodges; . . . he may revoke the charter of any district or local lodge found guilty after trial by the Executive Council of a violation of the constitution.[23]

In many ways the president's authority to appoint national representatives, organizers, deputies, and staff assistants is the most important of his enumerated powers. The Ladies Garment Workers' constitution has a good brief description of the work that national organizers or representatives do in most unions:

It shall be the duty of the general organizers to organize new locals, visit existing locals, adjust internal differences, assist local unions in the conduct and management of strikes and lockouts and, in adjusting threatened strikes and lockouts, cause to be audited the accounts of locals and generally to supervise the conduct of affairs by the local unions . . . each organizer shall render a report to the President at least once a month.[24]

[23] Constitution (1946), Art. IV, p. 14. [24] Constitution (1940), Art. IV, p. 25.

This constitution also makes plain that these employees are to be controlled by the president in carrying out his own functions as chief executive officer and chief organizer.

The President shall perform all necessary organizing and other work usually attached to the office of president. He shall have the right to employ any executive or other personnel necessary for the administration of his office . . . [and] shall have the right to engage or dispense with the services of any general organizer, subject to approval by the General Executive Board.[25]

Though all constitutions are not so specific, this is the general pattern of the chief executive's authority to appoint and control the manpower employed by the national union to carry out its functions. The president generally selects the organizers from among local leaders and outstanding active members, and approval of his appointments by the board is largely a formality. As representatives of the president they function like officers, their duties being similar to those of vice-presidents with whom they often work in conjunction. This led to frequent proposals that they should be elected rather than appointed, but the vice-presidents and other officers were strongly opposed, and such proposals have generally been defeated.

In addition to organizers or representatives, the president also employs staff executives and assistants, and the number and variety of these have greatly increased during the last two decades as the unions felt the need for experts to advise and help them in dealing with government labor boards and mediation and arbitration agencies, as well as in bargaining with employers when working agreements began to include such subjects as incentive plans, job evaluation, productivity allowances, insurance pensions, health, welfare plans, etc. Today there is hardly a union of any considerable size that does not have a research and educational director, and the staffs of many include lawyers, economists, statisticians, time-study men, accountants, and other specialized experts. These do not ordinarily come from union ranks, though some constitutions make them eligible for membership. But more and more the tendency is for the president to employ lawyers and

[25] *Ibid.*, Art. III, p. 16.

other professional experts to assist in dealing with government agencies and arbitration boards, as well as to do the necessary research and work out details of new proposals for bargaining with employers. At the same time many unions are specializing their organizers, representatives, and others from their own ranks as staff experts, and increasingly they are sending promising young leaders and junior officers to universities for special training to qualify them as staff experts.

The jobs of organizers, representatives, and staff assistants are patronage at the disposal of the president, and their security as employees of the union depends mainly on him. By delegating his power to his numerous agents, he controls them as well as the vice-presidents and other officers who, though they are usually members of the executive board, are also subject to his direction as part of his executive staff.

The concentration of power in the hands of the president comes pretty much as a matter of necessity, for unions must constantly carry on struggles with employers to share with the workers' organizations their original right to govern their employees unilaterally. Thus while their constitutions lodge "sovereign powers" in their conventions, unions still have "monarchs" to deal with— employers who have the managerial right to make regulations for the government of their employees. To limit the employer's governing powers over his employees and to force him to subject them to rules or laws embodied in collective working contracts, the unions strive to build and maintain their strength at least equal to his bargaining power. For this reason, also, union constitution makers do not fear building too powerful a union government as the founders of the U.S. government feared building too powerful a national state. The development of the national union as the basic unit of union government with complete powers over its local union governments and over its individual members came as a matter of necessity because this was the only means by which workers could free themselves from the absolute governments of industrial monarchs or hierarchies of industrial managements.

But union governments are not necessarily undemocratic for

this reason. They are in many respects similar to the governments of Great Britain and other European democracies which still have monarchs as heads of state and lodge all basic governmental powers in their parliaments. Union presidents and executive boards function much like the prime ministers and cabinets of such governments. As the former are delegates to the union convention, so the latter are members of parliament, and this body like the convention serves also as the assembly for making constitutional changes. Such governments have proved as capable of providing democratic rule and safeguarding the rights of individuals as the government of the United States with its coordinate executive legislative and judicial branches checking and balancing each other, and with its constitutional provision for a bill of rights.

Most countries with this form of government, however, have developed an independent judicial system for determining rights and controversies under their laws, the lack of which seems to be a fundamental weakness of union governments from a democratic point of view. But democratic traditions are strong in union organizations, and as we shall see in the next chapter something like due process of law is provided for in their constitutions and in practice for settling internal disputes and protecting rights of individual members. These traditions also led to the attempts to check the powers of the president by subjecting them to the superior authority of executive boards and to the convention, though in practice this has not proved very effective. Similar due process is also provided for in the constitutions to safeguard the rights of local and district government units which, though they are created by and may be abolished by the national union, nevertheless are given a large measure of home rule by the laws of the union.

Moreover, unions as private governments are subject to the courts of the land, and if national officers deny due process to members or subordinate governmental units, or otherwise abuse their powers, the aggrieved may and sometimes do take their cases to the public courts to have their rights adjudicated. With the courts thus open to correct wrongdoing, the necessity for an independent judiciary within the unions may not be as vital as in public governments; but for the individual member the cost of a law suit is usually prohibitive while the officialdom of the union has the resources of the organization to defend its actions. Also, the judges generally apply the constitutions and laws of the union in deciding such cases, and unless these have been violated, or are discriminatory, or fraud or arbitrary action is involved, they usually hold that the member has bound himself to obey the laws of the union and do not upset judgments of union officials based on the laws.

There are indications, however, that unions are becoming aware of the need for a judiciary that is independent of the executive officers. Partly this is due to a provision in the Taft-Hartley law of 1947 authorizing the National Labor Relations Board to decide jurisdictional disputes between the organizations which cause or threaten strikes. To avoid decisions by a government agency affecting the right of unions to determine the work over which they claim jurisdiction, the building trades were the first to agree to employ an impartial arbitrator to decide any such disputes which could not be settled by mutual agreement, and later many of the organizations both in the CIO and the AFL entered into so-called "no-raiding agreements" which provide for similar impartial arbitration. For many years too, a considerable number of unions have resorted to the "Honest Ballot Association" or other outside persons to supervise their elections in order to assure the membership that these will be fairly conducted.

THE QUALIFICATIONS prescribed in the constitutions for candidates for president and other executive officers are simple and normally not discriminatory. Most commonly the basic requirement is only good standing membership in the union for a specified period which is usually short, one to three years, and not over five years. There may be an age qualification for the presidency, generally thirty-five years, and where a union has different classes of members, the requirement is full membership, such as that he shall be a journeyman member, or a "beneficial member" where a union has an insurance system. Employment at the trade or by the union is often a requirement; at least originally before being elected to any office the candidate must have worked at the trade or in industry over which the union has jurisdiction.[26] Many unions also require candidates to be citizens of the United States or Canada, or they must have declared intent to become citizens. Some constitutions specify that only delegates to the convention may be elected to national offices, and most unions now make Communists, Fascists, and other subversives ineligible to hold office.

Union office is thus open practically to all loyal union members, but the constitutional qualifications have little to do with the actual selection of the president and other executives. They do not describe the union executive, but rather say who can not be one. Some degree of outstanding activity, experience, ability, leadership, and attachment to the union or sacrifice made for it are generally required. These actual qualifications are judged on the basis of the candidate's record and personal traits. The president usually has a record of previous office holding, and other national executives have had experience as local or district officers.

The first step on the road to the presidency is local union activity. This distinguishes a man. There are many who work quietly, but there are others who stand out, impressing their names on the membership by some form of public appearance, usually by talking, but often also by taking some leadership part in local strikes and picketing. They thus put themselves in line for election as business agents or local union presidents. From this point they move to activity in a wider sphere, among a number of locals that make up the district or regional organizations. They are elected as delegates to district councils, to the national convention, and become familiar with national union affairs. They come to the attention of the national officers and may be appointed as organizers or national representatives. As their names become well known to the memberships of local unions throughout the country, they try for election as vice-presidents or members or the national executive board.

[26] At the 1944 convention of the Miners' Union, John L. Lewis disqualified a rival candidate for the presidency on the ground that he was not employed in or about a mine or working for the union.

Many of the present national union presidents were elected to their positions when they were presidents of district organizations or business agents of large local unions. In recent years, however, the tendency has been to select the chief executive from among the other national office holders, though in some unions district and local leaders still control the selection of the president. As the organizations have grown in size and extended their collective agreements to cover great mass-production industries, the administrative policies of the national unions required more uniform application throughout the country than was possible when the district organizations were largely autonomous governing units operating independently of the national administration. In one way or another, the president and the national executive board freed themselves from control by powerful district officials, and membership in the circle of incumbent national executive officers has in effect become a final qualification for the presidency in many unions. Through their powers of appointment to fill vacancies, the officials add to their group and promote those within it, subsequent elections, whether by the convention or by referendum voting, generally confirming their selections.

When John Lewis became president of the United Mine Workers, the union functioned like a federation of autonomous districts. He converted it to a highly centralized national administration without changing the constitution but by using his powers under it. Subject to approval by the executive board he had the authority that constitutions usually give their presidents to revoke the charters of district organizations and "to create a provisional government for the subordinate branch whose charter has been revoked." The board was composed of elected representatives from the autonomous districts in addition to principal executive officers. One by one he either suspended the charters of the districts or the requirement that their officers be elected by the district membership, and he appointed his own designees in their place. He continued this until a majority of the executive board members came from districts whose key officers had been appointed by him.

At each Miners' convention since 1934, there have been some

delegates demanding the return of district self-government, but Lewis denounces them, cites inefficient and dishonest practices of district officers, points out that they fail to carry out the policies of the national union as adopted by the convention, and the delegates continue to uphold him. At the 1944 convention he summed up his position in part as follows:

I am sick and tired of some of these elected officers in some of these districts, when we ask them why they don't do this or why they don't do that, and have them tell me "why I am autonomous." What the hell do I care whether they are autonomous or not? I want action, I want service, I want loyalty, and I want to protect the rights of our people, and if you want John L. Lewis to be your president I want to have your support—and I think I am getting it.

National executives of other unions have compromised their differences with powerful district leaders, but generally constitutions now give the presidents and the executive boards sufficient direct authority to supervise the affairs of district and other subordinate governmental units to enable them to enforce national policies as adopted by the convention uniformly through all branches of the organization. Many elect vice-presidents who are designated to have charge of districts or give district directors the status of national officers.

In striking contrast to the methods used by Lewis to control district organizations was the manner in which Sidney Hillman managed the Amalgamated Clothing Workers, especially in the latter part of his incumbence. At the 1946 convention of this union, the last at which he presided before his death, an old experienced delegate was asked to explain the absence of debate and virtual unanimity of the delegates in adopting the measures submitted for their consideration. He said:

Well, you see, whenever a new matter comes up the President takes it to the Executive Board and talks it over with them, making whatever modifications he thinks necessary to win the approval of the Board. With these adjustments, the President then takes it to a number of key locals and finds out their reactions. Through this process, agreements are reached behind the scenes and there are no differences which need to be resolved at a convention. Oh, there used to be, back years ago, when new policies were adopted, such as over production standards and stabilization [of wages].

In the office of the president of a building and construction workers there was a sign hanging a few years ago which read: "Open to all members; prior experience in officeholding necessary; incumbents preferred." This sums up well the actual qualifications for the presidency, and it makes plain that the period or term for which a president is elected relates merely to the mechanics of the elections, and the same is largely true of other officers as well. The terms range from one to five years and more than 60 percent of the unions hold elections every two years or less. There are provisions in the constitutions for removal of the president by recall elections or impeachment by the executive board, but the frequency of the elections makes resort to these devices largely unnecessary, and they are rarely used.

The experience in previous officeholding that is necessary to qualify for president is acquired by successful union activity. What this means was described by a delegate at the Miners' 1944 convention, and it is significant that he spoke in opposition to district self-government in conformity with the national administrative policy of John Lewis and his associated executives. But he emphasized the opportunities that union activity affords to younger members to move up in the scale of officeholding and the training they receive on the way.

As far as the coal miner having a chance to move up, I got out of high school and went to work in a coal mine as a slate picker, the lowest classification around the mine. Do you know what I am now and have been for the last seven years? I have been president of my local union two years, I have been Chairman of the Mine Committee for five solid years. I have been handling the treasury and I have possibilities of going higher. I know there is room for ambitious men to go along with the International Union.

It is such ambitious men as this one who have been broken in on the established customs of lower officeholding that the circle of incumbent officers pick to add to it and to promote within it, and thus they become part of the official family and in line for the presidency when the opportunity comes. The younger active leaders model themselves on the president; they learn the game and the rules from him and from their experiences in applying his policies and decisions to the problems of the subordinate governmental units. Loyalty to the president, which is commonly identified with loyalty to the union, is one of the most important lessons younger leaders must learn. But the men who come forth are also drawn by the ideal of the common good to overcome the injustices and exploitation of workers they are familiar with or have themselves suffered.

The men who reach the top as union executives are much like their rivals, the captains of industry. A research director who has dealt with many union presidents describes them as "the same type physically and temperamentally; the muscular sort of person, the man of motor activity, the operator." Aggressiveness and a measure of ruthlessness are common traits among them as they were among the early industrial leaders who had to fight their way to the top from humble beginnings. Union presidents rise from the ranks, but unlike business executives, they do not move from one organization to another. Their careers are usually confined to one union; they may not hold membership in more than one, though they often help in organizing new unions. The exceptional circumstances of the organization of mass production workers in industrial unions by the CIO, however, led leaders from the older unions to become executives and presidents of some of the new unions. One of these, the CIO Packing House Workers, shocked the trade-union world by electing their lawyer to the presidency.

Union leaders rise to the top by their natural talents. Their will to power and experience develop the skills which help them to attain it. Most of them have had little in the way of formal higher education, but many are studious men who have supplemented their primary or high-school education by taking evening courses or by their own studies. In recent years some have had a year or two of college. But however little formal education they may have had, they are generally not uneducated men. They learn from experience rather than from the printed word, from attending and addressing meetings and conventions, from dealing with employers, politicians, government officials, and other public figures. They learn to understand and how to handle people both in and outside their union. They learn the law of the union and become adept in interpreting it and in applying it to particular factual situations. They learn that their abilities match those of business executives and other capable people with whom they deal, and they learn how to develop those abilities. Most of all, they learn how to use the symbols, the myths of unionism, and how to express their feelings in terms of union ideals.

Perhaps because of their lack of formal education, they are particularly insistent that proper respect be paid to the important positions they hold, and employers who ignore this do so at their peril. Some years ago the chief executives of five railroad unions sent a joint telegram to the president of one of the largest trunk-line railroads of the country requesting an interview to discuss certain claims for back pay involving hundreds of thousands of dollars. He replied that his "Vice-President in charge of Industrial Relations" would arrange to meet with them. They promptly wired back they would send vice-presidents to meet with his vice-president. The latter told the railroad president this was a mistake, who then advised the union presidents he would see them. When they did meet on an equal level the claims were adjusted on a compromise basis.

In the main it is the responsibilities of officeholding, the hard work involved, and the competition for advancement from lower to higher offices that bring out the latent abilities and train and educate union leaders. Indeed it is the opportunity that unions provide for otherwise suppressed leadership talents among industrial workers that is one of the main sources of the energy and vitality of the trade union movement, and the human energy they thus release also feeds the industrial and political life of the nation. What the responsibilities of union office at the lower levels mean to a local union president and how he feels about them was told to a Machinists' convention by one serving as a delegate. He said that his lodge paid his expenses and time lost from his job. "But," he went on, "we deserve it. We get kicked around during the year. It's like being a minister, everyone with a complaint loads it on to you, and there's always someone who complains he isn't getting service."

At the top level, we have the testimony of President Broach of the Brotherhood of Electrical Workers who resigned his office in 1933, and wrote to its executive council in part as follows:

Nearly four years ago when former President Noonan died, I wrote in our *Journal* that "I know something of the wear and tear of the work, how quickly it takes effect. . . . The atmosphere of controversy, the smoke, the poison filled conference rooms, little sound sleep, . . . traveling on trains when ill and worn, piles of mail filled with documents, requests, pleas, complaints and troubles of all sorts—all take their heavy toll, almost before one knows it. No line of work produces more shattered nerves and broken health. . . . Former President McNulty died a young man. Ford at forty-seven was a nervous wreck and could no longer carry on. A long list of other cases . . . could be cited. . . . The crowds see us only from the platform and the printed page."

It is not so much the hours worked. It is the ever present tension, worry, uncertainty, expectancy, the life of controversy. Responsible labor leadership keeps a man "keyed" up most of the time. He never knows when he will be called out of bed, what will break next. Things are always coming unexpectedly, suddenly. Always he is the object of hostility, trickery, flattery, and the meanest most vicious stories and misrepresentations. . . . I feel no other work levies such an emotional tax. . . . Naturally some men stand up under the strain better than others. I suppose it's largely a matter of temperament. One man can laugh off a thing that almost breaks the heart of another.

This is not an untypical picture of the gruelling work and life of a union president, and while many break their health under the load of responsibilities and some die in offce, few resign. Most of them learn to conquer the problems of their jobs, however, regard them as a challenge to their abilities, develop their talents, and rise in stature as they continue in office. There are, of course, weaker men who become presidents, but they are fewer in number. An example was President Muster of the CIO Furniture Workers in 1943 who when he was reelected to the presidency that year told the convention delegates:

In return I dedicate myself to the work ahead. I don't find it arduous. Those who are amazed at the amount of stamina I seem to have, don't be surprised because it comes very easy. . . . I like to work with people. I like the labor movement. I think it is the greatest movement in the world. That is what gives it initiative, that gives it impetus, that gives it salt that makes everything tasty to the work. I enjoy nothing better than to hear and rehear, and it never gets stale to me, the experience of the four o'clock in the mornings, of the picket lines, of the negotiations of the struggle and the strife, because it comes into my mind like a kaleidoscopic picture that all these things bring us to Cleveland [the convention] legislation which insures the continued growth of the union. That is so important. That is so vital.

Actually Muster was a loquacious, ineffectual person who accepted the power conferred on him by a faction which used him as a front for its control of the union. He did not try to impose his will on the faction leaders, but later he fell out with them and resigned, though, as he said, he liked the work and "don't find it arduous." Such men of weaker will and easy-going temperament are more often chosen president when two factions are about equally divided; someone with not too strong a will who has been neutral in the conflict between them is supported by both.

Salaries of union presidents generally are not high; most of them now fall below $20,000 a year. But some presidents do very handsomely, their compensation comparing favorably with those of the executives of good-sized business corporations. One was recently raised to $75,000 and some get $40,000 to $50,000. But relative to the total number of presidents, these are still comparatively few. With the expense allowances all presidents receive, most of them now get fairly adequate remuneration, and it can no longer be said that they are grossly underpaid as was generally true up to twenty or twenty-five years ago.

One of the first well-paid presidents was Daniel Tobin of the Teamsters' Union. Speaking of salaries at its 1925 convention, he said:

Payment? Yes, we get paid and paid very generously by our organization—I am speaking now of our local and international officers—but there is more in this work than payment in dollars and cents. There is no payment sufficient in money, and those of you who are business agents understand it. You understand the meaning of my words—there is no payment sufficient in money to recompense the men of labor for the things they do.

As a guest speaker at the 1927 convention of the Typographical Union, he offered some advice about salaries and union management generally, and from the discussion with President Howard of that union that followed, we can gather some idea of two common types of union presidents, their attitudes toward salaries and toward other problems of union leadership. Said Tobin:

One of the things we don't agree with you on [is] you change your presidents too often. I started in working for nothing, but I get a salary now three times equal to your intellectual presidents. [The Typographical president's salary at that time was $5,000.]

The salary we pay our men is not too much, and I want you to take this message home. If the referendum holds you back from progress get rid of the referendum. It is the progressive idea to talk about the referendum, the thing you stand for in national elections. If it is not, or there is any other cancer which is helping to destroy your organization, get rid of it.

To this President Howard replied:

The time has not arrived in the affairs of the ITU where we accept the same emblem for inspiration that is accepted by the capitalists of this country and have no apologies to make for the salaries paid to the officers of the ITU, because I believe it is the wish of the working printers of this country that the men and officers who represent them should remain in the atmosphere in which they received their education in the trade union movement. . . . We do not accept the dollar mark for inspiration for service in the International Typographical Union. . . . The record of accomplishment of this organization stands for itself as evidence of those who have served in minor positions . . . and of those who have served in honored positions; they could not one and all give any greater service had they received $100,000 a year as do the presidents of many insurance companies or organizations or associations of men.

Let me say to you just as frankly as you have given your advice that printers differ from you on the fundamental questions you have raised in your remarks. We recognize that the power in this organization, the inherent power comes from cooperation and association, . . . everything that has been accomplished for the benefit of the printers . . . has come as a result of the recognition that the inherent power in this organization rests in the hands of the men and women in the composing and mailing rooms . . . and when difficulties and great problems arise, we should appeal to those who hold the inherent power in this organization.

Money is one measure of the gap in the level of living between the union executives and the members of the organizations, though in a few highly skilled craft unions (Pattern Makers, Die Sinkers, newspapermen, and some of the smaller building mechanics' organizations) the men at their work have no reason to envy the pay of their officers. But pay is not the most important measure. There are other rewards and amenities that go with the positions of officers, and especially with that of the president. They meet and do business with government officials, industrial executives, journalists, politicians, university professors, and other labor leaders from countries throughout the world. Their lives touch the world of many points, their activities broaden, educate them, develop their capacities, while the work and existence of their members contribute little to their personal growth. It is these rewards and the power that their offices give them than attract men with the will to power to the gruelling work and responsibilities of union office holding, as men of similar character are attracted to the responsibilities of top office holding in the business world and in the governments of states and nations.

XI

THE JUDICIAL PROCESS
WITHIN THE UNIONS

IN THE EARLY HISTORY of the United Automobile Workers when the question whether it would affiliate with the CIO or the AFL had not yet been decided, its president, Homer Martin, suspended twelve of the seventeen members of the national executive board. The remaining board members, holding themselves to be the legitimate authority of the union, ratified Martin's action. The "suspended" members, claiming to be the lawful majority of the board, then suspended Martin and his colleagues. Here was a factional dispute, not unusual in a newly formed union before a majority of active members has had time to build an electoral machine for stabilizing its government, but this one taxed the judicial process beyond the breaking point.

The UAW's constitution at that time had been largely copied from other constitutions and did not contain many of the detailed provisions that its experience since then has taught it to include. But it did contain the usual provisions that the convention shall be the highest tribunal within the union, that between conventions the executive board shall be the highest tribunal, and that between meetings of the board its powers shall be exercised by the president. The constitution also provided that any elective officer could be impeached and removed from office on proven charges, and that in an emergency the president may suspend a national officer subject to approval by the executive board. In such cases the president was required to call a meeting of the board to give the suspended officer a fair and just trial.

The constitution thus supplied at least the outlines of judicial procedures for dealing with this crisis. Both factions attempted to move within the constitutional framework. Each gave the other formal notice of charges and confirmed the suspensions at trials conducted in accordance with the constitutional provisions, except, however, that those accused did not show up for trial. Rival law suits were also brought in the courts.

Meanwhile the CIO intervened in behalf of the anti-Martin faction and the AFL supported Martin. Locals and the membership lined up on one side or the other. But the dispute was finally settled neither by the judicial process within the union nor by the courts. It was resolved by National Labor Relations Board elections in the auto plants giving the employees a choice between the "UAW-CIO" and the "UAW-AFL." The CIO group won decisively in the larger plants, and Martin shortly thereafter disappeared from the ranks of professional union leaders.

This episode in the history of the UAW is not typical of cases arising for adjudication under union governments, but it illustrates an important fact about the judicial process within unions. Although this process is always available and is generally used in resolving disputes about rights and powers of officers and of the national union and subordinate governmental units, it can be supplanted or supplemented by the electoral process. Frequently, both before and after judicial determinations have been made, such controversies are settled by elections. In this respect union judicial procedures differ essentially from those of the public courts in the United States.

This difference is due to the fact that union constitutions do not provide for a separate set of officials known as the "judiciary," who in our public governments are normally independent of the executive officers and the representative legislative bodies. Those who make the union laws and those who administer the laws also sit in judgment on controversies arising out of the interpretation or application and enforcement of the laws. As a consequence, the judicial process is often intermingled with elections and with other governmental processes. Such intermingling makes analysis and evaluation of the judicial process difficult, but it is nevertheless clearly identifiable.

Union governments provide for official interpretation of their constitutions and laws or rules, for disciplinary proceedings against officers and members, and for resolution of conflicting claims of members and subordinate governmental units. The constitutions establish procedures for complaints, prosecution, hearings, and trials. In these judicial proceedings, the extent to which what the courts call "due process" is provided for either by the constitutions or by the officers who conduct the trials varies widely. So also there is wide variation in the effectiveness of union judicial processes in resolving the various kinds of controversies. Nevertheless there are certain common denominators among the judicial problems and procedures in all unions which make generalized descriptions possible, and from which reasonable conclusions may be drawn. In every union there is one system of courts established by the national constitution. The local unions are the lowest courts, the president, the national executive board and sometimes also district councils serve as intermediate courts, and the convention is the supreme court.

THE OFFICIAL INTERPRETATION of a union's constitution, laws, and rules is commonly vested in the president, subject to review by the executive board. Most constitutions contain a provision similar to the following from the Miners' fundamental law: "He [the president] shall interpret the meaning of the international constitution, but his interpretation shall be subject to repeal by the international executive board." Some say that he shall "decide all constitutional questions." Appeals from the executive board to the convention are usually authorized, but the Order of Railway Conductors' provision skips the review by the executive board, appeals going directly from the president to the convention. "The president shall interpret all laws of the Order, subject to appeal to the next session of the Grand Division." In some unions the interpretation power is formally lodged in the executive board rather than the president, but in practice he may nevertheless make initial rulings. A few constitutions do not mention interpretation, but some of them provide that "the president shall have such further powers in addition to those enumerated herein as are usual to his office." As a power of the president, interpretation is usually distinguished from other judicial powers such as those over disciplinary proceedings, trials, and settlement of controversies.

There are no procedural details set forth in the constitutions as to how the president's interpretations are to be made, though some prescribe that he shall keep a record of his interpretations and submit a report thereon to the executive board. (Some unions publish the decisions of their executive boards in their monthly circulars or journals.) Union laws require interpretation day in and out; the executive board meets infrequently, so that the president is the logical authority to make quickly needed decisions. Numerous requests for interpretation come to the president from local or district unions or their officers, or from members or groups of members. He may ask for more information, and his interpretations of provisions of the constitution and laws are largely based on such correspondence. He may consult the executive board members to get their approval for a ruling, and this too may be done by correspondence or even by telephone conversations. If any such decision is formally appealed to the board or to the convention, the regular appellate procedures provided in the constitutions must be followed. The need of disputants below for prompt decisions so they can go on with their affairs is enough to give finality to the president's rulings in most cases: and once he has interpreted a provision of the constitution, this usually becomes a precedent to be followed in future cases.

In most unions it is difficult to separate the judicial function of interpretation from the day-to-day executive and administrative duties the president must perform. In public governments, interpretation of the constitution and laws is among the highest of judicial functions; under union governments it is an incidental responsibility of the chief executive and his associated officers on the executive board. The omission from the constitutions of any procedural specifications in connection with the president's authority to interpret the meaning of the constitution, especially the lack of a requirement for hearings, is one of the factors that tends to build up the power of the chief executive. But this is more or less inevitable so long as so important a judicial function is joined as an integral part of the president's normal executive duties and responsibilities. Moreover, an astute president can make interpretations with confidence that they will stand up on appeal. He has many ways of gauging the sentiment of executive board members and even of forthcoming conventions.

As previously mentioned, the executive board was designed to check the powers of the president, and in controversies where it serves as a trial board or must provide for a hearing and a trial, these do serve as safeguards against arbitrary action by the president. But in exercising his general power to decide all constitutional questions, he develops an expertness in union law which the board members usually lack and they are not inclined to challenge his authority. Also, as we have seen, the circle of elected officers who constitute the board in most unions tend to act in unison and become a more or less self-perpetuating body, while in others the president controls the board rather than is controlled by it. The president's authority to interpret the constitution contributes in no small degree to these results.

In some unions where appeals from the president's interpretations are appealable not to the executive board but to a separately elected appellate body, the president may find himself in an embarrassing position when his decision is reversed. Some years ago a joint collective agreement was negotiated by four railroad brotherhoods with a carrier, and though it was signed and approved by representatives of the employees and national officers in accordance with the unions' laws, the employees of one of the organizations (Locomotive Firemen) later decided that the agreement was unfair to them, and they petitioned the president to release them from it so that they could negotiate a new agreement. He ruled against them, holding that the four organizations would have to join in serving notice of a desire to change the agreement, to which the other three were not agreeable. The Firemen covered by the agreement then appealed to the board of directors, the appellate body of their union, which reversed the president's ruling. Under the union's laws, the employees then had the right to ask the employing railroad company for a separate agreement, and they served the necessary notice. The company insisted, however, that without the approval of the other organizations involved, it could not negotiate such an agreement. The Firemen then petitioned the National Mediation Board to mediate the dispute with the carrier in accordance with the provisions of the Railway Labor Act. The Board met with parties, but, after hearing their contentions, advised them and the Firemen's national organization that it had no authority to mediate changes in the contract with one of the four organizations when the other three desired no change. The union did not process the dispute further, and the Mediation Board thus in effect overruled the decision of the union's board of directors.

A few examples must suffice to illustrate how a president may use his power to interpret the constitution and the kind of questions that are submitted to him for interpretation. John Lewis ruled that Philip Murray could not retain his position as vice-president of the Miners' Union and take a full salary as president of the United Steelworkers. Prior to this ruling Murray had held this office, but received his pay from the Miners as their vice-president. So too, at the 1944 Miners' convention Lewis ruled that a rival candidate, Ray Edmundson, having been disqualified as a delegate to the convention was likewise disqualified as a candidate for president or for any other office. This ruling as reported in the convention proceedings is a good illustration of how the interpretation power is exercised with judicial trappings. Said Lewis:

Article IX, Section 7, of the International constitution gives to the president . . . the authority and makes it his duty to interpret the meaning of the constitution, subject to proper review.

The president has noted that on Friday, September 15, 1954, the convention took an action . . . denying a seat to one Edmundson, purporting to represent Local Union No. 764. . . . The convention held that [he] was not eligible to be seated . . . for the reasons: (a) that he is not a member in good standing, and (b) that he is not employed in or around the mines as provided by the . . . constitution. . . .

The president holds that the action of the convention in ruling that the said Edmundson was not eligible to be seated . . . as a delegate for the reasons aforesaid given also operates to prevent [him] from being a candidate for an office in this union.

Lewis asked whether any delegate cared to appeal to the convention from the ruling of the president. Hearing none, he inquired whether the convention desired to affirm his ruling. A motion to affirm was then made and seconded, and the proceedings state: "The motion is carried unanimously," but they go on to quote a written request of one delegate which read: "I hereby wish to have my name registered . . . as voting in opposition to concurring in the ruling of the president, denying Ray Edmundson the privilege of being on the international ballot."

An interpretation by the president of the Glass Bottle Blowers Union was challenged at its 1944 convention. A local union had suspended a member for being absent from more than three consecutive meetings. A rule in its by-laws authorized expulsion of a member by a two-thirds vote for missing three meetings and also provided a fine of 50¢ for each absence. The by-laws had been submitted to the national union for approval as required by the constitution, and no exception was taken to the absentee provision. The local union had a closed-shop agreement and notified the management to discharge the offending member. The plant superintendent refused the union's request stating he would not fire a man for the reason given. The local then referred the matter to the president and he sent a representative to investigate. The representative met with the local people concerned, and upon learning the issue he telephoned the president and secured a ruling from him on the spot that the local by-law was unconstitutional. Accordingly, the member was not to be disciplined or discharged. The local appealed this decision to the convention, and though the appeals committee recommended that the president's decision be reversed, the delegates after a vigorous debate upheld the ruling of the president.

The Woodworkers' 1944 convention considered an appeal from the president's interpretation of a clause in the national constitution requiring expulsion of any member who belongs to the Communist Party. Charges were filed in a local against two members alleging that they had openly declared they belonged to a "Communist Political Association." The local was apparently reluctant to expel the two members and did not try them on the charges. Instead it asked the president for a ruling whether the Political Association was included in the ban against belonging to the Communist Party. He replied by letter that the Association was the same as the Party and directed the local to expel the members. The local refused and appealed to the national executive board which sustained the president. When the final appeal came to the convention, it was not referred to a committee for a report and recommendation which is the normal procedure, but was presented directly for consideration on the convention floor. The president's interpretation was the major issue debated by the delegates, and on a roll-call vote they sustained the rulings of the president and the executive board by two to one.

These examples make plain the informality of the president's procedures in interpreting the constitution or laws of a union and the more formal prescribed procedures which are followed by the appeal tribunals. But the vast majority of the president's interpretations are not appealed, and these, like the decisions of the executive board and convention, become law, for the precedents they set are held binding in subsequent cases involving the same clauses.

DISCIPLINARY PROCEEDINGS within the unions are the most distinctive examples of the judicial process under union governments. A member joining a union pledges himself to obey the constitution and laws of the national organization and of the local union where he holds membership. He thus subjects himself to the disciplinary powers of the organization. Since national officers have the responsibility of enforcing all laws, they may make charges against individual members, or they may direct the local officers to file the charges. But one member may also charge violations against another and proceedings against individual members may also be ordered by vote of the membership at a local union meeting. Most frequently, however, the charges are filed by officers, and the constitutions generally provide that the accused shall be given a trial.

Normally the courts of original jurisdiction are the local unions, for while trial boards in each local hear and pass judgment on the guilt or innocence of the accused, their decisions are in the nature of recommendations, and the final verdict is made at a local union meeting by vote of the membership present. Some constitutions, however, authorize trials by district authorities (the districts being composed of representatives of local unions in the area), and in certain types of cases the national union may assume jurisdiction and conduct the original trials. But ordinarily a man is tried in the local where he holds membership, and the verdict may then be appealed, sometimes to the districts, but most commonly to the national executive board, though there may also be a preliminary appeal to the president. Where the accused's membership is at stake, he always has the right of final appeal to the convention, and in most unions this right of appeal applies to other cases as well, but some constitutions make decisions of the executive board final in cases not involving expulsion.

The offenses for which a union may punish a member are widely varied. Often they are described vaguely, as "conduct unbecoming a union member," the commission of any "disreputable act," engaging in action which brings "reproach" or "discredit" upon the union, or "creating dissension" or "slandering" officers or the union. But many offenses are defined with precision. A member may be fined, suspended, or expelled for making a false statement in his application for membership, for misappropriating union funds, for "scabbing" in strikes, for working in violation of the union wage scale or in nonunion shops or with nonmembers, for disclosing union affairs not publicly disclosed by the union, for dual unionism (i.e., adhering to a competing union), for belonging to a subversive organization, and for other reasons of a like nature. Penalties are usually prescribed in the constitutions.

Traditionally, unions have insisted on requiring employers to impose the additional penalty of discharge or denial of employment to their suspended or expelled members. The original trade societies in the latter part of the eighteenth century bound themselves not to work with nonmembers, and the prohibitions against working with nonmembers in a good many current constitutions continue the tradition. Since collective working agreements have become customary, however, practically all unions strive to include in them provisions for closed or union shops. Where they succeed in thus making union membership a condition of employment, the employers are obligated to discharge suspended or expelled members and to deny employment to those who will not join.

But when Congress adopted the Wagner Act of 1935, which compelled employers to bargain collectively with representatives of their employees, and union agreements spread widely through the main industries of the country, public feeling developed that workers' opportunities to earn a living were seriously impaired by closed or union shops. Then, in 1947, the Taft-Hartley law revised and amended the 1935 Act in many respects. Among other restrictions it placed on unions, it substantially reduced the severity of suspension or expulsion as a penalty for violation of union law by limiting the right of the employer to refuse to hire nonunion employees and to discharge them for failing to become members or to maintain membership. This law banned closed shops entirely (providing that a worker does not have to be a union member in order to be hired); and though it authorized union-shop agreements which obligated employees to become members within sixty days after being employed, it provided that discharge of an employee for nonmembership pursuant to a union shop clause shall be illegal if the employee is denied membership for any reason other than failure to tender dues and initiation fees uniformly required of all members. Thus a union cannot require the employer to discharge an employee who loses his membership for violation of its laws, except those relating to dues paying.

For certain types of cases, union constitutions provide automatic disciplinary action, that is to say, a member loses his membership without a trial. Almost without exception, failure to pay dues or to meet other financial obligations to the union operates to drop a member from the rolls of the organization, although provision is usually made for giving him due notice of his delinquency. Summary discipline is also authorized for certain other violations of specific rules. In some unions power is vested in national authorities to suspend a member pending a hearing on charges against him. Normally, however, an accused member is given ample opportunity to defend himself before being fined, suspended, or expelled. The constitutions provide that he shall be duly notified of charges against him and that he has a right to a trial. Also, there may be a fixed time limit from date when the offense occurred within which charges must be filed.

In most unions pre-trial procedures are provided. The charges must be in writing, but rarely is the accused required to submit a written answer. In some unions charges are investigated and passed upon by the local union before they are submitted to a trial board. The investigation may be by a committee or it may be done by the local executive board to determine whether the charges should be submitted to a trial board or not. Upon consideration by the board or by a membership meeting, charges may be dismissed as unfounded. Frequently, when the charges have substance, they are settled without a trial; the offending member in effect pleads guilty in whole or in part, and arrangements acceptable to the responsible officers are made for redressing whatever wrong was done. The pre-trial settlement procedures are thus comparable to indictments by grand juries and consent decrees.

An accused member is normally tried in the local union where he holds his membership. Most commonly a special trial board is appointed or elected from the membership for each case. In some unions the local executive board serves as the trial board, in others a standing trial committee is appointed or elected, and these as well as the special trial board may also include officers. A few unions vest trial powers in the local union membership meeting, but trial by the membership is found only among small locals. Persons with a direct interest in a case are normally disqualified from sitting on trial boards. Some unions send national representatives to conduct local trials.

The trial procedures are laymen's imitations of the methods used in courts of law, but without the technicalities. Informality is the general rule, though laymen who present cases (derisively referred to as "sea lawyers") sometimes argue at length about details of procedure, evidence, and interpretations of union law. The charging party acts as prosecutor, and the accused may designate another union member to represent him or may conduct his own defense. Attorneys are commonly barred by constitutional provisions. Evidence is presented by introduction of documents and testimony of witnesses. The right to cross-examine witnesses is highly regarded, and postponements or adjournments for cause are expressly authorized and granted. Special provisions are made for default judgments. A record of the trial is kept in the form of minutes or a summary. Rarely is there a stenographic transcript, but either party may have one if it is willing to pay for the stenographic service.

When all the evidence has been presented and arguments have been concluded, the trial board meets in executive session and prepares its decision on the guilt or innocence of the accused with respect to the specific charges, and, if guilt is found, what penalty, if any, shall be imposed. But its decision is a recommendation, not a determination of the issues. It is made in the form of a report to the membership of the local union, and the actual judgment is made by the rank and file members—at least those who attend meetings. The report must be considered at a regular meeting of the local, and those present vote either to accept or reject it, or they may modify it or send the case back for a new trial. Usually this is done by majority of those present, but sometimes more than a simple majority is required, especially when the penalty is expulsion from the union. It is the local union's decision that is the binding judgment, and this must be obeyed as a condition for filing appeals to the higher judicial tribunals of the national union. The constitutions also usually provide that no member may resort to court action outside the union until he has exhausted all his remedies within the union.

The quality of the trials varies widely. Sometimes the proceedings are perfunctory; the accused are presumed to be guilty on the basis of preliminary investigations or pre-trial consideration of the charges at local union meetings, and the actual trial is a formality required by union law or by the defendant's ultimate right of appeal to the courts. At the other extreme are long drawn-out and bitterly contested trials marked by irrelevant argumentation, bickering, and disorder, in which the need for determining the truth or falsity of the charges is all but forgotten. Normally, however, the principal elements of order and fairness are present. The fact that the trial board merely makes a report to the local union members, who are the real judges in each case, stimulates care to maintain orderly procedures and to assure fair and just treatment to those on trial.

The constitutional requirements that charges shall be in writing duly served on everyone involved in a case contribute to the same end. These are essential elements of due process. They make certain that charges shall not be vague or general, but specific and based on cited provisions of the union's laws, and they provide a guide for the further proceedings. They safeguard the rights of the accused, and serve as a check on hasty or ill-considered disciplinary action. Union members often have differences or quarrels, and in the heat of argument verbal charges may be made freely, but to file them in writing gives pause and time to cool off. Thus a member sometimes can put an end to attacks by challenging his opponents to file charges against him or "shut up." It is also common for officials to warn members of violations or they will "bring him up on charges." The time limitations within which charges must be filed after knowledge of an offense is an additional safeguard to the individual member against stale claims, as is the common provision that no serious penalty may be imposed without a trial.

As in the courts, however, the fairness of trials depends greatly upon the fairness of the presiding judges. Quite aside from deliberate unfairness, the fact that in some unions the officers who constitute the local executive boards are authorized to conduct the trials while officers often also serve on special trial boards and standing trial committees places them in an ambivalent position, for as officers they have the responsibility of enforcing union laws. Thus the traditional police and prosecutor functions are combined in the trial boards with those of jury and judge functions. It is not uncommon for an accused member to complain that he was tried by a "hanging" judge or jury. Although the trial boards' decisions are only recommendations to the local union members, their findings of fact and determinations of guilt or innocence are comparable to the hearing officers' reports of such governmental bodies as the Interstate Commerce Commission, the Federal Trade Commission, or the National Labor Relations Board.

That officers with prosecuting functions sit as trial judges emphasizes the lack of an independent judiciary as well as the absence of systematic separation of judicial powers from the executive, administrative, and legislative powers of union governments. Although most constitutions do not delegate legislative powers to the executives, and reserve final judicial powers to the convention, this legislative body serves as the supreme judicial court. The same is true also of the local union membership meeting which though not a representative body does adopt local laws and policies, and the members sit as judges, reviewing the report of the trial board and determining the guilt or innocence of the accused and the appropriate penalty to be imposed.

These arrangements by which local membership assemblies and convention delegates function as courts is perhaps the most important difference between the judicial process in unions and the judicial processes of public governments in the United States. Court verdicts are not referred to the body politic or to the legislative branch of the government for review and final decision. Even New England town meetings do not sit in judgment of law violations; independent judges and courts perform this function. The arrangements for popular voting on the truth or falsity of charges resemble rather the so-called "peoples' courts" of soviet governments. They are defended as a form of direct democracy, but the lessons of history are clear that independent courts and judges are as essential to protect individual rights and liberties against popular majorities as against executive officials and the legislative bodies of governments.

When the members of a union first consider the charges in a case and decide not to dismiss them as unfounded but refer them to a trial board, the majority ordering the action may well believe that there is *prima facie* support for the charges and that they are serious enough to warrant disciplinary measures. There is likely to be a certain amount of prejudgment, therefore, when after the trial, the board submits its report and recommendations to the union meeting for the decision that must be made by the members. If disciplinary action is recommended, this tends to confirm the prejudgment, with consequent inclination to approve the trial boards recommendations as made. This is particularly true when the accused member is quarrelsome or otherwise unpopular, has been critical of union policies, or has been in opposition to a major faction that controls the local union. On the other hand a popular active member, especially if he is a good speaker, may persuade the membership to dismiss charges against him and refuse to order a trial.

In evaluating union disciplinary procedures, however, it must be borne in mind that normally it is almost impossible for the local union membership not to have formed an opinion on the merits of charges against a member before his trial, and that this may work to his advantage. This is commonly the case because the charges, true or false, grow out of the daily relationships of the members at their work or in their participation in union affairs, and the accusations are discussed in shops as well as at local meetings before they are submitted to a trial board. The members are also likely to be familiar with the facts in the case. In these respects union trials differ greatly from law suits where juries and judges have no such established relationships with litigants and might be disqualified if they had.

Since officers of the union are usually the prosecutors, the members also have a certain common interest against the officials or "bureaucrats," for they may find themselves defendants in similar cases. When they sit as judges and vote the verdicts in union meetings, therefore, in most cases they are likely to sympathize with the accused and to give him the benefit of doubts, while the number of cases in which they may be prejudiced against an unpopular defendant who has made himself obnoxious to a large portion of the membership is bound to be relatively small. Nor can we ignore the common sense of justice normally found among a body of men who work together and are associated in an organization to promote their common interest. By and large the relationships among union members are friendly, and ordinarily the judgments of local union meetings are no less fair and just than those of local or municipal courts.

The weaknesses in the local union disciplinary proceedings are due mainly to the failure of most members to attend union meetings. Usually only a small percentage are in attendance, and in the appellate tribunals there is the basic weakness that these are generally composed of executive officers who exercise their judicial functions as part of their regular administrative duties. A separate set of officials specialized to exercise only judicial functions is not provided; and the convention which acts as the supreme court is a legislative body, essentially political in nature.

APPEALS from local union disciplinary decision go directly to the national executive board in most unions. Some constitutions provide for appeals to district councils or "joint boards" as they are sometimes called, while in others the first appeal is to the president and then to the board. A few, such as the Bricklayers, establish a standing board of appeals and give no appellate jurisdiction to the executive board. It is composed of nine regional vice-presidents, and is distinct from the executive board. Like the other national officers, the members of the appeals board are elected for four-year terms. It does not hold hearings on appeals, but renders decisions on the record and briefs.

An appeal is taken by filing notice with the local, the other parties, and the appellate body. In most cases the record is put together by the executive officers of this body by correspondence and investigations; a few unions require the parties to make up the record. After the first appeal a record emerges, but it is not strictly binding on later appellate bodies. Usually cases appealed to the national executive board are decided upon a record, though a hearing may be granted if requested. The whole board may hear the parties or it may appoint a committee to conduct the hearing, and it decides the case after considering a report of the committee. Where appeals go first to district councils or joint boards, decisions are generally made on the basis of oral arguments and documents. The final appeal to the convention follows a pattern of review and opportunity for a hearing by a grievance or appeals committee with a vote of the delegates on the committee's report and recommendations.

Throughout the appeals procedure the decision of the lower tribunal remains in effect. Constitutions usually condition the right of appeal on obedience to the decision, and normally no relief is given pending appeal. Most appeals to the convention from the executive judicial tribunals are denied, as previously explained, partly because of precedents set by the delegate body and partly because of constitutional provisions for making decisions of the executive board final in certain types of cases. The number of convention appeals generally declines as a union grows older. But the system of appeals affords opportunities for settlement of cases out of court so to speak. Not infrequently, appellate executive officials act in effect as mediators between the appellant and the local union which decided against him, and similar adjustments are sometimes made also when convention grievance committees are considering appeals.

Although members are generally tried in the local unions, the entire judicial process is governed by the constitution and laws of the national union. The local trial boards are not a separate system of local courts established by local laws, and where districts conduct trials, these too are governed by national law. The constitutions of the national union include forms of constitutions for local and other subordinate governmental units, and while these are authorized to adopt by-laws, all local and district laws must conform to the constitution and are subject to approval by the national union. Thus local trials and appellate procedures are part of a single national judicial system.

The appellate procedures are substantially the same in other types of cases than those involving discipline of members. But the national constitutions provide special procedures for trying national officers and sometimes also they require that trials of local officers shall be conducted by the national union similar to the manner in which national officers are tried. Some constitutions, however, provide for special trials of local officers within the local unions, with the customary right of appeal to the higher judicial tribunals of the national union. Other types of cases, such as charges of one local union against another, and charges of national officers against locals, are necessarily not tried within the local unions but by national trial bodies.

THE RIGHT TO FILE CHARGES against a national officer is usually restricted to other national officers or to a specified minimum number of local unions. Significantly, most constitutions also provide penalties for filing false accusations against officers. Trials are provided for, and the national executive board commonly serves as the trial board; but some constitutions provide a special trial body for handling proceedings against a national officer. A few require the charges and defense to be submitted to a referendum of the membership. Generally, also, union constitutions empower the executive board to remove or suspend any national officer, including the president, subject to a trial. Appeals from convictions by the executive board or special trial boards may be taken to the convention, and in a few unions they are referred to a special referendum.

Judicial procedures, however, are not as commonly used for disciplining and removing officers, as they are in the cases of rank and file members. Officers are not only required to comply with union laws, they are also responsible for their executive acts and administrative policies to the convention or to the membership and the constitutions provide other ways of holding them in compliance with laws and punishing them for failure to carry out their responsibilities. Control over officers is more of a political problem than a judicial one. The final test depends on the sentiments of the membership, expressed either directly or through delegates at the convention, rather than upon a painstaking search of the facts at a trial to ascertain guilt or innocence. Moreover, the judicial process is not effective for controlling officers and more political methods are preferred.

The restrictions on filing charges against national officers and the penalties for false charges make plain that the judicial procedures are expected to be used only in cases of very serious offenses, and that ordinary disputes between officers and general dissatisfaction of members with their services are to be dealt with by the electoral process. A good many constitutions provide for recall of officers by special elections, and in the few unions where charges or appeals from convictions are referred to a vote of the membership, this is but a step removed from a recall election. In most unions, however, the periods between regular elections of officers are short enough to make resort to the judicial process unnecessary. About half hold elections either annually or every two years, and those that elect every four or five years also hold their conventions at the same intervals, so that the delegate bodies cannot dispose of appeals from convictions by the executive board or a special trial board any sooner than it can condemn or exonerate an accused officer by defeating or returning him to office in an election. From another point of view, the executive board, which is usually composed of all the national officers and which has the right to suspend any one of their number pending a trial, can as easily manage to defeat him for reelection as they can have his removal from office sustained by the convention.

A rare case of a removal of the president by the executive board occurred in the Rubber Workers' Union in the spring of 1949. As in the case of the Auto Workers described earlier this grew out of a factional dispute within the board, and the president was suspended from office by a majority after a trial on charges filed by an officer of a local union. This union's convention meets annually so that the president was able to get his appeal to the delegate body considered at its regular session in September, 1949. The convention adopted a special order of business to hear the case directly rather than to refer it to the appeals committee for a hearing and report. The union's official journal stated: "In order to avoid partiality, prejudice, or a slanted attitude, the controversial issue was trotted out onto the floor of the convention . . . so that all of the delegates could hear all of the facts and decide the case upon its merits." Each side was allowed three hours for direct presentation and a half hour for rebuttal. The removed president was reinstated by a majority of 100 votes out of a total of about 1,500, and the following day he was reelected for another term by a majority of 140 votes. He has continually been reelected president since that time.

Equally rare are trials of officers on charges filed by a sufficient number of local unions as required by the constitutions; but while judicial proceedings against national officers are seldom used, they are significant for another reason. They serve in effect to distribute power among the national officers. Where the president is given the right to suspend any officer whether he is a member of the executive board or not, his power over all other elected officials is confirmed and strengthened, and he has control over the individual members of the board. On the other hand, though the board as a body may remove the president as well as other officers, his suspensions are usually subject to a trial by the board, and as a court of appeals it is empowered not only to reverse his judicial decisions, but many of his executive acts are also made subject to its approval. Thus while there is some overlapping of powers, it is clear that the president is boss over all elected national officers, but when sitting as members of the executive board, they may overrule him by majority vote. Final authority, however, is in the body of convention delegates who, though not generally referred to as officers, are elected constitutional officials. When conventions are in session all powers, executive, legislative and judicial, are lodged in them, except as some constitutions provide for final decisions by referendum of the membership.

The use of judicial proceedings to discipline local officers is more common than trials of national officers. Local officers are subject to discipline both by their local unions and by the national organizations. When the charges arise within the locals, trial procedures follow the routines used in disciplining members. Some constitutions, however, provide separate and distinct procedures for trial of local officers within the locals. The authority of the national union to initiate action against local officers is usually lodged in the president, subject to approval by the executive board. In such cases an accused officer may be tried in his local union by direction of the president, but more commonly the constitutions provide for trials outside the local by district officers, or by special trial boards composed of national officers. A local officer may be suspended upon the filing of charges, and there are certain offenses which may bring an automatic penalty such as failure to attend meetings or to file reports. Appeals are to the national excutive board and the convention.

Disciplinary proceedings against local officers conducted by the national union, though in some respects similar to trial of members by the local unions, are less judicial in nature. Summary suspension without notice or hearing are not uncommon, and many constitutions provide no precise or detailed procedural requirements. These constitutional deficiencies, however, are now frequently corrected in practice because some local officers have obtained relief from the courts when they were removed from office without a hearing and due notice. Apart from the lack of procedural safeguards, there is a more important judicial shortcoming in connection with the disciplining of local officers by the national union. The hearings or trials are usually conducted by the same national officers who exercise both executive and judicial powers. The proceedings are therefore more in the nature of administrative enforcement of laws rather than judicial trials. And the authority of national officers both to file charges and to sit as members of trial boards is a hanging sword over the heads of local officials who are critical of national officers or their policies.

To the extent that local unions have authority to discipline their own officers, they are expected to do so when the officers engage in conduct warranting proceedings against them. When the local union memberships fail to act in such situations, the national union has the authority to initiate proceedings against local officials, or it may direct the local to file charges and give the accused officer a trial. That it becomes necessary for national officers to start proceedings against local officials may be due to the inertia of local union members, but sometimes national officers discipline local officials over the strenuous objections of the membership. The check against abuses by the national officers in this respect then becomes a political problem. If the members continue to support their officers, the consequence to the national union may be loss of the entire membership of the local rather than removal of officers.

UNION CONSTITUTIONS vest in national officers not only the power to discipline local officers, but also the authority to discipline the local unions as entities. This latter power is usually lodged in the national executive board or in the president subject to approval by the board. The offenses for which a local governmental unit may be disciplined are varied. They include violations of the national constitution or laws, failure to hold regular meetings or to submit financial and other required reports, lack of effort to organize eligible works or to act against corrupt officials, or failure to comply with orders of the national executive board or decisions of the national convention or to conform to policies adopted by the convention. A common penalty imposed on local unions is that they may be put in "receivership" or under a "trusteeship." The president or the executive board is authorized to appoint a national officer or "governing board" to administer the affairs of any local. A local union may also be suspended or expelled. If suspended, it loses the right to be represented at the national convention; if expelled, its charter from the national union is "lifted" or revoked. Under a trusteeship, the administrators of the local may appoint its delegates to the convention instead of the members electing them.

Judicial procedures are least used in disciplining local unions. There is little that resembles the judicial process when a local union is placed in "receivership" and an administrator or trustees are appointed to perform the functions of local officials. When a local becomes delinquent in paying per capita taxes or assessments on its members to the national union, the constitutions provide that it shall stand suspended and be denied representation at the convention. While delinquent locals are often carried along by the national union, no specified proceedings are required in suspending such locals. Summary suspension may also be used where locals fail to hold regular meetings as required by the constitutions or do not meet their obligations to submit required reports to the national organization.

For other offenses charges must usually be filed and hearing held by the national executive board before it can be either suspended or expelled, and something like judicial proceedings are followed in such cases. But proceedings to expel local unions are rare, as the national unions do not want to lose the memberships of offending locals, especially if they are of any considerable size. When a problem of disciplining a local arises, the national officers must decide initially whether to proceed against the local as an entity or only against its officers, and charges against the latter are more frequent than against the local itself. Most frequent, however, is the method by which the national union takes over the administration of a local union and appoints its agent or agents to govern it in place of officials elected by the members. The preferred use of this device reflects the reluctance of national officers to use judicial proceedings in controlling local unions, and the constitutional provisions generally authorize direct control of the locals by the national union. It may merge local unions, transfer members from one local to another, and abolish locals quite aside from disciplining for offenses against union laws.

The power lodged in national officers to supervise and discipline local unions, their officers, and individual members includes authority to settle controversies between locals or other subordinate governmental units. The methods used are more often mediatory than judicial, but even though local and national officers may adjust differences by agreement, there are provisions for appeal to the higher judicial tribunals of the union, and the appellate procedures provide a measure of judicial process.

In the early days of the Typographical Union two units at Montreal, one English-speaking and the other French, engaged in a bitter quarrel. The language demarcation could not be kept distinct because a number of printing shops did work in both languages, and printers moved from shop to shop. In their warfare the locals cut wage rates, blacklisted each other's members, and otherwise engaged in the worst excesses of jurisdictional disputes. After attempts at an amicable settlement by agreement had failed, the English local filed charges against the French unit at the 1876 convention of the union. Upon recommendation of its committee on appeals, the convention voted that a referee should be assigned to investigate thoroughly the matter in Montreal and render a decision that would be final and binding on both locals.

The referee submitted a report to the national president in which he found the French local guilty of the most aggression, and he decided that this local should be dissolved and its members should join the English unit. The president set aside this decision and advised the French local that it need not comply. He reported to the 1877 convention that the referee had made a careless, one-sided investigation and had exceeded his powers by ordering dissolution of a local governmental unit. In place of the referee's decision, the president urged setting up a special five-man committee to dispose of the controversy at the convention session.

The convention approved the president's action and accepted his recommendation. The special committee was elected by the delegates. It met with representatives of the two locals and the next day reached a decision acceptable to both locals and the convention. The committee upheld the referee's report on the facts in the case. Like him it ordered the dissolution of the French local, but provided guarantees that the government of the English local would be shared equally by French and English members by apportioning and rotating officers between the two groups, by equal delegations to the national convention, and by publication of all official actions of the single local in both languages.

The causes of inter-local conflicts have changed with the years, but the methods of settling them remain much the same. The variety of situations in which local unions come into conflict with one another has made establishment of standard procedures for dealing with such controversies impractical. A good many unions had language locals in the United States as well as in Canada prior to World War I, but immigration restriction laws adopted since then have greatly reduced their number, and some national constitutions now require that meetings of local unions shall be conducted in English. Nevertheless disputes between locals occasionally still arise out of nationality differences. A few years ago two locals of a building trade union in adjoining communities in Massachusetts got into a quarrel because the Irish business agent of one charged that the Italian business agent of the other was continually placing Italians in jobs within the area that belonged to the Irishman's local. The national officers were unable to adjust the differences, and this dispute too was taken to the convention and settled there in a manner similar to the settlement between the two Canadian locals of the Typographical Union.

The primary cause of the dispute between the Massachusetts locals was the alleged trespassing of one local into the territory of another. Similar disputes also arise where local unions are established on a craft or occupational basis and one claims that members of another local have been placed at work that belongs to its members. Such differences about the areas and occupations over which they have jurisdiction are the more common causes of conflicts between locals today. The disputes are complicated by personal differences between ambitious officers of different locals, and the situations out of which conflicts arise vary so widely that the organizations have not found it possible to devise standard judicial procedures to govern the processing of differences between local unions. The procedures are commonly improvised as each case develops. These disputes are similar to the troublesome jurisdictional controversies between national unions, each of which claims "sovereign" rights, but there is ample authority in the officers of every national union to decide controversies between its locals, though they often end up at the convention whose decisions are final and binding.

THE JUDICIAL PROCESS within the unions also includes adjudication of certain types of claims of members that arise in connection with disputes between the organizations and employers involving the application or interpretation of collective agreements. In performing its main function of collective bargaining, a union establishes rights and benefits for the employees covered by agreements, and also obligations. The agreements generally contain provisions for handling grievances, and with rare exceptions create judicial machinery for arbitrating disputes that cannot be settled by the parties themselves. But often union members make conflicting claims as to their rights under the agreements, and grievance committees or union officers may disagree with members as to the merits of their claims. In such cases the conflicts and differences of opinion must be resolved by the union before it can take a position with the employer. For this purpose unions have special judicial procedures which are similar to disciplinary proceedings against members in some respects and in others are like those by which the union's constitution and laws are interpreted.

The constitutions of the railroad brotherhoods contain the most specific provisions for settling such differences within the union. They provide for a local adjustment committee at each lodge, similar to the grievance committee found in local unions of most labor organizations. In addition, however, they establish a general adjustment committee on each railroad system, and authorize local lodges on two or more smaller railroads to join in maintaining a single general committee to serve the employees on the different roads. The members of the general committee are elected by the local lodges, and its officers, usually a general chairman, secretary, and on the larger roads sometimes also a vice-chairman, may also be elected by the lodge members, but more commonly they are chosen by the members of the general committee. On most railroad systems, the officers are salaried and devote full time to their work. The costs are covered by assessments on the memberships of the lodges represented on the committee; the grand lodge or national union does not finance the general committees out of the regular dues of the members.

A member claiming that he has not been properly paid in accordance with the terms of a collective agreement, or that his seniority rights were ignored in assigning him to a job, or that he was otherwise treated contrary to the provisions of the agreement, is required to submit his claim to his local lodge or its adjustment committee in order to have it processed against the employer. If there is any doubt as to the validity of the claim or if other members have conflicting claims, the general chairman of the system committee is usually consulted. If the local committee or lodge then refuses to support the claim or in any way modifies it, and its position is supported by the general chairman, the complaining member has the right to appeal to the general system committee. Precise arrangements are established for submission of the case and its consideration by the general committee. On questions of fact the findings of this committee are final, but on questions involving interpretation of the contracts with the employer or the laws of the union, its decisions are further appealable to the national president, and from him there is a final appeal to the convention.

Most other unions have similar procedures, but they are not so clearly prescribed in their constitutions or laws. Grievances of members arising out of the employment relations established by collective agreements are first handled informally by shop chairmen or stewards, and if these representatives in the places of employment find no merit in an alleged grievance, or that the claim of one member affects the rights of other members, or if for any other reason a steward refuses to process a member's grievance under the procedures set up by the collective agreement, the matter is referred to the grievance committee of the local union. In the local, the grievance is handled in much the same manner as charges of violations of union laws. The grievance committee decides whether the member's claim against the employer should be processed, and its decision is then voted on at a meeting of the local, which may approve or reverse the action of the committee, or order that the matter should be dealt with in some other way. Thereafter, the local union's decision is subject to appeal to the regular appellate tribunals of the national union, except where constitutions provide for the initial appeal to go to district authorities.

Thus the procedures for handling claims within the union to determine its position in disputes to be processed under the judicial machinery set up by agreements begin with nonjudicial action, and end with formal hearings on appeal. The lack of judicial process at the beginning is due to the fact that such claims do not arise within the scheme of union government until there has been a decision by a shop chairman or other union official, or by a committee of the local union. Sometimes such claims result from action taken by the employer alone, sometimes joint action taken by union and management representatives give rise to the claims, and sometimes they are a by-product of the action of union officials who are charged with responsibility of "policing" collective agreements and seeing to it that their provisions are applied by managements in accordance with the union's views of their intent.

Illustrative of how claims arising under collective agreements may cause differences between members and union representatives or officials, and how such disputes are adjudicated within the union, is a case considered by the 1944 Glass Bottle Blowers convention, to which it was appealed for a final decision. The employer in the case transferred a group of female employees from the packing department to the end of the production line, thus eliminating an operation that had previously been performed by men on the factory floor. He continued to pay the women their old rate of 44½¢ an hour, although the men whose jobs were eliminated had been paid 61¢ per hour. The women claimed they were entitled to the higher rate and the local union supported their claims. Local representatives of the union were unable to settle the dispute in conferences with the management, and a representative of the national union was then called in. He ruled that the employer's position was right, that the agreement required payment of only 44½¢. The local union then appealed to the national president who ordinarily would decide the issue subject to a further appeal to the convention.

The president happened to be abroad on union business, however, and a vice-president referred the appeal to a national wage conference of union representatives and the employers of the industry then being held. (Collective bargaining in this industry is largely industry-wide.) Although the case was not strictly within the scope of its business, the conference heard the parties and then affirmed the judgments of the employer and of the national union representative. This was appealed to the convention as if it had been a ruling of the president, and the convention's committee on grievances held a full hearing. The committee reported to the delegates upholding the position of the local union, and after a long debate on the convention floor a roll-call vote was taken which approved the committee's decision. The effect was to authorize the local union to prosecute the women's claims against the employer under the procedures provided by the collective agreement.

XII

LOCAL UNION GOVERNMENTS

ALTHOUGH MANY existing national unions were formed by self-governing local unions joining to establish national governments, the locals of each union now have only such measure of home rule as the national constitutions grant them. The relations of local unions to the national organizations are similar to those between municipalities and our state governments. As municipalities are subject to the constitutions and laws of the states, so the locals are subject to the constitutions and laws of the national unions of which they are subordinate branches; and, as some states grant more home rule to their cities than others, so some national unions grant more home rule to their local unions than others do.

American unions originated as self-governing local trade societies in the latter part of the eighteenth century. National unions such as we are familiar with today were not formed until about a hundred years later. Earlier the societies, each representing a different trade, joined in establishing local federations in various cities which they referred to as unions of trade societies, and the word "union" was first used to designate these city-wide ogranizations; newspapers referred to them as "Trades' Unions." These were the progenitors of the present-day city federations of labor, central labor unions, and city industrial councils. The local societies did not give up their self-governing rights when they joined such "unions," and they also remained autonomous governing bodies when they organized the first national labor federation in 1832 known as the National Trade Union, which lasted about five years. Printers' locals pioneered in setting the pattern for nationally governed unions. They formed the International Typographical Union in 1852, and it has maintained a continuous existence since then. Other trades followed their example in the succeeding decades, and since the beginning of the present century most local unions have been subordinate governmental units of national organizations.

Locals are chartered by their national unions, and the jurisdiction of each is usually defined, though often vaguely. The earliest national organizations followed the policy of issuing a charter to only one local in each city or urban area. They were craft organizations, and all members working in the area were required to belong to the one local. Later, as the cities grew in size and specialized branches of a craft developed or a union organized two or more related crafts, this policy was changed to charter locals in portions of a city and to establish separate locals for different branches of a trade or craft. The coal miners' union, which was organized as an industrial union, usually included all members working in or about a mine or in several nearby mines belonging to one company in their locals. The Brewery Workers, established as an industrial union before the AFL was formed, similarly provided for a local at each brewery, and this policy of organizing locals at each factory or plant is now common among all industrial unions. For the smaller plants in a city, however, they also have so-called "amalgamated locals," to which members working for different employers belong.

In the miners, clothing, textile, and other unions with large numbers of immigrant members speaking different languages, it used to be common to charter separate foreign language locals. Some of these were organized by the immigrant workers themselves and later became locals of national unions. Similarly where unions admitted Negroes at all (sometimes also Mexican workers), they generally placed them in "colored locals." These, however, functioned as subordinate branches of the white locals, for in dealing with employers and in sending delegates to union conventions they were required to be represented by white members. As immigration restriction laws were enacted by Congress and the foreign born learned English, the language locals were gradually abolished, and the number still in existence is quite small. In recent years, too, all but a few national unions have amended their constitutions to admit Negroes and Mexican workers on the same terms as all other members. They may be in separate locals, as is still common in Southern states, but the members and locals have the same rights as all other members and local unions.

A union worker holds his membership in a local union, and all the members of a national union are normally distributed among its locals. As citizens of the United States are also citizens of the states in which they reside, so a union member is a citizen of both his national union and the local to which he belongs. He becomes a member by joining a local union, and when he is initiated he pledges allegiance both to the national constitution and laws and to the local constitution and by-laws. A local normally must secure approval of its constitution and by-laws from the national union and national constitutions fix initiation fees and at least the minimum dues each member must pay. The national generally also prescribes the locals' bookkeeping system and regularly audits their accounts.

THE TYPICAL form of government in the locals is direct democracy; all governing powers are lodged in the membership meeting. The meeting elects the officers, and their actions are subject to its approval. It determines policies, adopts local laws, and serves also as a judicial body. The local union is the only unit of union government in which the members govern directly. All other units, the national, district, and various regional organizations, are representative bodies composed of delegates elected from the locals; the delegates normally adopt constitutions and elect the governing officers, but in some unions referendum voting by the members in the locals is required.

A local union has two main organs of government—the meeting and the officers. Like the national union it has a president and an executive board, but the powers of the meeting are not delegated to them between its sessions as in the case of the national union. Membership meetings are usually held at least once a month, and the officers including the executive board are directly responsible to the meeting. The main types of local officers are the president, a vice-president to serve as alternate, a secretary, treasurer, a specified number of executive board members, and commonly also a business agent who handles grievances and who is responsible for enforcing union rules and agreements with employers covering the local's members. The duties of the other officers are those traditionally associated with their titles; and there are also minor officials like trustees who control the local's finances and property and the sergeant-at-arms who checks attendance at meetings.

The business agent is usually the only full-time officer with a salary generally equivalent to the earnings of the most skilled men in the local. Other officers serve without pay or receive nominal salaries; they are generally reimbursed for any time they lose from their regular jobs in performing official duties. Because of the direct control of officers by the meeting, the local executive board functions more as an advisory committee to the other officers than as a superior executive and judicial authority like the national executive board. All official action of the officers must either be authorized or approved by the membership meeting, and the meeting is the court of original jurisdiction in the judicial system of the national union.

Thus, although the local union's governing powers are derived from the national constitution, which often contains a standard form for local constitutions, the specific authority of local officers flows from the membership meeting. Formal authorization or approval at a meeting is required for nearly every item of the local's business, from the payment of bills and answering of letters to the settlement of grievances and the negotiation of working contracts with employers. The membership meeting is also authorized to draft and adopt a local constitution and laws, provided these do not contravene the national constitution and are approved by the national union. The power of the membership is supreme over local affairs; majority votes of the membership at regular meetings are binding, though decisions may be modified or reversed by higher authorities of the national union.

The method of electing local officers and terms of office are usually prescribed in national constitutions. The most common method is by secret ballot. The older method of choosing officers by voice vote at meetings is now rare. Some constitutions provide that delegates to a national convention shall be elected at the same time as the local officials and for the same terms; others leave the locals free to decide these matters. Arrangements for conducting the balloting are generally left to local control, and these vary in different locals of the same national union. In some the secret vote is taken at a meeting in which case the polling place is in the union hall and polls are open only for an hour or two. In others the ballot boxes are at the union office with polls open all day. Local unions with membership from a single factory or plant often have union offices not far from the plant gates or they may establish polling places at several places near the building of a large plant. Another method is to place ballot boxes at convenient places within the shops or to send a team of election officials through a plant to distribute and collect the ballots. Some locals provide for mail balloting.

A local union's choice of election procedure indicates to some extent whether its government is controlled by the membership or by the officers. Some balloting systems are designed to secure maximum participation of members in the elections, while others are little concerned with stimulating a big turn-out of voters. When the voting is done at union meetings, the number of voters is generally smaller than when polling places are provided in or near shops and plants. As previously noted, only a small percentage of members attend meetings, and a minority commonly determines the elections. Membership interest in the government of local unions is better measured by the size of the vote in elections than by meeting attendance, but in most locals only a minority participates both in elections and in meetings.

The business of a local union meeting is largely routine; its function of passing on all actions of officers involves reviewing many trifling details, boring to most members. The active members who attend meetings regularly like the routines and the discussions; to them the routines have the same interest as household details to neighborly housewives. To participate actively a member must have some public speaking ability and at least a rudimentary knowledge of parliamentary procedures—qualities that most members do not have. Hence the small percentages of members who attend local meetings, and the ease with which groups of active members can get and maintain control of local union governments by attending meetings regularly and making advance preparations. These groups form the basis of the machines that control the policies and elections in many national unions. Many locals have grown so large with members working in numerous plants in various parts of an urban area that it is difficult for the opposition to organize on a city-wide scale to elect new officers. At any given time, however, local union offices are likely to be occupied by men who were elected because they were critics of their predecessors.

Both national and local officials often deplore the failure of large majorities of the members to attend local union meetings where they can govern directly and most effectively control the activities of their officers. On the average less than 10 percent of the members appear at the meetings. Occasionally when special subjects like wage negotiations or plant-wide grievances or possible strike action are to be discussed, the percentage increases, but not infrequently at regular meetings the number attending is not enough to make a quorum. Observation at particular meetings support the above estimate. A Boilermakers' local with 360 members had an attendance of 65, or 17 percent. At a Metal Miners' local only 30 out of 1,300 members attended—less than 1 percent. At a Teamsters' local of bakery drivers 84 percent were in attendance—400 out of 480; but another local of this union (freight drivers) had only 6 percent present—150 out of 2,700. At a Steelworkers' (fabricating) local there were not enough to make a quorum, and normal attendance was estimated by an official at 5 percent. Only 2 percent attended the meeting of Shipbuilders' local, 65 out of 3,000. A Printing Pressmen's local with around 1,000 members had 55 at its meeting, about 5 percent. According to officials of three Typographical Union locals their normal attendance ran as follows: a Birmingham, Alabama local 20 percent—about 60 out of 300 members; a local at Cleveland with 1,000 members—about 10 percent; and the Washington, D.C. local with 1,500 members—

also 10 percent. Generally, it appears, the larger the local the smaller the proportion attending meetings.

Sparse attendance at meetings and failure to exercise voting rights are weaknesses of democratic government which unions share with other organizations both public and private. State primary elections designed as a remedy for machine-controlled nominating conventions are notoriously participated in by small proportions of the eligible voters in both the Republican and the Democratic parties, and even in national elections for President and Vice-President of the United States only from 50 to 60 percent of the electorate take the trouble to vote. Similarly, the active participants in Chambers of Commerce, trade associations, fraternal and citizens' organizations are relatively few compared with their total memberships, and usually control their policies and offices. Safeguarding democratic control of local unions, however, is not so much a matter of getting full attendance at meetings as it is of making sure that free speech is guaranteed. One outspoken critic is often enough to hold officials to account and to prevent them from abusing their power. A corrupt officialdom has to suppress meetings to get away with booty.

Like the officers of such organizations, local union officers are usually persons who feel a sense of civic responsibility, enjoy dealing with people, and do not mind the strains of officeholding. They usually have some leadership qualifications and an urge to power, and they find more satisfaction in their union positions than in their regular jobs. Union politics has a certain fascination for them, and many of them look forward to careers as union officials in the national union or other positions in the labor movement. As officials they are constantly beset by complaints from members. The rank and file are often suspicious that the leaders are too friendly with managements and that they have easier jobs than the workers in the shops. Most local officers accept these things as part of their jobs and as good training for higher offices in the union. From among them the national officers are usually recruited. But the less ambitious are content to serve as local officials, to remain what they are, big fish in the smaller ponds. Some who are elected to local offices, however, find the duties and responsibilities onerous, and it is true in a good many locals that the office seeks the man rather than the reverse. Sometimes when a member criticizes the officials, his fellow members say: "Well, if you can do better, why don't you run for the office?"

Just as growth in population and development of nation-wide industrial enterprises have forced changes in the relations of the federal government to the states and municipalities, so the relations of local unions to the national and district or regional organizations have changed with growth in union membership and size of the locals. As matters once considered purely local affairs have become concerns of state and national governments because municipalities were no longer able to deal with them effectively, so some of the functions formerly performed by local unions have been largely taken over by district councils, joint boards or other regional organizations, and by the national union. The councils and joint boards are delegate bodies representing the local unions in an urban area or larger region, and most unions have such intermediate governmental units between the locals and the national organization. How they function in the system of national union government is described in the next chapter.

In times past local unions did almost all the bargaining with employers of their members. This and the handling of grievances arising under collective working agreements were their most important functions aside from governing their internal affairs. Many locals in various unions still have this responsibility. But as industrial development made the collective bargaining problems broader in scope than the jurisdiction of any one local, it became necessary in many industries and areas for the locals to act together in dealing with employers. To bring about sufficient unity among the locals to meet the broader problems, unions adjusted their governmental structure to give more power to district councils or joint boards and to make them primarily responsible for handling relations with managements. As corporation-wide bargaining became necessary and employers organized associations for bargaining with unions, the areas covered by district organizations were extended to include more locals. In some unions delegate bodies were formed to cover broader regions, to deal with divisions of large corporations that have plants in many states, and to accomplish other purposes than bargaining. Similarly, the growth of industry-wide bargaining has led national unions to take over the main responsibility for negotiating agreements with the industries from both the local unions and the district or regional organizations.

Another original important function of local unions was "organizing the unorganized" who were eligible for membership, and this too has largely been transferred from the locals to the intermediate governmental units and to the national. With the role of the local in collective bargaining reduced to participation through a delegate body, some of the local union autonomy was lost; and when delegate bodies or the national union assume the main responsibility for the organizing work, more is lost. However necessary these developments may be, they remove elements of local union vitality, and the role of the local has depreciated in many unions. Another factor that has contributed to this depreciation is the relatively recent development of union agreements which require employers to "check-off" union dues and turn the amounts over either to the national union or to the intermediate organizations. These take their share of the per capita dues and remit the rest to the locals. A few unions without such check-offs require that dues be paid to the joint boards or district councils which assign the respective shares to the various locals affiliated with them.

Nevertheless, local unions enjoy a large measure of self-government when they are strong and experienced enough to function without reliance upon national union officers or the intermediate governmental bodies. The strength of the local and the measure of autonomy it has depend more on its ability to settle as many of its affairs as possible than on the legal powers it gets from the constitution of the national union. A local which can successfully handle most of its business in the shops and all its internal affairs is largely self-governing, despite the supervisory authority the constitution vests in the upper governmental units. Such locals, if they have large memberships, are also able to influence the conduct of the national union's affairs to a considerable extent.

The collection of dues has been the chief and habitual routine point of contact between a union and its membership. Many members never come to the local union offices except to pay their dues, or they meet the business agent or shop steward regularly only when these come to the shops to collect dues. This monthly contact with the local union or its officers is increasingly being lost as the check-off system spreads. But some national unions have a policy of not asking employers to check-off dues; they prefer to let the locals do the collecting in order to maintain this regular communication with the membership and avoid becoming dependent on the employers with whom they have contractual relationships. In unions which adopted the check-off policy at their conventions some opposition usually developed among delegates representing locals which likewise preferred to collect all dues from their members rather than have employers do the collecting.

Local unions acquire property and bank accounts, and with these they also acquire some of the property owners' traditional conservatism. Like the national unions, many of which have built imposing headquarters buildings in Washington and other cities, locals are proud of the buildings they own in their communities, and of the fact that they no longer have to hold their meetings and do their business in rooms above saloons as was common a few decades ago. But some local unions have grown so large in recent years that their meeting halls are not big enough to hold all their members. The property and funds of a local give it an identity distinct from the members that compose it. The officials are the custodians and protectors of this entity, and it is in the local union that the outlook and point of view (though not so much the standard of living) begin to separate, which then extend and widen in the higher units of the national organization. As in the national union, the officers of the local union are responsible not only for its property and funds, but also for its security, for maintaining its continuous existence and keeping it strong, regardless of the changes or turnover in its membership. In this, factional groups among the members play an important part, for some factions are based on ideologies and on the national origins of members, as well as on personal preference for particular leaders, and each group strives to elect an officialdom that will keep the union as an entity true to its ideals and traditions of trade-unionism.

The need to keep the local union secure and strong is shared by the membership, and this often affects the attitude of locals toward new members. Once a local becomes well established, it commonly has less zeal to acquire new members, and this has been one of the reasons for the national union taking over the work of organizing. The national is also able to do a more effective organizing job, for it has the finances to employ full-time organizers who make more or less of a profession of this business. But as locals have been losing their former responsibilities for organizing, for bargaining with employers and collecting dues, they have had to develop other activities to build up and maintain the interest of the members in local union affairs and to strengthen their hold on their memberships. To further these purposes, many locals have been promoting social activities among the members and establishing facilities for recreation and adult education. The locals have also become much more active in community affairs than they were in the past; they contribute to community funds, encourage their members to do the same, and encourage both officers and members to participate actively in welfare and other community organizations.

For the most part, however, social activities of a recreational and educational nature have only a limited place in the local union life. Many well-established locals do very little about the social life of their members. Some content themselves with an annual dance or picnic. But the interest of local unions in community affairs is commonly better organized than the social pursuits of the members. This interest is not confined to cooperation with welfare, educational, and similar organizations. More important is the working together of the locals of each national union in the communities in which they function and also cooperation with the locals of other national unions for common purposes, both economic and political. This is commonly done through the district organizations of the various national unions, and to some extent these delegate bodies have also taken over the organization of the social affairs of the locals. The district councils and similar bodies of each union and the city or area federations of the locals of the various unions thus are joined to represent the interests of the labor community in the locality just as merchants, manufacturers, and other trade associations are joined in local chambers of commerce to represent the interests of the business community.

The support of the labor community is a source of strength to a local union whether it bargains directly with employers or indirectly through a district council or joint board or the national union. Lack of such support sometimes makes the difference between success and failure in achieving a union's bargaining program. Because what one union wins or loses has an impact on the whole labor community, the bargaining program is a matter of concern not only to the locals of the same union, but on all the locals of the various unions in the area. If one of them finds it necessary to strike to enforce its demands, the others are often called upon to aid financially and to help in maintaining picket lines. But if a local engages in a strike for objectives the labor community deems unsound it must fight alone, and its pickets may be ignored by the officers and members of other locals. Similarly, the various unions have political programs for which their locals seek each others support and form cooperative committees. As the chambers of commerce concern themselves not only with legislation in the interest of the business community but also in the interest of the public generally, so the organized labor community promotes political programs and legislation in the interest of citizens generally. Less frequently the two organized communities work together on programs of common interest.

BACK OF EVERY LOCAL UNION is the organization of its members in the shops or other places where they are employed. These are essentially continuations of the informal shop governments in non-union shops described in Chapter II; when a union organizes the employees, it unites the informal governments in a single organization subordinate to the local union. Much of the informality is retained in these organizations, and strictly speaking they are not governmental units of the national union, for they are regarded merely as administrative subdivisions of the local union governments. They have no constitutions, by-laws, or rule-making powers, but are subject to the rules, by-laws, and constitution of the locals. Their main function is to deal with shop problems of the employees. They take the preliminary steps in presenting grievances to foremen or other supervisors, and they are generally responsible for seeing to it that the rules of the union's collective agreement are properly applied by the shop managements. They can make no decisions binding on the members without the approval of the local union.

The shop organizations are usually referred to as "units" of a local union. They have little formal power. They may collect dues for the local but not for themselves, nor may they levy assessments. What finances they have are assigned to them from the dues paid to the locals. They are not authorized to legislate or adopt rules, and they have no authority to punish members for violation of union laws or rules. The constitutions of most national unions contain no specific provisions for shop units; those of Auto Workers, printing trades, and the American Newspaper Guild are among the few that describe them. The Typographical Union calls its shop units "Chapels," and describes their functions in its laws. The Newspaper Guild constitution provides:

A unit shall consist of the members in an individual shop in which there are not fewer than seven full-time employee members or in a shop having a contract with the Guild. Within the discretion of the local, a unit may consist of members in more than one shop where one or more of the shops involved employs less than seven members or where the shops are under one management. The officers shall consist of a chairman and a treasurer and such other officers as the unit may desire and as the local by its by-laws may permit. It shall exist only for administrative purposes and for representation of its members within the local unions. It shall not have a separate constitution or by-laws. It shall not enter into any agreements. It shall not have relations with any person or organization outside the ANG without permission of the local or the local governing body.[1]

Like the local unions, the shop organizations hold meetings and elect officers, but the shop meeting often assembles irregularly on call of a chairman or a committee when important problems arise on which the views of the employees are desired. Some units, es-

---

[1] Constitution (1946), Art. VIII, p. 21.

pecially the larger ones, are more formally organized and schedule regular meetings. In neither case, however, does the shop or unit meeting have governing powers comparable to the local union meeting. It is not a legislative assembly but serves as a means of registering the consensus of the members on shop problems and to advise unit officials on questions that arise in handling of grievances and on improvements they seek in wages and working conditions. The meetings may also plan programs for social activities of the unit members. Attendance at unit meetings, especially when they are held in the shops, is usually greater than at local union meetings; but the larger part of the membership rarely attends.

The principal officers of a unit or shop organization are a shop chairman and one or more stewards; the larger units also have a secretary and sometimes also a treasurer. In its most rudimentary form the shop organization is headed only by the shop chairman who may also be known as steward. In shops which are departmentalized each department elects a steward, and all the stewards constitute a shop committee, presided over by the shop chairman who is often referred to as the chief steward. In large plants with numerous buildings, each may be established as a separate unit of the local union; in smaller plants with a few adjacent buildings there are plant committees with a plant chairman. The terms of office of chairmen or stewards are usually the same as those of the local union's officers, except in the construction trades where the term is for the duration of the project.

It is through the shop chairmen, stewards, and shop committees that a unit carries out its functions in the shops. The laws of the Typographical Union prescribe:

In all offices [shops] in which three or more members are employed a chapel shall be organized and a chairman elected. In case of failure or refusal of a chapel to elect a chairman, it shall be the duty of the local president to appoint a member as chairman. The chapel chairman shall be recognized as the representative of the union in the chapel over which he presides and it shall be his duty to report to the president of the local union any violation of union law or provisions of the contract. Failure to perform the duties of his office shall render a chapel chairman liable to such penalty as the local may apply in accordance with the laws governing charges and trials.[2]

[2] Book of Laws (1945), By-Laws, Art. III, p. 24.

Although this refers only to the chapel chairman, it applies equally to the body of stewards in large plants and describes the duties of shop committees and shop chairmen in most unit organizations, all of whom are commonly referred to as stewards. It also makes plain the normal relationship of the shop units to the local union. The reference to failure to elect a chairman reflects a common problem in shop units of many organizations. Members sometimes refuse to serve as chairmen or stewards, and it is necessary for the local union to appoint them. These unit officers serve two masters: the group of members in the shop or department from which they are selected, and the local union authority. Some men find it a satisfying experience to receive complaints from fellow workers and try to adjust them in accordance with provisions of agreements with employers and rules of the union and at the same time meet the expectations of the union's authorities; often they have to tell employees that their grievances are not justified. Other men find this a frustrating and thankless job. Stewards are ordinarily not paid for their services but are reimbursed for time lost from their regular work. Usually, however, a steward has seniority ex-officio over the group of employees he represents, and a shop chairman has top plant seniority. The reluctance of members to serve as stewards has led a few unions to rotate the office among the members, but the position is too important to be filled in this manner. Even when they are elected or appointed, inexperienced or unstable men sometimes impair relations with the employer at the expense of the membership. The unwillingness of members to serve as stewards or chairmen and the use of volunteers to fill the jobs have weakened the effectiveness of a union in many a shop and plant.

In small locals whose members all work in one shop, there is little differentiation between the shop organization itself and the local union. The shop meeting is the same as the meeting of the local union, and the shop chairman may also be president of the local union. In larger locals whose members work for different employers, there may also be units with only a single steward or shop chairman and irregular shop meetings assembled at his call. In the huge "amalgamated" locals of industrial unions, the units are more formally organized, hold regular meetings, and have a full set of officers including stewards in all departments. Amalgamated locals are so called because in industrial unions a local ordinarily consists of the employees of one employer or plant. The Auto Workers' constitution authorizes such plant or factory locals to petition the national union to combine; and they are chartered as amalgamated locals, the old locals becoming units of the new locals. The units function much like local unions. The general meeting of the members in a manufacturing establishment under the jurisdiction of an amalgamated local is the highest authority for handling problems within the manufacturing establishment in conformity with the by-laws of the local union and the international constitution. A member may be tried on charges by his unit; if found guilty, he may appeal to the next meeting of his amalgamated local. The constitution also authorizes a unit to secede from such a local by majority vote of its members at a specially called meeting, after which the national union establishes it as a separate local union. There have been such separations, mainly caused by factional disputes between the units and the locals.

Sometimes the relations of shop units to their parent local unions approximate those of the locals to district councils or joint boards, the area governing bodies composed of elected representatives from the locals. The Auto Workers local at the River Rouge Ford Company plant has adopted a representative council form of government with the approval of the national union, the council taking the place of the usual local membership meeting. This local has about 60,000 members, which exceeds the memberships of approximately 15 percent of the national unions. A typical unit includes the employees of a separate building of the plant, but some units are departments, like transportation, that cut across buildings. The units elect delegates to the council which has the functions and powers normally lodged in the local union meeting, but the local's officers are elected by referendum vote of the members.

Another example of a local with an elected council is Local 65 of the Retail, Wholesale and Department Store Workers' Union.

This has around 25,000 members distributed among 100 units scattered over a large mercantile section of New York City. It includes wholesale units in dry goods, secondhand clothing and other apparel, garment supplies for fabrics and millinery, hardware, footwear, food and drugs, paper products, needle processing, and also warehouses of chain stores and general warehouses. Its top executive officers and executive board are elected at large. It has a sizeable treasury, owns a substantial building, employs a large staff, and publishes a bi-weekly paper "The Union Voice." It conducts a full program of social, cultural, educational, and political activities which for a number of years were Communist oriented. For some years the left-wing officers who controlled the local successfully defied its parent national union, but after the CIO expelled a number of Communist-dominated unions, in 1950, the national took steps to expel the local's top officers, and they announced plans for merging with some of those expelled organizations. Subsequently, however, the local leaders were reported to have renounced the Communist line, and they made their peace with the national union.

Such locals with a representative council substituted for the membership meeting are rare. Generally, however large the membership of a local union may be and however numerous the shop organizations or units, the local union meeting is the chief organ of government both for the local and the units. But because the portion of the members who attend the meeting is usually smaller in the big locals and ample treasuries enable their officers to employ large staffs to service the members more effectively, the governing powers of these locals tend to concentrate in the hands of top local officials without much check from the membership meeting. This is true not only in amalgamated locals of industrial unions, but also in large locals of craft organizations whose constitutions generally do not give their shop units the self-governing authority over shop affairs granted by industrial union constitutions. To overcome this tendency most large locals provide for election of officers by referendum vote of the members, and some amalgamated locals require that each unit shall have a representative on the local executive board, but with little success.

Local 12 of the Automobile Workers in Toledo is a more typical example of how an amalgamated local union functions. It has about 35,000 members and many units in metal working plants as well as in shops or stores whose employees the UAW does not make eligible to membership and who ordinarily belong to locals of other national unions. These employees are attracted by the size, strength, and prestige of the big local, as well as the services it provides for its members, which other unions with small memberships cannot make available to them in the city. Local 12 calls itself the biggest and the friendliest UAW local in Ohio. It does not have a representative council, and its rule-making and other governmental powers are lodged in the membership meeting as in ordinary locals of smaller size. Only a small proportion of the members attend the regular meeting; inquiry brought a response from an officer who estimated the normal attendance at less than one percent. But if most members came to the meeting, it would require a stadium to accommodate them—hardly a place for orderly exercise of the local's legislative and judicial powers or review of the administrative actions of officers.

This local owns its headquarters building, a roomy old apartment house; it provides meeting halls for units and facilities for servicing units and members. Its services are not confined to handling grievances but include assisting some units in bargaining with employers, helping members in their personal affairs, and providing opportunities for recreation and education. It organizes classes for instruction in various subjects and provides the instructors. It runs an active sports program. It has built an auditorium with bowling alleys. Members can pay their utility bills at its dues window. The local provides an income tax service and keeps a lawyer available to members. It publishes a weekly newspaper and runs a summer camp for children. It is governed by a smooth-running machine and is a power in local politics.

The UAW has other such huge locals, though most of them have fewer thousands of members, and amalgamation of smaller local unions into larger ones is a growing tendency in the Steelworkers and other national unions. Both craft and industrial union constitutions authorize their national executives to combine locals whose membership declines with changing economic trends and becomes too small for effective administration and for other reasons. But amalgamation of stable local unions requires the consent of the locals involved. Such merging of local unions are less common in craft unions, and their constitutions do not use the term "amalgamated locals" or make special provisions for them. Many of them do have large local unions comparable in size with the industrial amalgamated locals, but these have usually become big by normal growth of membership and active organizing work rather than by merging of locals, though some absorption of small locals is not uncommon.

An example of such a local union that functions much like UAW Local 12 is New York Local 3 of the Brotherhood of Electrical Workers. It has 30,000 members and is the largest building trade local in the United States. Professor Neufeld of the New York School of Industrial and Labor Relations at Cornell University, who made a detailed study of its government and administration in 1950, refers to it as an "industrial federation." [3] The local, like the national organization, is primarily a craft union, but its members also work in electrical manufacturing plants and other industries; it is in fact a combined craft and industrial union. The members elect the usual officers found in local unions and also a business manager who largely functions as the chief executive of the local, though it has a full-time salaried president. The local executive board consists of the president, a vice-president, and five elected members. To assure integrity in election procedures a former chairman of the State Labor Relations Board has been called in to conduct and supervise elections; he is assisted by a large staff, and voting machines are used.

For servicing the members in collective bargaining, handling grievances, and making sure that contracts with employers and union rules and property applied in shops and on construction jobs, the members are grouped in three divisions, each headed by an assistant business manager appointed by the business manager. There is a construction division with 8,000 members, a main-

[3] Maurice F. Neufeld, "Day In, Day Out with Local 3, IBEW," in *New York State School Bulletin 17* (June 1951).

tenance, manufacturing and supplies division with 18,000 members, and a smaller marine division. The men in the construction division took the lead in organizing the maintenance and manufacturing workers, and are the most active group in the government of the local. Each division does the bargaining for its members; the two larger ones have contractual relations with many hundreds of employers. Members' grievances arising out of the application or interpretation of contract provisions are handled by "business representatives" employed by the divisions.

Headquarters of Local 3 are in a seven-story building in Manhattan. There the affairs of the local are administered under the direction of the business manager. In the building is a hall where unemployed members congregate and are referred to jobs. There is a school for apprentices, a library with books supplied by the Public Library for which the local pays a rental charge, a Workmen's Compensation Service for advising members injured on their jobs, and facilities for carrying on a wide variety of social, recreational, and welfare activities, as well as the business offices of the local's officers. The Local's bi-weekly paper *Electrical Union World* is edited in the building, and there are offices for the business representatives to which members may bring their grievances. The welfare features of the local include a "Pension, Hospitalization, and Benefit Plan" jointly supported and administered by the union and employers which provides various kinds of insurance and disability pensions as well as for retirement. Also jointly with employers are several housing projects, with occupancy not limited to members.

THE LIFE OF A NATIONAL UNION depends on the virility of its local unions and their governments. These in turn depend on the vitality of the less formal shop organizations, and particularly on how well the shop chairman, stewards, or shop committees perform their functions. The roots that give health to the union and vigor to its organs are in the shops and other places where the members work. If they are not well tended, the organization shrivels. When the government of a union falls into the hands of a dictator, he usually makes sure the roots are well cared for. The roots are a complex of human relationships centered on the jobs and work opportunities in the places of employment. They involve relations between worker and worker, between each worker and his foreman, between departmental sections of employees, between employee groups and their supervisors, and between the whole body of employees and the employer's management hierarchy. Then there are the relations of the employees to their local and national union and the relations of both of these with the employer.

A shop or factory is not only a place of employment; it is also a social meeting place for conversation and companionship. Employees talk to others who work next to them and in small work groups. Even the fastest assembly lines have breaks when workers can chat as machines are being set or repaired or the flow of material slows. Building and construction workers talk as they work, and so do bench workers in small shops. Lunch time is a period for talking as well as eating, as are the relief periods or "coffee breaks" that have become customary in factories as well as offices. Workers congregate to talk in lavatories and washrooms, and it was one of the cruelties of some nonunion employers that they policed plant toilets to prevent employees from talking about their grievances or union organization. But unions too complain about restroom talk. An official of the United Steelworkers remarked: "If we could do away with the bath-house meetings, we would get more members out to the regular union meetings." And a shop chairman who could get no comment at a shop unit meeting after submitting a report on new contract terms to be submitted to employers by the union, reproached the members, saying that he knew there would be no lack of discussion in the factory washrooms. One does not have to know parliamentary law to discuss a subject in a washroom.

Shop talk and the companionship which it engenders led to the organization of sub-rosa groupings of employees in nonunion shops by which they exercise some control over the terms and conditions of employment that the employer determines unilaterally. In unionized shops the union tries to channel the talk into shop or unit meetings to get the consensus of the whole body of employees on important matters. Members who do not attend meetings hear in the shops what happened at the meetings from those who were there, and the shop chairman and stewards tell employees about the meetings as they get opportunities in touring the shops. Workers form their judgments as much from the talk of the shop as from discussions at union meetings. This is one reason for the sparse attendance at meetings, and it is a form of participation in union affairs that many members prefer. A local union of 2,500 telephone workers held a referendum on a proposal to affiliate with a reorganized and strengthened national union. Only 30 percent voted, but the provisions of the new constitution were thoroughly discussed by most of the members. The operators and clerks talked about them in the restrooms, at lunch, and in snatches of conversation on their jobs, the repair and installation crews in two's or three's as they worked and traveled from one location to another. Their judgment was formulated in such random discussion and the referendum merely registered a sentiment that had fully developed. Many members did not vote because they knew what the result would be.

Though a union organizes the specific union interests that are present and immediate in the shops and on the jobs, the topics of shop talk covers everything in which employees are interested. Union affairs, grievances, contract provisions, and union politics are only some of the common subjects of conversations, ranking in importance with sports, shows, and personal gossip. The union topics, set in a background of general varied talk, strengthen rather than weaken the binding force of union organization. Samuel Gompers believed that the Cigarmakers of which he was a member took the lead in organizing the American Federation of Labor because they could have books read to them and discussions as they rolled tobacco leaves.[4]

In small shops, the intimacy and companionship of shop talk continues into the shop meeting, but in the more formal meetings of the larger factory "units," much of this intimacy is lost. In these, too, we see the beginning of the gap between the member-

[4] *Seventy Years of Life and Labor: An Autobiography* (New York, Dutton, 1925), I, 81.

ship and the officers which continues to widen with each step upward in the hierarchy of governing officials. The office of steward marks the first point for the exercise of skills and talents opened up by unions to men who need more than their jobs for self-expression. It is the first step for ambitious men who want to rise to union power. The gap is not wide at this point; the distinctions and privileges are small, and the steward lives among the workers in his constituency, as do shop chairmen who preside over committees or larger bodies of stewards. There is hardly a phase of union life which does not rest upon the shop steward's experience. The rapid expansion of union membership stimulated by the national and state labor relations acts of the 1930s and 1940s has made the training of stewards the principal concern of union or "workers' education," just as industrial managements have had to develop programs for training foremen and other supervisors in methods of dealing with unionized workers and their shop officials.

Many unions now have formal training classes for stewards, and they run summer schools in cooperation with colleges and universities for them and for ordinary members. The classes and schools are supplemented by manuals of instruction or hand books for stewards. Union publications repeatedly emphasize the importance of the shop steward. Typical is the following excerpt from the monthly bulletin issued by the Hotel and Restaurant Workers Research and Education Department (August, 1955):

CONSIDER THE STEWARD—HE MAKES THE UNION WORK

Number One key to a successfully operated labor organization is the union shop steward . . . a post which involves great responsibility and trust. . . . The steward, as the average organized worker's direct contact with the union, handles a job of vital importance to the entire organization. . . .

Many top officers in the American Federation of Labor started as stewards and worked their way up. This dream encourages many a young man or woman to make the required sacrifices in time and effort on the chance that he, too, will emerge as a leader of men and a power on national and, sometimes, in international affairs.

These stewards greatly influence the attitude of the general membership toward their union, because they are the union officers in close daily contact with every member.

The importance of the steward in the union scheme of things is clearly shown by the amount of attention, instruction, and printed literature that is directed solely at him and his colleagues. Very few unions prepare material for the guidance of the local union president, vice-president, or similar official, but the first, or close to the first, pamphlet that an International Union publishes is for the guidance of stewards.

The handling of grievances on the job is perhaps the single most important function of the steward. The contract negotiated between the employer and the union is only the blueprint for harmonious relations, but it is the steward who makes the agreement work, and if the agreement works smoothly, then the union machinery is in fine condition, also.

The CIO Textile Workers' "Manual of Instruction" says:

The steward is the cornerstone of the union. . . .

The union depends on you and your fellow stewards for future leadership. The men and women who will represent labor in industry-wide conferences and at national policy making conventions will come from the ranks of those who are today adjusting grievances.

Management also depends on you for good industrial relations. It is a recognized fact that a union steward who successfully performs the responsibilities with which he is entrusted is an asset to the company as well as the workers he represents.

In some of the older craft organizations, however, the steward function has less vitality than most unions, both craft and industrial, ascribe to it. In these, the stewards are usually appointed, while the business agent is an elected full-time salaried officer; and the latter performs most of the duties of the shop or job steward. He has the responsibility of policing union contracts and rules in the shops; and he has some discretionary authority over stewards. An Ironworkers' local business agent restricts the steward to non-contract grievances of a strictly shop nature. He allows some shops to elect their stewards if he considers them competent; otherwise he appoints the steward. A business agent of the Operating Engineers appoints the stewards but entrusts them with a good deal of responsibility over shop affairs; the same practice is followed by the AFL Electricians' local in Washington, D.C. The business agent of a Teamsters' dairy worker local appoints the stewards; but he has a practice of polling the members and usually accepts their advice. Another business agent allows shop pressmen to elect their steward if they insist on it. "Otherwise," he said, "if the shop chairman turns out badly, I would get blamed; but if the chairman is elected, I leave it to the shop to watch him, and if any trouble happens, I tell them it is their fault." A steward or shop chairman is closer to his constituency than the business agent of a local union with members working in many different shops; he is tested by the personal knowledge of the members he represents in the shops where he is a fellow employee.

The formal distribution of power and responsibility between the shop organizations and the local unions and between the locals and the national union, as provided by the constitutions, only partially explains their relations to each other. The actual relationships vary in different unions depending on the direction of the flow of power, whether it is up from the membership in the shop units and local unions through the district and regional councils to the national union government or down from the top. This is determined not so much by the constitutional provisions as by the capacity of the membership to judge the services the officers render and the ability of the officials to manipulate membership judgments. The pioneer unionists who had to fight employers and the police to establish their organizations cherished their self-governing rights in the local unions they formed. The later membership and new locals organized by well-financed national unions and under the protection of favorable laws are more accustomed to have things done for them. After a local union has won security for itself and its members with the added strength of the national organization, the members like the national officials are unwilling to risk the gains the union has achieved by internal divisions of opinion, and the locals are more inclined to submit to higher authority. Thus the flow of power from the membership tends to be reversed.

The Machinists' Union is commonly regarded as a vigorous, democratic union. One of its vice-presidents discussing democracy in unions explained how its democratic character is maintained. Democracy in his union, he said, depends upon the local and district business agents who are elected to office. He went on:

Sometimes people think that the Grand Lodge [national] officers and representatives form a political machine which runs the union and the business agents, but that is not the case. The fact is that if we did not have the support of the business agents, we, the national officers, could not last in office. We have to face a referendum election periodically by the entire membership, and the extent to which we survive depends upon the extent to which we satisfy the business agents and the other local union officers.

The shop steward looks to the business agent for help, for service, and if he does not get it, that business agent is through. The business agent in turn looks to the Grand Lodge representative, and if he fails to give service, the Grand Lodge representative is replaced. The Grand Lodge representative looks to me and the other national officers, and we must give him the help he needs. All the service and training we develop flows back to the steward on the job and whether he can satisfy the membership. If he cannot, he will be changed, but before that test is made, all the officials along the line up to the top are tested. I don't say this happens in every case, but it does happen in enough cases so that the officials are responsible to the membership of the locals for the performance of their duties.

XIII

DISTRICT AND REGIONAL GOVERNMENTS

UNION CONSTITUTIONS commonly provide for intermediate governmental bodies between the national governments of the organizations and their local union governments. These are variously designated in the constitutions as district councils, district lodges, joint boards, joint councils, and by other names. They are not membership organizations like local unions. They are invariably representative bodies composed of delegates elected by the locals where a union has a number of them in a city or larger area within a state or covering portions of several states.[1] But the districts governed by a council or joint board are not exclusively territorial. The locals of a union whose members work for an airline or a railroad or in an industry may constitute a district. Some unions whose members work at different trades have locals organized on a trade basis, and there may be more than one joint board or council of the same union in a single city or district—a separate one for each trade.

The Machinists' constitution makes plain the multiple character of the intermediate governing bodies:

[1] Small national unions which have only one local union in each city ordinarily do not provide for such intermediate governing bodies, but the Asbestos Workers Union, with only 118 locals and a total membership of about 9,000, does charter "conferences" when the locals voluntarily establish them; and the locals of other small unions sometimes organize them informally. Some of the larger unions (e.g., Typographical Union, Musicians, Operating Engineers, Brotherhood of Electrical Workers) also follow a policy of not chartering more than one local in any city. And, though the Brewery Workers' constitution provides for only one local for each trade or branch of the industry in any city, nevertheless several separate locals of brewers, bottlers, and keg drivers are represented in the local joint executive board of New York City.

District lodges shall be established upon railroads, in industries where mutual shop interests require it, and in localities where two or more local lodges exist, for the purpose of securing mutual protection, harmonious action, and close cooperation in all matters relating to the machinist craft. . . . A district lodge is a delegate body made up of representatives duly elected from local lodges within the railroad system, industry, or locality in which the district lodge is established.[2]

The constitution of the Ladies' Garment Workers refers to its trade councils as joint boards, others as district councils, and makes the establishment of the former mandatory and the latter permissive:

Whenever there are two or more L.U's located in the same city or locality and engaged in various branches of the same trade, they shall organize a joint board. . . .
All of the local unions . . . of any one city or locality, not represented in a joint board, may organize a district council, which shall consist of an equal number of delegates from each local union.[3]

Similarly the laws of the Carpenters' Brotherhood require locals of building tradesmen to form district councils and authorize locals whose members do not work on building materials to establish separate councils.

Where there are two or more local unions located in a city they must be represented in a Carpenters' District Council. . . . Local unions other than those working on building material shall not have a voice, vote, or delegate in any district council of building tradesmen, but may establish district councils of their own. . . . District councils may be formed in localities other than in cities where two or more local unions in adjoining territories request it, or when in the opinion of the General President the good of the United Brotherhood requires it.[4]

The Hatters, Cap and Millinery Workers simply provide that "wherever there are two or more local unions in the same city or locality engaged in the same trade they shall organize a joint board." But some unions make no provision for separate joint boards or councils by trades. They authorize establishment of only one such body in a city or district, though the locals over which it has jurisdiction may be organized on a trade or industry

[2] Constitution (1946), Art. XXI, p. 48.
[3] Constitution (1940), Art. VI, p. 34; Art. VI, p. 37.
[4] Constitution (1944), *General Laws*, Sec. 26, p. 23.

basis. Typical of these is the Hotel and Restaurant Employees Union; it provides for a single local joint executive board "wherever more than one local exists in any one city or vicinity" though cooks, waiters, and other crafts are organized in separate locals, but its railroad locals belong to a "Joint Council of Dining Car Employees." The Teamsters' Union also charters separate locals in the larger cities for bakery drivers, milk drivers, general truckers or miscellaneous workers, and all are required to affiliate with the one joint council covering the city and surrounding area. Its constitution directs:

> Whenever three or more local unions are located in one city they shall form a joint council, but where there are only a few local unions in small cities or towns adjoining or adjacent to large cities, they shall affiliate with the joint council in the large cities.
> In localities composed of small cities and towns, the General Executive Board shall decide when, where and by whom joint councils shall be formed.[5]

In addition, this union provides for regional conference boards which perform some of the same functions as joint councils, but these are not delegate bodies elected by local unions. The national union organizes them, and they are composed of representatives appointed by the national president and the business agents of the locals in the region. They cover large geographical areas like the Central, Southern, Western, or Eastern States.

The Railroad Brotherhoods base their intermediate governmental units not on cities or other territorial districts but on the separate railroad properties. On each road or railway system they provide for a "General Committee of Adjustment" (or Protective Committee) which is made up of delegates from the lodges or locals whose members work on the particular lines. The locals of a number of roads may be combined to form a single general committee, and those of a small railway company may affiliate with a committee on a larger road. The Hotel and Restaurant Employees have a council of dining car employees, while the Machinists organize district lodges on railway systems as do other unions which function mainly in other industries and also have

---

[5] Constitution (1940), Art. XV, p. 46.

locals on the railroads. The Boilermakers and Blacksmiths reduced the number of their railroad district lodges from 38 to 7 in 1956; thus each general committee will include representatives from locals on many railroads instead of being confined to one railroad system.[6] Though named adjustment or protective committees, they also negotiate the working agreements with the railroads, and the committee chairman signs them in behalf of the locals and their members. In railroad parlance, they are referred to merely as "general committee."

Like the rail transportation brotherhoods, large industrial unions in the mass production industries provide for intermediate bodies composed or representatives of locals whose members work for particular employers or corporations. These are known as corporation councils or conference boards, and they differ from the Teamsters' conferences in not being confined to regions; the locals they represent may be from any part of the United States where a corporation's plants are located. Thus the United Electrical, Radio and Machine Workers Union constitution provides that conference boards may be established for the purpose of coordinating the collective bargaining activities of local unions which deal with employers having many plants, or are located in more or less well-defined segments of the electrical, radio, and machine industries.

The Auto Workers' constitution empowers the executive board to form its corporation councils:

> In cases where there are a number of locals involved in negotiations and bargaining with a major corporation or an association of corporations, the International Executive Board shall set up an intra-corporation council. . . . When the large corporation or national association has widely scattered branches, the intra-corporation council shall set up sub-corporation councils.[7]

---

[6] "The present thirty-eight district lodges chartered by the International will be dissolved. The entire United States has been divided into seven proposed geographical areas and the railroad systems in each of these areas have been grouped together to form seven new district lodges" (Boilermakers and Blacksmiths *Journal*, February 1956). This was done because a large number of lodges were not able to finance their activities with increasing unemployment among the union's railroad members due to substitution of diesel for steam engines.

[7] Constitution (1944), Art. XX, pp. 52–53.

Such corporation councils and conference boards are not given governing powers over other activities of the locals they represent. In the Auto Workers they convene prior to the opening of negotiations for new agreements with the corporations to coordinate the demands of the different locals. The same article of the constitution states that it "shall be understood that such intra-corporation council is not a legislative body . . . and shall not deal with policies . . . other than those concerning their own immediate corporation problems." This union also authorizes the calling of national and regional wage-hour conferences for discussion of common problems in "competitive shops" to assist in establishing uniform standards within a competitive group and in organizing unorganized shops. If in the judgment of the executive board such conferences prove inadequate, it may establish national and regional councils for these purposes, but neither the councils nor the conferences have legal powers over the locals represented in them, nor do regional conferences like those of the Teamsters have such legal powers.

The unions in the mass production industries also provide for district councils, but these councils generally have very limited governing powers over their affiliated local unions. In some they are merely advisory bodies. The districts are broad geographical areas rather than cities or "localities" where a union has two or more locals, though a district may cover a large metropolitan center or only a portion of it. Not all the districts have councils. Usually a majority of the locals within a district must request formation of a district council, and it is established if the national executive board agrees that there is need for a council. In some of these unions, the district councils function in the judicial process within the organizations; others also grant the varying degrees of limited authority over their affiliated locals. Although the Steelworkers' constitution also provides for geographical districts, it makes no provision for district councils, and the union is opposed to them even on advisory basis.

Many unions outside the mass production industries also provide for state councils composed of delegates from locals within the states. The functions of these are to promote state legislation and administrative policies by state officials which the particular unions or organized labor generally favor. They also lobby to oppose legislation considered anti-labor.

The national unions have the same powers over district, regional, and industry-based units as they have over local unions. The constitutions fix the boundaries of districts, and the national executive board may change them, but usually not without approval by a vote of the membership in the districts. In some unions the district organizations may be abolished in the same manner. The district councils, joint boards, and similar bodies are authorized to adopt by-laws which must not conflict with the national constitution or laws and must be approved by the national union; any change in by-laws must likewise be approved. All the different types of intermediate governing bodies are normally financed by per capita taxes levied on the members of the locals subject to their jurisdiction, and some unions also permit levying of special assessments upon approval by a majority or two-thirds vote of the local members in a district.

THE VARIETY OF TYPES of district and regional organizations differ not only in the governmental powers they have over affiliated locals, but also in the purposes for which they are established and in the methods provided for their creation. Some unions require the local unions to form the intermediate governing bodies. Others lodge the authority to create them in the national executive board or the president. Still others leave it to the national officers to decide whether there is need for such bodies or make it optional for the locals to establish them if they so desire. A union with more than one type of intermediate body may make establishment of some obligatory while others are left to the discretion of the locals or to national officers if they have the authority to create them. By whatever method a council or board may be established, all locals within their areas are usually required to affiliate with them.

In the Amalgamated Clothing Workers, the executive board decides whether or not a joint board should be created. The general executive board has power to organize two or more local unions in the same city or area into a joint board. The Teamsters' executive board has the same power in small cities and towns, but in larger cities the locals must form joint councils. The authority to set up corporation councils in the Auto Workers is also lodged in the national executive board, and the conference boards of the United Electrical, Radio and Machine Workers were established in the same manner. The Asbestos Workers' Union leaves the locals free to form such bodies or not as they prefer; its constitution provides that "Local unions which organize among themelves either intrastate or interstate shall be granted conference charters."

The Machinists provide that district lodges must be established by the locals in all localities where two or more exist as well as on railroads and in industries, and a majority of the unions make it mandatory that the intermediate bodies be formed whether by the national or the locals. But in the Ladies' Garment Workers, locals engaged in various branches of the same trade "shall organize a joint board" while those not represented in such a board "may organize a district council." Similarly, Carpenters' locals working on building material "must be represented in a district council," but those not working on such material "may establish district councils of their own." Where district councils are merely advisory bodies or have restricted governing powers, the locals usually decide whether a council should be established or not, subject to approval by the national executive board.

Although the councils are delegate bodies composed of representatives of the locals, not all unions set forth in their constitutions how delegates shall be selected or how the voting strength shall be apportioned among the locals. The Hatters, Cap and Millinery Workers, for example, do not mention the composition of their joint boards, saying only that they shall be formed by the locals, and other unions do the same. Most frequently, however, the constitution does provide some guidance even if it is only to leave the matter to the district organizations. Thus the Boilermakers specifically provide that the district lodge itself shall decide the method of choosing delegates. The Teamsters provide that the seven executive officers of each local, excluding business agents who are not considered officers, constitute the delegation to the joint council. This arrangement provides equal representation to each local regardless of size of the memberships. A few unions (e.g., Bricklayers, Hotel and Restaurant Employees) also require equal representation on the district council, but allow for elected members, and local officers are eligible. The Ladies Garment Workers distinguish joint boards from district councils by requiring equal representation in the latter. More commonly, representation is in proportion to membership, but some constitutions do not go beyond providing that the delegates shall be elected by the locals.

Many unions set forth in their constitutions broad statements of the purposes of their intermediate governing bodies with accompanying statements of their powers. Thus the Machinists: "District lodges shall be established for the purpose of securing mutual protection, harmonious action, and close cooperation in all matters related to the machinist craft," and further provide that the district organizations "shall have authority over and control of all [locals] within their jurisdiction." The Amalgamated Clothing Workers combine purposes and powers in the single statement: "Joint boards shall organize, coordinate and supervise the activities of their affiliated locals."

Some constitutions state the purposes without the powers, but make specific grants of authority or imply them in various sections of the constitutions dealing with particular subjects, such as collective bargaining, strikes, assessments, trials, and punishment for offenses. The Boilermakers thus distribute the powers, and their statement of purposes says only: "District lodges may be formed for mutual protection and to provide harmony between different [local] lodges and shops." Where the purposes are limited to a single activity broad powers may be given within that purpose. Thus a "caucus" is provided for by the Longshoremen's and Warehousemen's Union in each occupational group or geographic area "with full authority to set up such machinery as it deems necessary and appropriate for dealing with its collective bargaining problems."

Other union constitutions make no general declarations as to purpose, but do as to powers. The Teamsters, for example, without mentioning the purposes of their joint councils, authorizes them to make such by-laws as they deem proper, require all local unions within the jurisdiction of a council to "comply with its laws and obey its orders," and specifically grants the council judicial powers. Likewise the Carpenters' district councils "have the power to make by-laws, working and trade rules for the government of the local unions and the members working in their districts." The Miners' Union similarly declares no purposes but gives its district organizations specific judicial powers and authority to call local and district strikes; and they have general control of the locals much the same as in the other unions mentioned.

Both the purposes and powers of the Brewery Workers' joint boards are listed at length in their constitution, and the nature of the local union activities which the quotations above purport to coordinate and harmonize by cooperative action, as well as the nature of the powers to control or supervise the locals, are briefly explained:

The Joint Local Executive Board shall deal with all questions and transact such other business as may be in the interest of the local unions.

[It] shall be the controlling body in all local strikes or boycotts . . . to supervise and direct agitation against nonunion products, and manage the payment of regular strike benefits. . . .

The [JLEB] shall also enforce the strict observance of the existing contracts by both parties. . . . [Locals must submit their demands to the Board and it coordinates the bargaining with employers.]

[It] shall have control of the union labels . . . and shall decide which firms are entitled to them. In case of violating the contract [it] may withdraw the label from the respective firm with the consent of the General Executive Board.

The [JLEB] has the right to levy regular monthly assessments or temporary ones for the purpose of defraying the necessary expenses. . . .

In case of differences between the local unions, or between the [JLEB] and a local union affiliated, both sides shall submit their grievances to the [GEB]. . . .

Should differences arise between a local and its members, the [JLEB] then only has the right to interfere when so instructed by the [GEB]. The [JLEB] has no right to levy fines, but can make recommendations to locals to sustain, reduce or increase fines.[8]

The intermediate governing bodies of the unions cited above are typical of those which are given full governing powers over

[8] Constitution (1942), Art. V, pp. 32–33.

affiliated locals and all their activities, except that many unions do not grant judicial authority to these bodies. In two of the five unions cited (Machinists and Boilermakers) no judicial powers are granted, but the Brewery Workers, despite the provision above that joint boards may only make recommendations to locals as to fines, also provide that local union fines of between $5 and $10 are appealable to the boards and their decisions are final, while fines of less than $5 may not be appealed. Nevertheless a district council's "authority over and control of local unions" as some of the constitutions word it, may be as complete when it is without judicial powers as when it does have such authority. In some cases this control is so complete and the district organization performs so many of the functions of the locals, that if the affiliated locals disappeared they would hardly be missed.

The industrial organizations in the mass production industries limit the powers of their territorial and industry-based councils to particular activities or functions of the locals they represent, or give them no legal powers over the locals. Thus the authority of the Auto Workers' Corporation Councils and the Conferences of the CIO Electrical Workers are limited to collective bargaining. They may deal only with matters concerning relations with the employers, and do not have legislative or judicial powers. The Auto Workers' district councils, however, have only advisory functions, and their advice is given not directly to their affiliated locals but to national officers: "The purpose of the district council," says the constitution, "shall be to recommend to the regional director and the International Union constructive measures for the welfare of local unions and their members. It shall discuss competitive wages, rates, agreements . . . organizational problems." This union's wage-hour conferences and councils are similarly advisory.

The district councils of other such unions are not much more than advisory bodies. Their stated purpose in the Rubber Workers is "to promote activities and programs which will primarily benefit and advance the welfare of the local unions." Though the constitution grants "autonomy" to councils, it provides that this "shall in no way conflict or interfere with the autonomy of the local unions"; and it mentions no powers of the councils over the locals.

The Oil Workers' district councils are granted "full autonomy to function in the interest of such district" without the proviso against interfering with local autonomy, but they are given no specific authority over local unions, except that some judicial functions are implied in the statement: "It shall be understood at all times that any local union shall have the right to appeal from any decision of the district council to the International Executive Council"; but the provisions for handling "Charges and Trials of Local Members and Officers" require appeals from local union decisions to be made directly to the International Union." The Electrical Workers are more specific: "If found guilty, the defendant shall have the right of appeal to the district council." However, more commonly, the district councils of the big industrial unions are given no judicial powers.

In a few of these industrial unions, district councils do exercise some supervision over activities of locals other than adjudication of disputes, but the extent of their authority is rarely spelled out in their constitutions; and where a district is within the bounds of a city or metropolitan center, the council's powers to control and govern the locals may be substantially the same as those of the joint boards, district lodges, or councils in the Brewery Workers, Machinists, and the other unions cited above. As noted in the preceding chapter, the amalgamated locals in some of the large industrial organizations function much like these bodies, though the manufacturing units of which they are composed are guaranteed autonomy in strictly unit affairs.

AS THE purposes, powers, and composition of the district organizations indicate, their role as instruments of government is not to provide a measure of home rule for the members in geographical areas and urban centers, but rather to join the local unions in larger governmental units for cooperative action and to regulate and administer their joint activities. The most important of these are collective bargaining, strikes, handling grievances (often referred to as enforcing contracts) and adjudicating charges of violation of union laws and disputes between locals.

The role of the intermediate governing bodies in the judicial process within the unions has been described in Chapter XI. Many unions give them no judicial functions; the locals are the courts of original jurisdiction, the national executive board is the only court of appeal, and the national convention is the supreme court. In the unions where intermediate bodies do have judicial powers, they commonly serve as lower appellate tribunals before cases are taken to the national union. For example, the Joint Board of the Amalgamated Clothing Workers not only hears appeals from local union decisions, but may also assume original jurisdiction when charges are filed in a local union against a joint board officer, delegate, or paid representative such as a business agent. The Teamsters' joint councils have a similar mixture of functions. A member found guilty may take an appeal to a council, but the council may also try original charges brought by a local against a member of another local, if the accused member's local refuses to bring him to trial.

In a few unions the joint body has final authority to decide certain types of cases. Thus in the Mine Workers a member's right of appeal ends with the district executive board unless his membership in the union is at stake; and decisions of Brewery Workers' joint boards are final in cases of fines of $5 to $10. In the Brotherhood of Carpenters, district councils take over all the judicial functions of locals: "Where a district council exists all charges shall be tried before that body."

In the sphere of collective bargaining, as we have seen, the big industrial unions set up separate intermediate bodies for negotiating agreements with employers such as the corporation councils of the Auto Workers and the conferences of the International Electrical, Radio and Machine Workers. The locals represented in these bodies submit their respective demands to the councils which then formulate the bargaining program and policies, and the council may modify or reject proposals of the locals. A director is appointed for each council by the national president with approval of the executive board. With a committee of the council he does the actual negotiating, although the president or other national officer also participates. Agreements reached must be approved by vote of the local memberships. After a contract is made, the council is concerned with its administration. Grievances or disputes about interpreting contract provisions that cannot be settled with the managements are referred to the regional director for further processing. If he cannot adjust them, or if he rejects any of them, they are referred to an administrative department of the national union of which there is one for each large corporation with plants in many states. The chief of the department decides whether the grievances should be dismissed or submitted to the umpire who arbitrates differences arising out of the contracts.

On the railroads, the general committees are primarily responsible for handling all relations with the companies, though a national officer or representative is usually assigned to assist them in bargaining and also in adjusting grievances when many have accumulated. Frequently joint negotiations are carried on with the main trunk lines or with other groups of roads, and the general chairmen of the committees on the different roads usually headed by the national president constitute the bargaining committee. But separate working contracts are signed with each general committee as representatives of the employees, and indorsed by the national president. The Hotel and Restaurant Workers' Council of Dining Car Employees functions like the general committees on the railroads, but their local joint executive boards in cities operate differently, as we shall see later. Local unions of the railroad brotherhoods rarely act as bargaining agents, whereas in most unions, including the large industrial organizations, negotiating contracts with employers is one of their most important functions.

District councils and joint boards generally are empowered to coordinate the collective bargaining activities of their affiliated locals except in the mass-production industries where most of the district councils usually have no powers in this field. In the other unions, the extent of the councils' or boards' authority over negotiations and contractual relations with employers varies from complete control to merely advising or assisting affiliated local unions in doing their own bargaining. The Carpenters' councils, for example, are the sole bargaining agents for their affiliated locals. The council formulates demands on proposals for new agreements on the basis of information gathered informally by the delegates representing the locals as to desires of their members. The actual bargaining is done by a committee composed of one council delegate from each local, usually with a Master Carpenters' Association. Tentative agreements reached must be approved by a meeting of the council, and it signs the contracts.

The Brewery Workers' joint boards have less control of collective bargaining. Each of the affiliated locals formulates its own demands, which must be submitted for approval first to the board and then to the national union. Each local has the right to elect three representatives on the negotiating committee, though customarily regular delegates to the joint board are chosen. The committee reports back to the board which may require further negotiations or accept what the employer offers as a tentative agreement. Such tentative agreements must be submitted to a referendum vote of the local memberships, and if approved, the agreements are signed by each of the locals, by the secretary of the joint board, and also by the national union.

The Machinists' district lodges on the railroads and airlines also function like the general committees of the rail transportation brotherhoods, but their district lodges in cities do not ordinarily bargain for or make working contracts for their local unions. Commonly they help the locals do their own bargaining. They provide this service through their business agents who are elected at large by the members of the affiliated locals; and the national union as well as the locals share the expense of employing business agents. A shop committee of each local frames the demands served on employers, and the business agent together with this committee does the bargaining. Agreements reached must be approved by the local. The district lodge is a party to the contract, however, for it is signed not only by the local's president and the shop committee, but the business agent also signs it for the district. If the agreement or any provision of it is rejected by a local or the district officers, the matter is referred to the national union for adjustment or decision.

The joint boards of the Hotel and Restaurant Workers combine some of the features of the above unions in exercising their responsibilities for collective bargaining. Each board has an executive committee composed of all the local union business agents; though they are not members of the board, they may attend meetings and speak there. The locals submit their demands to the board meeting, and the delegates vote on the proposals. When these are approved, the business agent prepares them in the form of a contract which is sent to the national union for its approval. If any proposal is rejected by the board, it goes to the national as an appeal from board action. When the necessary approvals have been secured, the executive committee of business agents conducts the negotiations with employers. The contracts they agree upon must be approved at a meeting of the board and ratified separately by each local union, but ratification by a joint meeting of local union members is also permissible. Thereafter it is the responsibility of the locals to enforce the contracts and handle grievances. The board intervenes only when a question of contract interpretation is involved affecting all the locals.

In the vital field of strike activity, the role of the intermediate governing bodies varies in a similar manner. Thus the Carpenters provide: "Job and shop strikes are to be conducted on rules made by the district council or by the local union where a district council does not exist. . . . A district council . . . shall adopt rules for the government of strikes and lockouts." The Teamsters, however, require that a local must notify the joint council when it becomes "involved in a strike, lockout, boycott, lawsuit, or other serious difficulty, . . . and [the council] shall take such action as they deem necessary and report the same to the General President." The Brewery Workers make the joint board "the controlling body in all local strikes" and it also manages the payment of strike benefits. In the Hotel and Restaurant Workers, a local may strike on its own, but it is not entitled to the support of the other locals unless the strike has been approved by the joint board. The Mine Workers authorize their district organizations to "order local strikes" on their own responsibility, but where local strikes are to be financed by the International Union, they must be sanctioned by the International Executive Board. Most unions also require a vote of the membership, often more than a mere majority (e.g., two-thirds or 55 percent) to authorize a strike.

Sanction of strikes by the national officers as well as the district councils is generally required by most unions, and the financial aid or strike benefits are not paid if the strike is illegal: that is, not sanctioned by the national, by the district, or by vote of the members where this vote is required.

Intermediate governing bodies supervise or control other activities of local unions as well as strikes, collective bargaining, grievance handling, and disciplining locals and members. Often they have the responsibility of organizing nonunion workers in their districts. In some unions, they manage the payment of strike benefits; in others they administer supplementary Social Security benefits provided for in contracts with employers, or service local union members in connection with them. Some unions also provide mortuary funds or life insurance for members, and district councils may have charge of the payments or general supervision over them. They commonly furnish legal aid in Workmen's Compensation cases and other matters, and sometimes the political activities of the locals are centered in the district organizations. Local union educational and recreational activities are also often coordinated or managed by the district bodies.

But union constitutions are usually vague about the authority of the district councils or joint boards over these miscellaneous activities or do not mention them at all. The Ladies' Garment Workers have a rare provision that "Local unions may maintain labor bureaus alone or in conjunction with other local unions and may conduct libraries, reading rooms and lecture courses for the enlightenment of their members." When locals act in conjunction in such enterprises, the joint board may help to maintain them or they may be located at the district headquarters under the management of the district organization. But both the authority exercised by the intermediate governing bodies, and the services they render to locals and members, are subject to approval by the national union.

XIV

UNION FEDERATION GOVERNMENTS: THE AFL-CIO

LIKE SOVEREIGN NATIONS, national unions form alliances and confederations for mutual defense, for furthering interests they have in common, and to facilitate peaceful settlement of disputes among the unions. In Chapter V we traced the development of the major interunion organizations from the National Trades' Union (1834–37), a congress of local unions, through the struggle for survival between the Knights of Labor and the American Federation of Labor in the last two decades of the nineteenth century, down to the coexistence of the AFL and the CIO as rival confederations in recent years. In December, 1955, these two organizations merged and formed the American Federation of Labor and Congress of Industrial Organizations, commonly referred to as the "AFL-CIO."

Such an ending of the contest between the Knights of Labor and the AFL proved impossible seventy years earlier, for the Knights attempted to build an imperial form of labor union government with national unions as subordinate branches subject to a single centralized authority. In 1881, the growing national craft organizations formed a "Federation of Organized Trades and Labor Unions" which recognized the autonomy of each separate union and five years later they proposed a "treaty" to establish harmonious relations with the Knights in acknowledgment of "the solidarity of all labor interests." The Knights rejected the offer, and the federated trades then reorganized as the American Federation of Labor to combat the "menace" of the Knights more effectively. Its constitution from 1886 on was based on "strict recognition of the autonomy of each trade." By the beginning of the present century the AFL emerged victorious from this conflict, and the Knights of Labor disappeared shortly afterward.

Since that time, all major labor federations or congresses have been leagues of national unions comparable to the United Nations, the North Atlantic Treaty Organization (NATO), and the former League of Nations. Each union retains its self-governing rights, just as each country which holds membership in the United Nations retains its national sovereignty. When the CIO was organized in 1938, it similarly recognized the autonomy of each of its national industrial unions, and the constitution of the recently formed AFL-CIO provides that each affiliated national union "is entitled to have its autonomy, integrity, and jurisdiction protected and preserved." It also recognized "the principle that both craft and industrial unions are appropriate, equal, and necessary as methods of union organization."

Thus, unlike the federal government of the United States, union federations do not have direct authority over the individual members and internal affairs of affiliated national unions, though as we shall see below, they govern directly certain local unions and national organizing committees or councils, and the merged AFL-CIO is given limited powers over race relations, racketeering, and Communist activities within the unions which were not formally granted to previous federations.

In terms of citizenship a union member is a citizen both of a national union and one of its locals where he holds his membership. He is normally not a member of the federation to which his union belongs, the exceptions being the members of local unions and organizing committees that are directly attached to the federation. (These are temporary organizations preparatory to distributing the local members to appropriate national unions or establishing the organizing committees as new autonomous unions.) Generally, only unions are members of a federation as only nations are members of the United Nations. As the latter recognizes the independence and equality of the governments of its member nations, so does a labor federation recognize the independence and equality of the governments of its affiliated national unions.

BUT, while there is this similarity between federations of unions and alliances or leagues of nations, an important distinction between labor federations and international organizations must be borne in mind. Unions, whether affiliated with a federation or not, are parts of a movement of working people to organize as a class, primarily for compelling employers to give their labor forces a voice (through representatives of their own choosing) in determining wages, conditions of employment, and rules for the government of employees, but also for political and general welfare purposes. They have a common interest against employers, and since the earliest trade societies established themselves as continuous organizations, united action by the separate unions and a unified labor movement has been a constant aspiration of organized workers.

Thus as noted in Chapter III, J. R. Commons and Associates, in their *History of Labor in the United States,* placed "the beginning of American labor movements in the year 1827 at Philadelphia . . . [when] American wage earners for the first time joined together as a class regardless of trade lines, in a contest with employers." At that time there were no national labor organizations. The unions were local self-governing trade organizations, they joined together to support a Carpenters' strike for a ten-hour workday, and formed a "Mechanics' Union of Trade Associations," the first of what are now referred to as city federations of labor, central labor unions, or city industrial councils.

A year later, the *Mechanics Free Press,* earliest of American labor papers, published the preamble of this Association, and commented: "This is the first time that working men have attempted, in a public meeting, to inquire whether they possess, as individuals or as a class, any right to say by whom they shall be governed." [1] The Knights of Labor, as we have seen, tried to unify all labor organizations under a single centralized authority, and the AFL in 1886 proclaimed "the solidarity of all labor interests," while the preamble of the AFL-CIO constitution (published in January, 1956) states: "The establishment of this Federation

[1] Commons and Sumner: *Documentary History of the United States* (Cleveland, Clark, 1910), V, 21.

through the merger of the American Federation of Labor and the Congress of Industrial Organizations is an expression of the hopes and aspirations of the working people of America."

After the first association of unions in Philadelphia, similar associations were formed in other cities, and following the depression brought on by the panic of 1837, there were many such organizations in the late 1840s and early 1850s under names like Trade Assemblies and Trade Councils. When the national unions were organized in the last half of the nineteenth century, both the Knights of Labor and American Federation of Labor similarly provided for joining locals of different unions in cities in "Trades and Labor Assemblies," but the AFL soon changed these to "Central Labor Unions" or "City Federations of Labor." The CIO named its similar bodies "Local Industrial Councils," and the constitution of the merged AFL-CIO refers to both city federations and industrial councils as "Local Central Bodies."

Thus the original city associations of local unions were built into the federations of national unions, and remain essential parts of such federations today. As long ago as the mid-nineteenth century, there were also some state "Trade Assemblies or Councils," and later the AFL established state Federations of Labor patterned on these, while the CIO paralleled them with state "Industrial Councils." These "State and Local Central Bodies" are not to be confused with the district councils or joint boards discussed in the preceding chapter, though like the latter they are composed of delegates from local unions within a city or larger area which may be co-terminous with a state. District councils represent locals of a single union and are subordinate only to the national governments of their respective unions, whereas city and state central bodies join together locals from different national unions and are subordinate organizations of a federation.

It is this practice of establishing inter-union subordinate organizations at all levels, local as well as national and intermediate, that marks the distinction between the structure of union federations and of international organizations such as the United Nations. Although they are alike in being leagues of independent governments rather than super-governments, each union and each nation retaining its right to govern its own members or citizens and internal affairs, the international organizations do not yet reach down below the national level and have no dealings with local governments or other divisions of national states. Organized labor, being a movement to unite workers as a class for combatting or bargaining with employers and for political action, finds it necessary to intertwine in the federations local unions and intermediate bodies of their affiliate organizations. Nevertheless, each national union retains its governing powers over its own local unions and district councils or joint boards.

An important function of both union federations and international organizations is to maintain peace, one in the world of labor, the other in the world of national states, and in this respect they are also alike. Unions have disputes over their jurisdiction, they raid each other and carry on strikes or wars against each other much as nations do. Thus labor federations set up machinery for peaceful settlement of controversies among their member unions, as the United Nations does for adjusting international conflicts. But in the federations as in the United Nations, the powers to effect settlements are mainly mediatory rather than compulsory, for if either party to a dispute proves recalcitrant the only remedy a federation has is to expel the union which in any case is free to secede or withdraw its affiliation.

IN CHAPTER I, written when early attempts at uniting the AFL and the CIO had ended in disagreement, we remarked: "If history is any guide there are likely to be some independent unions, some dissident labor movements, so long as individual workers are free to retain freedom to choose and to form their own organizations." When the merger was consummated in 1955, the AFL had 109 affiliated national unions and the CIO had 32. But outside the AFL-CIO there remained 58 unaffiliated or independent unions. The larger unions remaining independent are the United Mine Workers, the rail transportation brotherhoods (Locomotive Engineers, Conductors, Firemen and Trainmen), the Longshoremen's Association expelled by the AFL for racketeering and four of the eleven Communist-controlled organizations expelled by the CIO, the rest having been consolidated with the four.

Among the smaller so-called independent unions, some have formed and are affiliated with minor federations of their own. These federations for the most part consist of directly affiliated locals, but a few have formed national unions whose autonomy is recognized by the national federation. The three principal federations are: the Confederated Unions of America, the Engineers and Scientists of America, and the National Independent Union Council. Little is heard of them, and they furnish no information as to the number of their affiliates or the total membership represented by them. The 1955 Directory of National Labor Unions says about these federations only that they "have some of the characteristics of a federation such as issuance of charters to, or the maintenance of affiliation among, autonomous labor organizations in more than one industry."

Although 58 or almost 30 percent of the approximately 200 national unions are "independent" (i.e., not affiliated with the AFL-CIO), the organizations joined together in the merged federation include nearly 90 percent of all organized workers in the United States. AFL unions had a combined membership of close to 10,800,000 prior to the merger, and there were about 5,200,000 in the CIO organizations. Thus the new federation represented approximately 16,000,000 members at the time of its formation out of a total estimated union membership of nearly 18,000,000, while the 58 independents had slightly less than 2,000,000.[2]

With more than 70 percent of the existing national unions and nearly 90 percent of the union members in its fold, the AFL-CIO appears to have achieved the highest degree of labor unity that the American trade union movement has ever had. But at the present writing (April, 1956) it has only laid the foundations for

[2] Of the total of nearly 18,000,000 members, a little over a million were in locals of the national or international unions outside continental United States, most of them in Canada, some in Hawaii, Puerto Rico, Alaska, and the Canal Zone. The combined AFL and CIO memberships include those in local unions and national organizing committees or councils directly attached to the federation (U.S. Department of Labor, Bureau of Labor Statistics, Bulletin 1185, *Directory of National and International Labor Unions in the United States* [1955].

such unity, and the actual building of a united movement has barely begun. Although all CIO and AFL unions are now members of the combined AFL-CIO, they have entered the new federation with the charters granted them by the former separate federations, and under these practically all the 32 CIO unions have jurisdiction over crafts and industries which conflict with the jurisdiction of AFL chartered unions. Moreover, in rival organizing campaigns between the different unions, many have extended their jurisdiction beyond the limits intended by the charters, and the integrity preserved to each national union by the AFL-CIO constitution includes the jurisdiction it actually exercised at the time of the merger.[3] Real unity within the new federation will not be achieved until these overlappings of jurisdiction are ironed out.

Uniting the two federations was a great achievement that took years to accomplish. Adjusting conflicting jurisdictions of the autonomous national unions is a much more difficult task that will take many more years. The problems involved are comparable to what the United Nations would face if almost half its member countries were claiming each others territory, as the Arabian nations and Israel are doing. But there is a steady trend among American national unions to combine in larger organizations. While such consolidations are usually made for more effective functioning of the unions, not infrequently elimination of jurisdictional conflicts is also one of their purposes. Within three months after the AFL-CIO was formed the former CIO Packing House Workers Union merged with the former AFL Meat Cutters and Butcher Workmen in a single national union. This is one way in which the difficulties of adjusting jurisdictional boundaries may be eased, but the formation of bigger and bigger unions may also have adverse effects on the government of the AFL-CIO by lessening the influence of smaller unions and concentrating powers of the federation in the officials of a few of the largest organizations.

[3] The new constitution states: "Each such affiliate shall retain and enjoy the same organizing jurisdiction in the Federation which it had and enjoyed by reason of its prior affiliation with either the American Federation of Labor or the Congress of Industrial Organizations." *Report of the Joint AFL-CIO Unity Committee*, First Constitutional Convention of the American Federation of Labor and Congress of Industrial Organizations (New York, December 5, 1955), Constitution, Art. III, Sec. 3.

Consolidations like that of the Meat Cutters and the Packing House Workers are apparently not to be forced by the AFL-CIO, for the constitution provides: "Affiliates of the Federation shall be encouraged to eliminate conflicts and duplication in organization and jurisdictions *through the process of voluntary agreement or voluntary merger* in consultation with the appropriate officials of the Federation, to preserve subject to the foregoing, the organizing jurisdiction of each affiliate" (italics added). But whether other powers granted by the constitution to the federation may not be interpreted to compel merging of affiliated national unions remains a question. There are certain voluntary agreements on which the merger of the AFL and CIO is based which it is well to consider first.

The basic agreement between the two organizations was worked out by a "Joint AFL-CIO Unity Committee." In this they agreed "to create a single trade union center in America . . . which will preserve the integrity of each national and international union," and set forth the principles by which the new federation is to be governed and the methods for effectuating the merger. The agreement was approved by the executive bodies of both organizations in February, 1955, after which the joint committee prepared a draft constitution which was likewise approved in May, 1955. Then in December, separate conventions of the AFL and CIO ratified the actions of the executive bodies, and thereafter the delegates of both conventions met in joint session and established the new federation by adopting the constitution as drafted, in which the merger agreement is incorporated as a part thereof.

Also a part of the new constitution is an "AFL-CIO No-Raiding Agreement" made in 1953 (but signed only by 77 AFL and 29 CIO unions) which provides: "No union affiliated with either federation shall attempt to organize or to represent employees as to whom an established collective bargaining relationship exists between their employer and a union in either federation." This was a preliminary step toward the merger, and it was to expire in December, 1955. The new constitution stipulates that the no-raiding agreement "shall be preserved and, with the consent of the signatories, shall be extended for a period of two years from its present expiration date." Coupled with this in the constitution are two other agreements, one made in 1951 between organizations within the CIO providing for settlement of disputes among them, the other a similar AFL internal disputes agreement adopted in 1954. As to them and the no-raiding agreement, the constitution directs:

A joint committee shall be appointed by the Executive Council to formulate the means for incorporating these three agreements into a combined no-raiding and organizational and jurisdictional disputes agreement which can be effective as between all of the unions becoming signatory to it irrespective of their former affiliation and for the purpose of extending, by voluntary agreement, such provisions to all affiliates of this Federation.[4]

Thus in settling jurisdiction controversies as in trying to eliminate them by merging of national unions, it appears that the ends sought are to be accomplished by voluntary agreements of the affiliated unions, with officials of the AFL-CIO acting as mediators or advisors. But the constitution also provides that each affiliate "shall respect the established collective bargaining relationship of every other affiliate and no affiliate shall raid the established collective relationship of any other affiliate," and provision is made for complaints of violation of this section to be filed with the president of the Federation. If such complaints cannot be settled in accordance with the no-raiding agreement or by voluntary agreement with the aid of the president, he is required to refer the matter to the Executive Council which, after a hearing, "shall make such decision as it believes to be necessary and appropriate." Should an affiliate fail to comply with a decision, the Council must submit the case to the federation convention "for such action as the convention may deem appropriate." This means that the guilty national union may be expelled from the federation for failure to comply.

Expulsion is not an effective remedy, for the expelled union can function independently and continue its raiding. Nevertheless, in interunion organization and jurisdiction disputes, the AFL-CIO does have power to decide conflicts between its autonomous national unions, and though voluntary settlements by mutual agree-

[4] Constitution, Art. XVIII, Sec. 2. See, also, statements by George Meany and Walter Reuther in *Industrial and Labor Relations Review*, Vol. 9, No. 3 (April, 1956).

ment are emphasized, they are not exclusively relied upon. But what makes this power particularly significant is the fact that both the separate AFL and CIO disputes agreements provide for final and binding decisions by a neutral arbitrator or umpire when controversies cannot be settled by voluntary means, and these umpires are still functioning. Whether the plan for combining the no-raiding and disputes agreements to be formulated by a joint committee of the executive council will retain the arbitration feature is not known. In any case, however, the AFL-CIO will have the authority to expel a union for not complying with an arbitration decision, as the separate federations had before the merger. Decision by umpires was a forward step to the extent that it brought an independent judiciary into the government of union federations, but, as the constitution of the merged federation now stands, it appears that the convention rather than impartial arbitrators will decide raiding, organizational, and jurisdictional disputes, and the convention's determinations are bound to be influenced by political considerations.

In addition to the authority of the AFL-CIO over such disputes the federation is also given certain powers over corruption and Communist or other subversive influences within its autonomous affiliated unions. To keep them "free from any and all corrupt influences and from the undermining efforts of Communist, Fascist or other totalitarian agencies" the constitution empowers the executive council to investigate "any situation in which there is reason to believe that any affiliate is dominated, controlled, or substantially influenced in the conduct of its affairs" by such agencies or by "any corrupt influences." It may make recommendations or give directions to the affiliate involved, and by a two-thirds vote may suspend any affiliate found guilty after such investigation. The suspension is appealable to the convention, but it remains in effect pending an appeal. With respect to civil rights within the unions, however, no such powers are granted to the federation. Although the constitution provides for a standing committee on civil rights, as it does for a committee on ethical practices to deal with corruption and Communism, the civil rights committee is limited to assisting the executive council "to bring about at the earliest possible date the effective implementation of the principle stated in this constitution of nondiscrimination." It is not backed up by investigatory and disciplinary powers of the council, as is the ethical practices committee.

AT THE FOUNDING CONVENTION of the AFL-CIO in December, 1955, there was practically no discussion of such problems as these or other issues that might arise from the provisions of the merged federation's constitution. The president of the Typographical Union was the only delegate who raised a serious question. He rose to urge a proposal to provide for nonintervention of the federation in the affairs of the national unions and lay more stress on their autonomy and independence. The convention referred the proposal to the executive council for study and a report to be submitted to the next convention in 1957. But the federation's president, George Meany, took the occasion to explain that the powers of the new federation over its affiliated unions would not even be as great as the powers the AFL exercised before the merger. He said:

I feel this constitution goes about as far as a constitution can go in preserving the integrity and unity of the affiliates. . . .

It has been said that this constitution gives more power to the merged federation than the constitution of the AFL. Just let me bring out one point—no organization can be compelled to merge with any other organization. The federation will have no such power.

He then went on to cite some AFL history. Between 1911 and 1939, conventions of the AFL had ordered six national unions to merge or amalgamate with other national unions. (Its constitution did not specifically grant the federation such authority.) And he concluded:

All of these actions . . . were taken by convention not by any Executive Council. . . . These are deeds and not words. I don't say the actions were right, but I do say under this constitution for the merged federation, the merged federation has no such right as exercised by the AFL on these six occasions that I have just cited.

The convention of a federation as of a national union is the supreme court in interpreting the constitution. Though the president and the executive council of the AFL-CIO may believe that the new federation has no right to order an affiliate to merge with another, the convention may well decide when considering an appeal submitted to it in a specific case that it does have that right and so order. Thus a precedent would be set which would be cited to justify such action in subsequent cases. This is substantially what the AFL convention did in the cases cited by Mr. Meany. Being the highest authority in the AFL-CIO, its conventions' decisions are final as to the intent and meaning of the federation constitution, as the Supreme Court's decisions are final in interpreting the constitution of the United States.

Moreover, the president and executive council of the AFL-CIO may also set precedents and interpret the constitution in exercising the powers it grants them. An interesting example of this is already available involving the conflicting jurisdictions of the United Textile Workers, formerly AFL, and the Textile Workers of America, formerly CIO. These two unions made little progress in organizing the great body of unorganized workers in the textile industry, especially in the Southern states. Since the new federation was formed, each of these organizations has separately applied to the AFL-CIO for assistance in carrying on organizing campaigns among the nonunion workers. But the answer given to both unions by officials of the federation was that neither financial aid nor organizers or other assistance would be given to either affiliate until they agree to end their hostilities by entering into a joint organizing jurisdictional pact or merge the two unions.

Thus the executive officers of the AFL-CIO have interpreted their authority to encourage voluntary mergers or jurisdictional agreements as empowering them to deny federation funds and organizers to affiliated national organizations in order to press them to merge or make agreements for carrying on unified organization campaigns, despite their preference for continuing as rival organizations. It is possible that this indirect compulsion on autonomous affiliates by the executives might be overruled by a federation convention, but this is not probable.

Until the convention does overrule it, the power will remain in the executive to use such pressure to force affiliated unions to amalgamate or to make jurisdictional and organizational compacts which the constitution states shall be "by voluntary agreement." And, as the convention of the AFL interpreted its constitution to authorize it to order merging of unions, the new federation's convention may well do the same despite its president's opinion that "it has no such right."

All governing powers including judicial interpretation being lodged in the convention, the powers of the AFL-CIO over its member national unions are likely to be whatever the convention determines they should be.[5] But in this convention (as in the conventions of the national unions) judicial determinations, policies adopted, and other actions taken are not products of the body of delegates alone. They are the result of power forces operating both within the federation and in its affiliated unions. What the convention does is largely influenced by the personalities of federation officials, by centers of power in the unions, by alliances among them or the officials that represent them in the federation, and also by the public opinion of the memberships of the various organizations. It is these forces that explain why the constitution of the AFL-CIO specifically grants the federation authority to deal with problems of corruption and Communist influences within its otherwise autonomous affiliates, while such authority is not granted in matters concerning civil rights of their members. We may expect, therefore, that the same forces will determine how these provisions will be interpreted and enforced when specific cases are brought to the convention for decision on appeal from the executive council.

The problems with which the provisions deal were, of course, not created by the merger of the two federations. They bedeviled the AFL and the CIO when they were separate organizations, and it is substantially true to say that the constitution of the AFL-CIO does not do much more than codify the practices of the two fed-

[5] In this connection it may not be amiss to recall the incident at the 1945 Machinists' convention cited in Chapter IX. To a delegate's question whether certain action that had been taken set aside the union's constitution, its president answered, "No, the convention violated it."

erations in dealing with the same problems. Corruption and racketeering were mainly problems of the AFL, and Communist-controlled unions were essentially a CIO problem. Both lacked specific authority to force their autonomous national unions to root out these evils. But both, after much hesitation, did take some action, and it is these precedents that led to the inclusion of the provisions against corrupt and Communist influences in the constitution of the AFL-CIO.

The AFL resorted to interpretation and unwritten law in expelling the notoriously racketeer-ridden International Longshoremen's Association. Explaining the expulsion, the AFL president said in an interview with the editors of *U.S. News and World Report:*

We have placed a new interpretation on the autonomous right in so far as it pertains to racketeering. We have said in effect: "All right, you've got your autonomous rights. But there is an unwritten law that you use those autonomous rights for the benefit of the labor movement. If you violate that unwritten law by using those autonomous rights as a cloak for illegal activity, then you can't belong to the AFL." That was approved by a convention vote of 72,000 to 750.

The CIO amended its constitution in order to expel Communist-controlled unions. It adopted an amendment authorizing its executive board to hear the cases of unions charged with being communist dominated and to take appropriate action. As previously mentioned, eleven organizations were found guilty and expelled.

With respect to civil rights within the unions, however, practically all the CIO affiliates provided in their constitutions for no discrimination among members or applicants for membership because of race, creed, or color; and most of the AFL unions that had limited membership to white workers changed their constitutions in recent years to prohibit such discrimination. This, of course, did not immediately abolish discrimination, but much progress toward that end was made. Hence, the constitution of the merged federation gives it no such powers over civil rights as it grants over corruption and Communist influences within the unions, but relies on the executive council and the civil rights committee "to bring about at the earliest possible date the effective implementation of the principle . . . of non-discrimination."

Although the AFL-CIO constitution also codifies the practices of the former separate federations in dealing with duplicate organizations and jurisdictional disputes, it officially sanctions "dual unionism" (two or more unions having jurisdiction over the same workers) which both federations previously discountenanced. In issuing charters to affiliated unions, each federation attempted to give exclusive jurisdiction to only one union over particular crafts, trades, or industries. Nevertheless, overlappings were common, but when disputes arose and federation officials or the convention had to decide them, the issue was which union was entitled to the jurisdiction under its charter; and theoretically at least, this was the basis of the decisions. Under the constitution of the merged federation, however, the established bargaining relationships of each affiliated union are protected regardless of how those relations may trespass on the territory of other unions, so that each may rightfully claim it is operating within its legal domain.[6]

Thus the constitutional provisions for handling jurisdiction problems may reasonably be interpreted differently by different unions and federation officials. Some may well contend that the AFL-CIO must rely on "the process of voluntary agreement or voluntary merger" to eliminate conflicts in organization and jurisdictions (Article III, Sections 3 and 10); and, as we have seen, President Meany gave assurance that it has no authority to order the merging of unions. But if a complaint is filed by one union that another has failed to "respect [its] established collective bargaining relationships," and the dispute is not settled by voluntary means, the executive council and the federation convention do have power to decide the controversy (Article III, Section 4); and in so doing, the convention might reverse President Meany's opinion that affiliates could not be ordered to merge as a means of settling jurisdictional conflicts.

Apparently, it was necessary to leave the powers of the AFL-CIO

---

[6] This applies only to the unions chartered by the AFL and the CIO prior to the merger of the federations. The former policies of the separate fedrations will be continued when additional unions become affiliates of the AFL-CIO. Section 7 of Article III provides: "Charters or certificates of affiliations shall not be issued to national or international unions, organizing committees, or directly affiliated local unions in conflict with the jurisdicton of affiliated national and international unions, except with the written consent of such unions."

over disputes between affiliated unions somewhat ambiguous in the constitution because otherwise the merger of the two federations would hardly have been possible. One of the main reasons for failure of previous attempts to unify the federations was the insistence of many unions that conflicting jurisdictional claims be settled before the merger, and officials of some unions still feel that this should have been done despite their assent to the compromise that was finally arranged. The compromise provided for maintaining the status quo through the no-raiding agreement (approved by conventions of both federations in 1954), which protects each union that signed it in the actual jurisdiction it exercises regardless of overlappings with other unions. Then, a year later, the two federations were merged at the top, with guarantees to the affiliated unions that their established bargaining relationships will be respected, and their integrity and autonomy will not be sacrificed on the altar of a unified labor movement. As a result of thus sanctioning the principle of dual unionism and at the same time empowering the federation to determine jurisdictional issues, the trend toward unification or consolidation of national unions will doubtless be accelerated, and some lessening of interunion disputes may be expected. But the smaller unions fear being swallowed by the large unions, and this is especially true of small craft organizations whose identity and ability to regulate their crafts may be entirely lost if merged with industrial unions. Nor are the smaller industrial unions without such apprehensions.

In the case of the craft unions, their obligations under the constitution of the AFL-CIO conflict with their rights under the National Labor Relations Act (Taft-Hartley). This law authorizes any group of employees who constitute a craft to seek and obtain an election, and by a majority vote they may be severed from an industrial union and established as separate "bargaining units" to make contracts with employers covering only the craftsmen. But by exercising this right they violate Article III, Section 8 of the federation's constitution, providing that "each affiliated union shall respect . . . and refrain from raiding . . . the established bargaining relationships of any other affiliate." Moreover, by including the provision against raiding in the constitution, the unions that have refused to sign the no-raiding agreement are in effect treated as if they were obligated to abide by it in the same manner as those that did sign.

In a proceeding before the National Labor Relations Board, the Operating Engineers petitioned for an election to separate off a group of operating engineers who were included under a contract of an employer with a local union of the Auto Workers. The latter contended that as an affiliate of the AFL-CIO there was imposed upon the Operating Engineers by the no-raiding provisions of the constitution an obligation "not to seek representation of the employees who are a part of the unit represented by the Auto Workers." The board ruled that this contention was without merit, "even if there was such an obligation." [7]

Thus the craft unions have less freedom as affiliates of the AFL-CIO than they have under the law, and the organizations (industrial as well as craft) which are not signatories to the no-raiding agreement, if they continue to refuse to sign, will apparently be doing so to no purpose. It is noteworthy, too, that the executive committee of the new Industrial Union Department established by the merged federation has recommended that vacant vice-presidencies in the Department should be chosen only from unions which have signed the no-raiding agreement.

THE GOVERNMENTAL STRUCTURE of the AFL-CIO follows the pattern of the two federations when they operated as rival organizations. This structure and how their governments functioned were briefly outlined in Chapter V. Like them, the new federation is composed not only of national unions, but also certain local labor unions and national organizing committees or councils, which it governs much as the United States governs its territories and island possessions. These directly attached organizations are temporary arrangements (resulting from the organizing activities of the federation) until the locals can be turned over to appropriate national affiliated unions, and the councils or organizing committees can be established as new autonomous national unions within the federation.

[7] North American Aviation & Operating Engineers, 115 NLRB (1956).

As in the former separate federations, the convention of the AFL-CIO is "the supreme governing body." Its functions are not confined to legislating and policy making, but include also electing the executive officers who are subject to its control. In addition, it is the supreme court of the federation, but it does not have the authority to hear and decide appeals from judicial tribunals within the national unions as the Supreme Court of the United States may review decisions rendered by state courts.

The convention is to meet regularly every two years after the founding meeting in 1955, whereas the former separate federations convened annually. Because of this change, the AFL-CIO constitution provides for annual meetings of the presidents of the national unions with the executives of the federation and sets them up as a "general board," described below. Each national affiliate is free to determine the method of choosing delegates to the convention, but the number of delegates varies with the size of the union, though not in direct proportion. Those with less than 4,000 members are each entitled to one delegate. For each additional 4,000 or portion thereof another delegate is allowed up to 12,000. Unions with memberships in excess of 25,000 get 5 delegates for every additional 25,000 up to 75,000. Then one more delegate is allowed for each 50,000 members up to 175,000, this number entitling a union to 9 delegates. Thereafter one more delegate is added for each 75,000 members. But local unions directly attached to the federation and state and city central bodies are each allowed only one delegate.

This amounts to some overrepresentation of the small organizations, but not enough to give them a predominating influence as, for example, representatives from rural areas commonly have in state legislatures, though they may represent smaller populations than those from urban districts. At the founding convention of the AFL-CIO there were about 1,500 delegates. It was the large delegations from the big unions and their leaders who dominated the assembly. This was evident from the way delegates from the smaller unions assented to provisions of the constitution they criticized in private conversations as threatening the security of their organizations but did not voice their apprehensions on the floor of the convention. Voting at the convention may be by division or show of hands, but upon request of 30 percent of the delegates present, a roll-call vote must be taken in which each delegate is "entitled to cast one vote for every member whom he represents."

When the convention is not in session the executive council takes its place as the "governing body of the federation." The council consists of the president and the secretary-treasurer who are designated as "the executive officers," and 27 vice-presidents. All are elected by majority vote of the delegates. Regular meetings of the executive council must be held at least three times a year, and an executive committee with more frequent meetings is provided for, consisting of the president, the secretary-treasurer and six vice-presidents chosen by the council. The council directs the affairs of the federation, is required to carry out the instructions and decisions of the convention, and enforce the provisions of the constitution, and it may adopt rules to govern the federation that are not inconsistent with the constitution. Like the convention, it is also a judicial body for settling disputes and interpreting the constitution, but between meetings of the council, the president has authority to interpret the constitution.

In addition to the specific powers of the executive council described above in matters involving corruption and Communist influences, it is also authorized to promote "the organization of unorganized industries," to assist affiliated unions in organizing work, to form new national unions, and the duty is imposed on it "to watch legislative measures directly affecting the interests of working people, and to initiate . . . such legislative action as the convention may direct." In carrying out these provisions, the council is required "to recognize that both craft and industrial unions are appropriate equal and necessary as methods of trade union organization and that all workers whatever their race, color, creed or national origin are entitled to share in the full benefits of trade union organization."

As chief executive, the president appoints and fixes the compensation of organizers, representatives, agents, and employees of the federation, directs their activities, and he may suspend or remove them. His salary is set by the constitution at $35,000 a year, and he is chairman of both the convention and the council as well as of a new body in the executive organization of the AFL-CIO, which the former AFL did not have, though the CIO had something similar. This is a "General Board of the Federation" created by the constitution consisting of members of the executive council and the presidents of all affiliated national or international unions, and also the presidents of each "Trade and Industrial Department." The board is to meet on call of the president at least once a year. It is given authority to "decide all policy questions referred to it by the executive officers or by the executive council," and voting by the board members is governed by the same rule as voting in the convention. Because the convention will be meeting every two years, the board's annual sessions (or more frequent ones on call) will provide opportunities for the chief officers of the autonomous affiliated unions and the officers and executive council of the federation to determine jointly important questions of policy whenever they arise between conventions.

Prior to the merger, the AFL had trade departments for each of the following trades: Building and Construction, Metal Trades, Union Label and Service Trades, Marine Trades, and a Railway Employees Department. These five are continued in the AFL-CIO, and a sixth is established, known as the "Industrial Union Department." The constitution states: "Each department is considered an official method of the Federation for transacting the portion of its business indicated by the name of the department." The departments, however, are composed of representatives of affiliated national organizations, and they manage and finance their own affairs. They may establish local councils, or railway system federations by the railroad department. They are in fact subsidiary federations of the general federation, elect their own officers and executive boards, and each department has its own convention. A union may affiliate with more than one department, and it must pay a per capita tax to each department on the number of members whose occupations come under the several departments.

Thus, though a condition of the merger agreement was that an industrial union department would be created to handle problems of former CIO unions and that it would be headed by Walter Reuther, then president of the CIO, not only CIO organizations are in the department, but about 40 former AFL unions have also joined it, so that it now has 72 affiliated organizations. Similarly, some of the CIO unions may now be members of the other trade departments. All the departments are open to any AFL-CIO affiliates who may appropriately belong to them. They govern themselves but must conform to the constitution and laws of the federation, and their actions and decisions are subject to appeal to its executive council and convention.

To be distinguished from these are the staff departments administered under the general direction of the president of the federation with the aid of "standing committees" whose members he appoints. The constitution directs him to appoint fourteen such committees, but with the approval of the executive council he may combine committees and create new ones. Both the former federations had many committees, but the merged organization has integrated them with the staff departments for more effective administration of its principal activities. The functions of the standing committees are indicated by their titles. Thus the duties of the Committee on Legislation are "to carry out the policies and programs of the Federation in Congress, in legislatures of states and in local governments"; the Civil Rights Committee is to aid the executive council in implementing the principle of non-discrimination in accordance with the constitution; the Committee on Ethical Practices has the responsibility of helping "to keep the Federation free from any taint of corruption or Communism." The other eleven standing committees are similarly concerned, respectively, with political education, international affairs, workers' education, social security, economic policy, community services, housing, research, public relations, safety and occupational health, and veterans' affairs. Some idea of the range of the AFL-CIO's activities and interests may be gathered from the committee titles.

Differing from both the staff departments and the Industrial and Trade departments is a separate Department of Organization in which is centered the responsibility imposed by the constitution for "organization of unorganized industries." This department is also under the general supervision of the federation's president, but it is headed by a director of organization appointed by the president after consultation with the executive committee and approval by the executive council. As in the case of the head of the industrial union department, it was a condition of the merger agreement that the first director of organization should be a CIO man, and the appointment was made accordingly. The CIO was spectacularly successful in organizing mass production industries, whereas the AFL usually failed because of the insistence of its craft unions that workers be distributed among them according to the trades or crafts at which they were employed. This experience doubtless contributed to the choice of the first director from CIO ranks. In the past, unions were commonly criticized for restricting admission of new members because they feared there were not enough jobs to go around, and wanted to monopolize the opportunities for employment. The establishment of a special department to give methodical direction to the organization of nonunion workers and the formation of new national unions marks the earnestness of the merged federation to bring all working people within the fold of organized labor.

The state and city central bodies described in a preceding section of this chapter completes the picture of the agencies through which the AFL-CIO functions and governs its affairs. These bodies, being composed of representatives from locals of the various national unions in the states and cities, have no collective bargaining responsibilities, nor do they have any administrative or policy-making powers with respect to contractual relations with employers. All such matters are reserved to the affiliated unions. The central bodies' functions are limited to watching and lobbying for or against state and municipal legislation, to participating in community affairs, and to promoting labor interests in the areas where they operate.

Spokesmen for employers and commercial organizations have expressed concern that the unification of the two federations will give the AFL-CIO a huge labor monopoly. With respect to collective bargaining, this charge is no more valid than it was when the two were separate organizations, for the combined federation as such has no authority to bargain or make working contracts with employers, except as it may control the bargaining of its directly affiliated local unions. As representative of many millions of working people, however, and as a lobbying organization to further their interests, there can be little doubt as to the increased influence and power of the AFL-CIO as a single labor center. But this influence and power depend on the willingness of its affiliated national unions to cooperate with it for common purposes, and as we have seen, many of them have conflicting interests.

THE FEDERATION is not a monolithic organization. It has no authority over the millions of members within the unions. It cannot try or punish them for offenses, nor can it tax them directly. It gets its funds by taxing the unions on the basis of the size of their memberships. Its guarantee to preserve the integrity and protect the autonomy of each national union is a strict limitation on its powers imposed on it by the union, not a delegation of its powers to them. The federation has only the limited powers enumerated in the constitution. This is made plain by the difference between the provisions for dealing with corrupt and Communist influences within the unions and the civil rights provisions. Apparently the unions were willing to allow the federation to intervene in their internal affairs to help eliminate corruption and Communism, but unwilling to provide implementing sanctions for discrimination on account of race, creed, color, or national origin. Significant also is the fact that the constitution deals only with those civil rights which involve such discrimination. It says nothing about protecting the rights of members against arbitrary or capricious actions of the governments of the unions to which they belong. Moreover, the national unions in their political and lobbying activities are free to endorse or oppose candidates from public office and federal legislation even though the federation takes a different position on the same candidates or legislation.

Groups of affiliated national unions and their leaders are also free to make alliances to protect particular interests, and centers of power are thus formed within the federation below the level of its top authorities. Even the industrial and trade departments of the federation may act as such power centers to oppose policies of the executive council. Thus the building trades department is holding up the merging of AFL and CIO state and city central bodies, which by constitutional provision must be accomplished by the end of 1957, because of disputes between some of the building organizations and some industrial unions. Late in April, 1956, this department, which is composed of the presidents of building and construction unions, adopted a resolution instructing their local unions not to agree to merging the state and city bodies until some agreement is reached with the industrial union department as to which unions have jurisdiction over construction work connected with industrial plants. The latter department, says the resolution, takes the position that "industrial unions have the right to install and service materials which industrial union employees manufacture . . . [and] to do construction work [which] is an extension of industrial plant operations." The AFL-CIO executive council condemned the building trades department for so instructing the unions that are represented in it, but the differences remain to be settled by voluntary means.

The arrangements provided in the constitution for financing the enlarged activities of the new federation is another indication of how its affiliated national unions have reserved to themselves the powers to govern their members and internal affairs, and how limited are the enumerated powers they have granted to the federation even over interunion relations. Before the merger, the AFL was authorized to levy a tax on each affiliated union to the extent of 4¢ per member per month. This yielded the AFL between five and six million dollars annually. The CIO's corresponding tax was 10¢ per month, and though levied on a membership less than half the size of that in the AFL unions, its yield was also over five million dollars annually, the combined yield being something under eleven million dollars. The tax fixed in the AFL-CIO constitution is the same as that formerly levied by the AFL, and this is estimated to yield only about eight million dollars. Thus, despite the expanded activities and functions of the new federation, its annual income will be several million dollars less than the income of both federations prior to the merger.

The numerous small unions in the AFL were doubtless opposed to raising the tax above the 4¢ they had been paying before the merger. Almost half the national organizations in the AFL each had less than 25,000 members, and about 60 percent had memberships of less than 50,000. The big industrial unions in the CIO could well afford to pay the 10¢ tax levied on them, and its small unions that could not support themselves were receiving aid from CIO funds. Although the compromise to maintain the tax at the lower figure will seriously hamper the AFL-CIO in carrying out its ambitious programs, it shows that the national unions who make up the federation not only retain their "sovereignty," as they often refer to their self-governing rights, they can also exercise control over the federation through the power of the purse.

What the unions and the federation will do with their powers, how they will meet the complexities of dual unionism, overlapping jurisdictions and other problems referred to above, and how democracy within the trade union movement will be affected, it is not possible to say at this writing, four months after the AFL-CIO was formed. But some of the possibilities are considered in the concluding chapter.

[AT THIS POINT the manuscript closes. Unfortunately, death intervened before the author was able to write the concluding chapter. See the editorial preface.]

INDEX